Business
Advantage

Student's Book
Upper-intermediate

Michael Handford, Martin Lisboa,
Almut Koester, Angela Pitt

CAMBRIDGE
UNIVERSITY PRESS

CAMBRIDGE
UNIVERSITY PRESS

University Printing House, Cambridge CB2 8BS, United Kingdom

Cambridge University Press is part of the University of Cambridge.

It furthers the University's mission by disseminating knowledge in the pursuit of education, learning and research at the highest international levels of excellence.

www.cambridge.org
Information on this title: www.cambridge.org/9780521132176

First published 2012
7th printing 2015

Printed in Dubai by Oriental Press

A catalogue record for this publication is available from the British Library

ISBN 978-0-521-13217-6 Student's Book with DVD
ISBN 978-1-107-42231-5 Teacher's Book
ISBN 978-0-521-28130-0 Personal Study Book with Audio CD
ISBN 978-0-521-13218-3 Audio CDs

Cambridge University Press has no responsibility for the persistence or accuracy of URLs for external or third-party internet websites referred to in this publication, and does not guarantee that any content on such websites is, or will remain, accurate or appropriate. Information regarding prices, travel timetables and other factual information given in this work is correct at the time of first printing but Cambridge University Press does not guarantee the accuracy of such information thereafter.

Business Advantage

success starts here

Business Advantage contains a wealth of expert advice from global business leaders, thinkers and specialists, and uses content taken from a corpus of business language as well as vocabulary from real meetings in real companies. This ensures that you benefit from learning the skills and the language that reflect the reality of working in business.

Dr Sally Hibbert
Associate Professor of Marketing,
Nottingham University Business School

Muhammed Yunus
Founding Director of Grameen Bank
and Nobel Peace Prize Winner

Dell

Renault-Nissan

Dr Jochen Runde
Director of the MBA Programme
and Reader in Economics, Cambridge
Judge Business School, University
of Cambridge

Suleyman Narimanov
Project Manager, Russian oil industry

Havaianas

Nokia

The case studies that accompany each unit of Business Advantage have been carefully selected, meaning you will benefit from seeing how business is done across a wide range of different industry sectors, in organisations of all sizes (both profit and not-for-profit), and from all around the world.

Thanks to the innovative Theory-Practice-Skills approach and the substantial input into the lessons and activities from the world of business, success starts with Business Advantage.

Upper-intermediate

Student's Book with DVD	978 0 521 13217 6
Personal Study Book with Audio CD	978 0 521 28130 0
Teacher's Book	978 1 107 42231 5
Audio CDs	978 0 521 13217 6
plus online material	

www.cambridge.org/elt/businessadvantage

Map of the course

Topic: Business environment	Lesson	Focus	Language	Input: Reading/Listening	Output: Speaking/Writing
Unit 1: Competitive environment	1.1 Theory	Concepts of competitive markets	Language to describe levels of competition	Interview with Professor Jochen Runde, Cambridge Judge Business School, University of Cambridge	Prepare and deliver a competitive analysis
	1.2 Practice / Case study	A highly competitive company	Past tense review	*Saint-Gobain* Extract from company website	Present to a potential distributor
	1.3 Skills	Building relationships across companies	Making your feelings understood	Recording of small talk in an international meeting	Develop a relationship with clients
Unit 2: Future uncertainty	2.1 Theory	STEEP analysis	Language of certainty/uncertainty	Interview with Dr Hans-Martin Beyer, ESB Business School	Conduct industry sector STEEP analysis
	2.2 Practice / Case study	Global consumer goods industry	Language to describe the consumer goods sector	*Global Consumer Goods Industry* Industry association report	Launch a new product
	2.3 Skills	Presenting a case at a meeting	Discourse markers to link speech	Recording of an IT meeting in a multinational bank	Present the benefits/stages of a future change
Writing 1	Preparing presentation slides	Creating a strong visual impact	Summarising information for presentations	Presentation materials from the Global Commerce Initiative	Design effective presentation slides

▶◀ **Watch Sequence 1 on the DVD to find out more about Business environment.**

Topic: Managing people	Lesson	Focus	Language	Input: Reading/Listening	Output: Speaking/Writing
Unit 3: Rewarding performance	3.1 Theory	Employee reward strategies	Vocabulary of pay and incentives	Interview with Professor Stan Siebert, Birmingham University Business School	Construct a pay package
	3.2 Practice / Case study	Performance-Related Pay (PRP) in practice	Compound nouns	*Nokia Corporation* Extract from company Executive Compensation Report	Make executive pay decisions
	3.3 Skills	Negotiating a pay rise	Language for negotiations	Recording of a performance appraisal in a business consultancy	Negotiate a pay rise with your employer
Unit 4: Fostering creativity	4.1 Theory	Creative thinking and creative management	Word formations	Extract from *Creative Management* by Dr Jane Henry, Open University Business School	Solve problems creatively
	4.2 Practice / Case study	Innovation in practice	Past modals	*Carnegie Wave Energy* Interview with Jeff Harding, Non-Executive Director	Make a product into a commercial success
	4.3 Skills	Decision-making	Evaluative metaphors and idioms	Recording of a meeting about contracts between two companies	Decide between two contracts
Writing 2	Describing a process	Describe a creative problem-solving process	Review passives; linking language	Creative problem-solving processes from the Open University MBA programme	Write a description of a business process

▶◀ **Watch Sequence 2 on the DVD to find out more about Managing people.**

Topic: Managing cultures	Lesson	Focus	Language	Input: Reading/Listening	Output: Speaking/Writing
Unit 5: Organisational cultures	5.1 Theory	Understanding organisations	Vocabulary to talk about organisations	Extract from *Understanding Organizations* by Professor Charles Handy, founder of the London Business School	Decide on an appropriate culture for an organisation
	5.2 Practice / Case study	Creating a successful culture	Ways of asking questions effectively	*Mundipharma International Ltd* Interview with Ake Wikström, Regional Director	Allocate budgets across departments
	5.3 Skills	Dealing with problems across departments	Language for making summaries in meetings	Recording of an inter-departmental meeting	Improve communication across departments
Unit 6: Working across cultures	6.1 Theory	Culture and individual strategies in business	Vocabulary for culture; reporting verbs	Interview with Professor Helen Spencer-Oatey, the University of Warwick	Maintain good relations in difficult situations
	6.2 Practice / Case study	Multicultural mergers	Vocabulary to make positive and negative judgements	*Renault-Nissan* Extracts from company website and an academic article	Manage an alliance between companies from different cultures
	6.3 Skills	International team-building	Metaphors of movement	Recording of a meeting between two international logistics departments	Develop guidelines for an international team
Writing 3	Argument-led writing	Arguments for and against	Vocabulary of reason, result and contrast	Arguments for and against privatisation from *BusinessWeek*	Write about pros and cons of private ownership

▶◀ **Watch Sequence 3 on the DVD to find out more about Managing cultures.**

Topic: Managing operations	Lesson	Focus	Language	Input: Reading/Listening	Output: Speaking/Writing
Unit 7: Change management	7.1 Theory	DICE theory	Cohesion and referencing language	Extract of article from *The Boston Consulting Group*	Plan and evaluate a change to study or work project
	7.2 Practice / Case study	Implementing change	Present perfect tenses; non-verbal communication	*Laird Technologies Beijing* Interview with Charlie Peppiatt, Vice-President of Global Operations, Laird PLC	Improve team performance and productivity
	7.3 Skills	External negotiating	Ways to organise spoken language	Recording of meeting between two multinational pharmaceutical companies	Negotiate issues in a joint venture
Unit 8: Project management	8.1 Theory	The principles of project management	Verb/noun combinations	Extract from *The Project Workout* by Robert Buttrick, Programme Manager at Cable & Wireless	Schedule a project
	8.2 Practice / Case study	Russian oil industry – Sakhalin-1 Project	Future perfect and future continuous tenses	*Sakhalin-1 Project* Interview with Suleyman Narimanov, Engineering Project Manager	Plan the goals and objectives of a project
	8.3 Skills	Maintaining relationships	Inclusive and exclusive language	Recording of a sales meeting between two IT companies	Negotiate sensitive arrangements
Writing 4	Describing graphs	Describing graphs	Compare and contrast figures and trends	Graphic information from *The Carbon Trust*	Describe graph showing carbon emissions across industries

▶◀ **Watch Sequence 4 on the DVD to find out more about Managing operations.**

Topic: Marketing	Lesson	Focus	Language	Input: Reading/Listening	Output: Speaking/Writing
Unit 9: E-marketing	9.1 Theory	The 4Cs of marketing and e-marketing	Vocabulary of marketing and e-marketing	Extract from journal article by Dr Charles Dennis, Dr Tino Fenec and Professor Bill Merrilees	Improve a company's e-retailing operation
	9.2 Practice / Case study	The benefits of selling on- and offline	Review of standard conditionals; introduction to mixed conditionals	*Dell Computers* Interview with Alastair Brown, Chief Operating Officer of Bizantra, London, and former Marketing Director, Dell, Asia	Conduct and report market research
	9.3 Skills	Organising a presentation	Language for introducing and linking slides	Recording of an e-presentation by Philip Weiss, Managing Director of ZN, a specialist e-marketing agency	Prepare and deliver an e-presentation
Unit 10: Branding	10.1 Theory	What is branding?	Vocabulary of branding	Lecture by Dr Sally Hibbert, Nottingham University Business School	Discuss own brand v. manufacturer's brand
	10.2 Practice / Case study	The Havaianas brand	Brand and product collocations	*Havaianas* Extract from Alpargatas Annual Report	Develop brand extensions
	10.3 Skills	Using persuasive communication in meetings	Use *if* to persuade and direct	Recording of the beginning of a staff meeting at a luxury hotel	Persuade staff to change
Writing 5	Persuasive communication online	Online persuasion	Language to change features into benefits	An online forum discussing benefits and features	Write persuasive copy for an internet site

▶◀ Watch Sequence 5 on the DVD to find out more about Marketing.

Topic: Accounting and finance	Lesson	Focus	Language	Input: Reading/Listening	Output: Speaking/Writing
Unit 11: Accounting	11.1 Theory	Activity-based costing (ABC)	Gerunds; financial vocabulary	Text on ABC accounting from *Guide to Management Ideas and Gurus* by Tim Hindle	Compare traditional cost accounting and ABC
	11.2 Practice / Case study	Cost and price	Vocabulary to describe different types of costs	*Ukrainian International Airlines* Interview with Richard Creagh, company Vice-President	Decide the pricing strategy for an airline
	11.3 Skills	Developing internal relationships	Polite language	Recording of the end of a staff meeting at a luxury hotel	Apply politeness strategies in difficult situations
Unit 12: Microfinance	12.1 Theory	The concepts of microfinance	*Used to, be used to* and *get used to*	Extract from United Nations Conference on Trade and Development website	Research microfinance
	12.2 Practice / Case study	Grameen Bank	Word formations about banking	*Grameen Bank* Presentation by Professor Muhammad Yunus, Nobel Prize-winning founder of Grameen Bank	Integrate conventional banking and microfinance
	12.3 Skills	Delivering a presentation	Good delivery techniques	Speech by Barack Obama, US President	Presentation about a project
Writing 6	Formal and informal emails at work	Functions of emails	Formal and informal email language	Business emails	Write an email to your manager

▶◀ Watch Sequence 6 on the DVD to find out more about Accounting and finance.

Topic: Strategies and decision-making	Lesson	Focus	Language	Input: Reading/Listening	Output: Speaking/Writing
Unit 13: Corporate Social Responsibility	13.1 Theory	Business ethics and Corporate Social Responsibility	Vocabulary linked to CSR	Extracts from business texts on Corporate Social Responsibility	Debate the part ethics has to play in business
	13.2 Practice / Case study	The business case for Corporate Social Responsibility	Phrases with dependent prepositions	*The BBC* Interview with Yogesh Chauhan, the BBC's Director of Corporate Social Responsibility	Present on how to improve CSR
	13.3 Skills	Supporting the speaker	Language for supporting a speaker	Recording of a telephone conversation between a manager and the owner of a travel company	Encourage speakers to communicate their ideas clearly
Unit 14: Strategic planning	14.1 Theory	Corporate strategic planning	Verbs used in strategic planning	Extract from *Strategic planning in non-profit and for profit organisations* by Carter McNamara, Developer and Director of Free Management Library	Create a strategic plan
	14.2 Practice / Case study	Planning within a company	Multi-word verbs	*Abercrombie & Kent* Interview with Justin Wateridge, Managing Director	Devise a strategy for a travel company
	14.3 Skills	Using narratives in interviews	Narrative tenses	Recording of an internal meeting at a medical company	Improve job interview skills
Writing 7	First contact emails	Analysing emails	Language tones	Business emails	Apply for a job via email

▶◀ **Watch Sequence 7 on the DVD to find out more about Strategies and decision-making.**

Authors' thanks

We are enormously grateful to all those people who contributed, supported and put up with us during the writing process. Particular thanks go to all the team at Cambridge University Press. To our editor Neil Holloway, who has played several roles in the project – a clear-minded editor, a motivating guide, a critical reader, and a solid supporter and helper. To Chris Capper, the commissioning editor, for being a firm guiding hand who led the project with skill and diplomacy. To Joy Godwin, who has been an enormous help with her experience and judgement of what will work and with her voice of calm and good sense. To Laurence Koster for being an excellent sounding board and a dab hand with technology. To Alison Silver for her sharp focus and attention to detail and layout. To Chris Doggett for helping to track down all the permissions that have retained the book's authenticity.

Our thanks go to all the interviewees, who kindly gave us their time and valued expertise: Dr Hans-Martin Beyer, Alastair Brown, Yogesh Chauhan, Richard Creagh, Jeff Harding, Dr Sally Hibbert, Suleyman Narimanov, Charlie Peppiatt, Tim Rabone, Professor Jochen Runde, Professor Stan Siebert, Professor Helen Spencer-Oatey, Justin Wateridge, Philip Weiss, Ake Wikström, Professor Muhammad Yunus.

We would like to thank our students, colleagues, friends and family, who have helped so much to make this book what it is.

Michael: Thank you to my wife Mayu and my children Julia and Maya for being so understanding and loving. Thanks to my students at the University of Tokyo and trainees at Isuzu and JCG, to Mike McCarthy, Ronald Carter and Hiro Tanaka for their support and encouragement, and to Graham Webb and Simon Gibbs for their insights. And to my fellow authors for such an interesting and educational journey.

Martin: A big thank you to my wife Manuela for her support, ideas and knowledge of the Havaianas brand. To my children, Max and Nico for their sense of humour and knowledge of life. Thanks are also very much in order to the numerous students, colleagues and friends in business and academia whose ideas and suggestions have added real value to the material.

Almut: Many thanks to Winnie Cheng, Seunghee Choi, Astrid Jensen, Ian McMaster, Anne Pauwels and Michael Pritchard for providing texts and data. Very special thanks to my husband Terry Pritchard for help with data, ideas and activities and his patience, support and encouragement throughout this project.

Angela: Special thanks to the staff and students at Neu-Ulm University; to Susan, Amelia and Mabel for their good-humoured intelligent sense; to Michael for his patience, and to all my family for reminding me that there is life beyond the keyboard.

Introduction

What is *Business Advantage* and how can it help you?

Welcome to *Business Advantage* Upper-intermediate. *Business Advantage* gives you the theory, practice and skills that will lead you to success in international business.

Business Advantage Upper-intermediate is the second book in the *Business Advantage* series. It is aimed at students who wish to progress through the B2 level.

How is the course organised?

There are 14 units in each book. The unit topics have been carefully researched and chosen to provide you with a comprehensive foundation in the main areas of business you would expect to find on a general management training course or on an academic Business Studies course. Each unit is divided into four lessons.

- **Theory**
  Presented by professors and lecturers from business schools and universities – you will gain new understanding of key business principles and ideas.

- **Practice**
  A case study based on texts and interviews with managers in *real* companies – you will learn how business theory is applied in practice in the real world.

- **Skills**
  Based on *real* recorded communications in companies – you will understand how business people *really* speak to help you perform successfully at work.

- **Writing**
  Based on authentic material which will enable you to produce a variety of effective written business communications (every two units).

What is included in each lesson?

Introduction
You are introduced to the main content in a user-friendly format. We use your personal experiences, visual images and quizzes to prepare you carefully.

Language focus
To improve and broaden your vocabulary and grammatical range. The language syllabus covers the main tenses and grammatical structures appropriate to your level plus key vocabulary and phrases. The language presented is drawn extensively from research and actual examples of English used in business taken from the Cambridge English Corpus ⊙ – one of the world's largest databases of authentic written and spoken language. You can be confident that the language presented is real language used in business today.

Reading or Listening
Introduces and develops theories, topics and ideas about business that are useful in both English and your own language. You also have the chance to improve your speaking skills through discussion questions at the end of each section.

Output

Each lesson builds to a final Output section. This is usually a group task where you have to *use* the language and ideas presented to solve a problem or deal with a business dilemma or issue.

Critical analysis and Intercultural analysis

Every unit also includes at least one Critical analysis and Intercultural analysis section. Critical analysis will help you develop questioning skills that are necessary in the academic and business world. Intercultural analysis will help you develop an understanding of your own culture and other cultures – a vital skill in today's business world.

Transferable skill

You will also find a Transferable skill section in each unit which will provide you with some very useful tools, such as speed-reading techniques, that will improve the way you learn and the way you work.

What is on the DVD?

The DVD in the Student's Book contains video case studies to watch after every two units. You can use the DVD for extra listening practice and to find out more about the business topics in *Business Advantage*. There are documentaries filmed at companies as well as round-table discussions filmed with MBA students from the Cambridge Judge Business School, University of Cambridge. When you see ▶◀ in your Student's Book, ask your teacher about watching the DVD sequence in class, or watch it at home on your computer or TV.

The video case studies are accompanied by worksheets available on the *Business Advantage* website: **www.cambridge.org/elt/businessadvantage**

What is in the Personal Study Book?

The Personal Study Book gives you extra practice of the grammar, vocabulary and skills you have covered in the Student's Book. There are also additional reading activities focusing on inspirational business leaders and thinkers, together with further case studies on a variety of organisations.

Where can I find more activities?

Ask your teacher about the Professional English Online website for extra activities to do in class: **www.cambridge.org/elt/pro**

We hope you enjoy learning with *Business Advantage* and wish you every success.

Michael Handford
University of Tokyo, Japan

Martin Lisboa
Foundation Campus, Lucca / University of Pisa, Italy

Almut Koester
University of Birmingham, UK

Angela Pitt
University of Neu-Ulm, Germany

1 Competitive environment

1.1 Theory: Concepts of competitive markets

Learning outcomes
- Learn theory, language and concepts of competitive markets.
- Learn mind-mapping and note-taking techniques.
- Prepare and deliver a mini-presentation using a mind map.

Introduction

1 Discuss the following questions.

- How competitive are you in your work or studies?
- Is it always important for you to be successful?
- How important is it to be ambitious in order to become successful?

2 There are many parallels between the worlds of competitive business and professional sport. Label the 'strategies for success' below (1–4) as follows (A, B, C or D).

A Appropriate for business   C Appropriate for both
B Appropriate for sport   D Appropriate for neither

1 Pay significant rewards to top performers
2 Maintain a large pay differential between best and worst performers
3 Fire the worst performers
4 Create a culture that focuses on winning at all costs

Discuss your answers and explain your reasons.

3 The following developments arguably make the business environment more competitive. What effect would they have on business in your country?

1 Manufacturers increasingly locate factories in low-cost countries.
2 A single global currency is introduced in all countries.
3 The government forcibly breaks up large companies that dominate their industry sector.
4 New competitors from emerging economies enter the world stage.
5 The speed of technological change increases.
6 The government cuts tariffs (import taxes) on goods and services from overseas.

4 How competitive is the environment you work in (or want to work in)? What makes it competitive (or uncompetitive)?

Language focus 1: Sport as a metaphor and analogy for business

1 Sport is seen by many people as an analogy for business competition. Complete the following sentences that link sport to business using verbs from the box.

acted	monopolised	regulated	invested	globalised

1 Different sports, like different industries, are largely _____ by a small group of teams or companies.
2 Some business people, like some sports people, have _____ illegally to 'win at all costs'.
3 Sport, like business, needs to be heavily _____ to ensure that competition is fair and equal.
4 Both business and sport are becoming increasingly _____ compared to the past.
5 Sports teams and companies have _____ heavily to attract top talent.

In pairs, tell your partner about any examples that illustrate some of the points above.

2 Underline the high-frequency collocations with adverbs in the sentences above. Then try to memorise them.

Example: *largely monopolised*

3 Look at the following sports metaphors that are commonly used in business and decide which sport they originate from. Then complete the sentences below with the correct metaphor.

> touch base   kick off   take it on the chin
> the ball's in their court   score an own goal

1 We've sent them our final offer, so now _____ .

2 We've arranged to have lunch first and then _____ the meeting after that.

3 That's a good idea. Let's _____ on that tomorrow.

4 If we're not careful here, we'll _____ .

5 It's hard to accept, but sometimes we just have to _____ .

4 What do you think these metaphors mean?

Business view

Professor Jochen Runde is Director of the MBA Programme and Reader in Economics at the Cambridge Judge Business School, University of Cambridge.

5 Listen to Professor Jochen Runde's definitions of the key terms below and put them in the order you hear them being described.

 1.02

- oligopoly _____
- perfect competition _____
- natural monopoly _____
- business environment _____
- monopoly _____

Listening 1: The competitive environment in sport and business

 1.03

1 Listen to Professor Jochen Runde describe some connections between competitive sport and the world of business, and note down the four sports he mentions.

2 Listen again and answer the following questions.

1 What lessons can business learn from the Oxford–Cambridge boat race?

2 What examples does he give of teams with 'market power'?

3 Why do these teams have 'market power' in his opinion?

4 Which sport has rules to ensure competition is fairer and more equal?

5 What metaphor does he use to describe a sport that has unfair rules that favour some teams over others?

6 What word or phrase that Professor Jochen Runde defined in Language focus 1 question 3 best describes 'level playing field'?

Critical analysis

1 What teams have the most market power in sports in your country? How do they use this power? How can sports governing bodies create a more 'level playing field' by reducing their market power?

2 What about business? What companies have the most market power in their industry sector? How do they use it? What can national governments and international institutions do to restrict this power?

Listening 2: Monopolies, oligopolies and perfect competition

 1.04

1 Listen to the second part of the interview and answer the questions.

1 What two things do monopolies do with their market power?

2 In what two situations does it make sense to have a natural monopoly?

3 How possible is it in practice to create perfect competition?

4 How can you make markets more competitive?

2 Professor Jochen Runde uses the term 'reduce entry barriers', which is also commonly expressed as 'reducing barriers to entry' or 'reducing market entry barriers'. Here, we are referring to barriers that companies build around their products and services to stop competitors entering the market.

Look at the following strategies that big companies can use to build barriers and categorise them as follows:

a Probably illegal in most countries

b Would probably be investigated by Competition Authorities

c Generally considered acceptable business practice

1 Make a takeover bid for a rival company _____

2 Agree common price strategy with rivals _____

3 Propose a merger with a rival company _____

4 Become a global company _____

5 Lower prices to below cost price _____

6 Register a lot of patents _____

3 Most countries or regions have institutions and laws to monitor monopoly activities and restrict their market power. Match the institutions below to their correct country or region:

1 Monopolies and Mergers Commission   USA

2 Federal Trade Commission   UK

3 Competition Commission   EU

What is the name of the corresponding institution in your home region or country?

Transferable skill: Mind-mapping and note-taking

Mind maps are useful for taking notes during meetings, lectures and presentations. They are also a good way of recording information that you can easily and quickly refer to at a later date.

1 Look at the outline of a mind map below and note how it is constructed with circles, lines, bullet points and summary titles. The main subject is always placed in the centre of the mind map. To ensure that you take down information quickly, you need to develop good note-taking techniques. Write down examples from the mind map.

		Examples
1	use abbreviations	_____
2	use shorthand	_____
3	use acronyms	_____
4	miss out articles (*a, an, the*)	_____
5	miss out prepositions	_____
6	miss out subject nouns	_____

2 In pairs, complete the mind map below without referring back to your notes or to the tasks in this lesson.

Output: Competitive analysis

In small groups, choose a well-known company or product from one of the industry sectors below. Think about this company in relation to other companies or products in its industry sector. Decide if you want to take a country, regional or global focus.

internet services	MP3 players	Formula 1	soft drinks
European football	computers	food retail	fast food

Stage 1

Discuss the following questions and then record your conclusions in a large mind map.

- Who is the competition?
- How strong is the competition?
- Why does the company or product enjoy such a strong position in its market?
- What examples are there of how they exercise their market power?
- How do you think the market should be regulated?
- Should the company be investigated for anti-competitive practices? Why/Why not?

Stage 2

Use your mind map to present the main points of your discussion to the class in a short talk (2 minutes). Conclude your talk by stating whether you think the company is monopolistic or not in its given geographical and industry sector market.

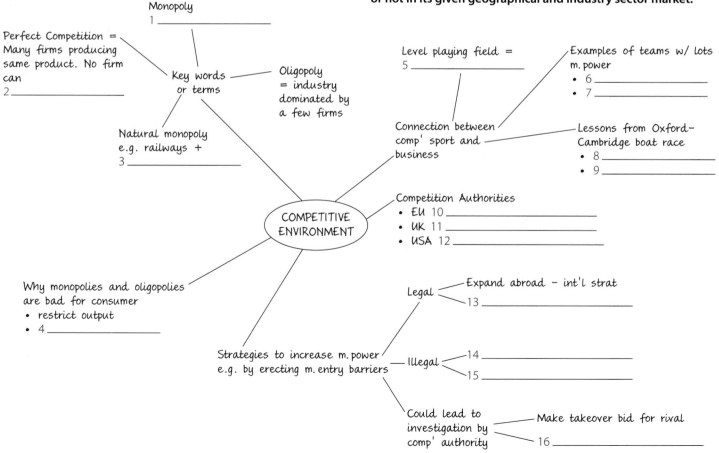

1.2 Practice: A highly competitive company

Learning outcomes

- Understand how a company with market power operates and remains competitive.
- Review tenses used to talk about the past.
- Persuade a potential distributor to accept a proposal.

Hall of mirrors, Versailles

Nanjing Olympic Centre, Nanjing

Polish Radio, Krakow

Glasinform, Vienna

Profile: Saint-Gobain

Saint-Gobain is a multinational group of over 1,000 companies, and is one of the oldest companies in the world. It was created in 1665, employs over 191,000 people, and is among the top 100 industrial companies in the world, as well as the Global 100 most sustainable corporations. It has built a presence in 64 countries, and is European or world leader in all of its activities; for instance, it is the world's largest producer of glass and other materials used in construction and home-building.

Introduction

1 Which large multinational corporations seem very powerful at the moment? What sectors are they in? Who are their competitors? Why do you think they are so successful? Is it only because their products are so good?

2 Would you like to work for any of these companies? Why/Why not?

3 What characteristics do you think a highly competitive company should have?

4 Look at the pictures above. What is the link between them?

5 Have you heard of Saint-Gobain before? If not, does the information in the profile surprise you? Do you think that Saint-Gobain is a highly competitive company? Why/Why not?

Reading 1: The history of Saint-Gobain

The following headings have been removed from the text which follows, which is from the Saint-Gobain website. Quickly skim through the text and put them in the correct place. One has been done for you.

Back to the future, or 20+ years evolving non-stop ✓
From legal monopoly to free competition
Industrial revolutions and modern times
An 'à la française' multinational, then nationalisation
A workshop goes industrial

1665–1789:

Louis XIV signed the letters patent establishing the *Manufacture des Glaces de Miroirs* in Paris in October 1665 — and founded another 25 such establishments that year.

Louis XIV's Chief Minister at the time was Jean-Baptiste Colbert. His underlying political and economic agenda involved undermining Venice's supremacy in Europe's glassmaking industry. He accordingly granted this manufacturer a number of tax breaks and advantages (including a temporary but renewable monopoly) to help it keep pace with the demand for mirrors in homes and royal buildings. The workshop nevertheless received an impressive and symbolic order in 1684: 357 mirrors for the Hall of Mirrors in the Palace of Versailles.

1789–1856:

The French revolution signalled the end of the legal monopoly, brought the days of privilege to an end, and forced the manufacturer to adjust its business model — and culture. Privileges were abolished and business competition was introduced. English and newer Belgian rivals took over half the European glass market when glassware casting technology became commonplace, and the legal and technical monopoly vanished. The company, however, reacted.

1856–1970:

Buoyant markets, international expansion and market diversification kept Saint-Gobain on an upward trend for three-quarters of a century.

The glass industry blossomed during the second half of the 19th century. Worldwide production grew practically 9% a year from 1850 to 1870, and Saint-Gobain started honing its strategy to stay on the move and thereby fend off foreign competition. It merged with its main domestic rival, Saint-Quirin, in 1858.

1970–1986:

The 1960s and 1970s brought deep-reaching changes across French society — and predictably sent ripples through a number of business sectors. Big industrial firms were trying to find the critical mass they needed to survive in the new 'economic world war'.

A political development promptly shelved those plans: a left-wing coalition won France's 1981 presidential election and the group was nationalised in 1982.

In 1986 it regained its freedom and took stock of the lessons it had learned over the previous decade.

1986 to the present day:
Back to the future, or 20+ years evolving non-stop

The 1986 privatisation initiated a careful reshuffle. The business portfolio it shaped as a result largely foreshadowed the group's profile today. It rolled out its transformation in two main stages (one each decade).

Saint-Gobain spent the bulk of the first decade striving to restore sustainable and profitable growth, and to establish worldwide leadership across its business lines. Then it redirected its strategy towards high-tech materials.

In those 20 years, from 1986 to 2006, Saint-Gobain saw its sales multiplied by 350%. New business acquisitions accounted for 54% of that growth.

It has recently refocused its strategy on the habitat and construction markets and set out to:

- build the homes of the future
- step up development in emerging countries
- further its operational excellence.

About 77% of Saint-Gobain's €40 billion in sales last year came from business lines associated with the housing and construction markets. The Group is active in 64 countries. It is still on the move today, and pushing ahead on three fronts — expanding in emerging countries, consolidating certain business lines with acquisitions, and stepping up its investment in R&D.

Reading 2: Sharing information about Saint-Gobain

Work in pairs.

Student A: Read the history of Saint-Gobain from 1665 to 1970. Why were the following important in the history of Saint-Gobain? Tell Student B about the people and events in your own words.

| Jean-Baptiste Colbert | the French Revolution | Saint-Quirin |

Student B: Read the history of Saint-Gobain from 1970 to the present day. Why were the following important in the history of Saint-Gobain? Tell Student A what happened in these years in your own words.

| 1982 | 1986 | 2006 |

Language focus 1: Adjective and adjective + noun combinations

Match the adjectives with the nouns below, following this pattern: *adjective and adjective + noun*.

Example: *legal and technical monopoly*

Adjectives: legal sustainable economic political impressive technical profitable symbolic

Nouns: order agenda monopoly growth

Quickly scan through the text to find the phrases and check your answers.

Critical analysis

Do you believe that the government should protect certain industries? Why/Why not? What about state monopolies? Do you think that they are a good or bad thing?

1 Match these sentences from the text with the tenses below.

Big industrial firms ¹**were trying** to find the critical mass they ²**needed**.

It ³**has** recently **refocused** its strategy.

It ⁴**took** stock of the lessons it ⁵**had learned** over the previous decade.

- past simple
- past continuous
- present perfect
- past perfect

2 Match the tenses above with their definitions.

1 The _____ is used to talk about single events, habitual events or states that happened at a definite time in the past.

2 The _____ is used to talk about events taking place in the past that connect with the present.

3 The _____ is used to talk about a timeframe leading up to a point in the past.

4 The _____ is used to talk about events in progress around a particular time in the past. It may refer to past time events occurring as a background to other events which interrupt them.

3 Certain time words and expressions tend to go with particular tenses. Match the following with the tenses (some are used with more than one tense).

in my life   last week   when it happened   this is the first time
for one year   recently   already   yesterday
one hundred years ago   this century   in the 1980s

4 Complete the sentences using the correct tense of the verb in brackets.

1 At the time she _____ part-time in a shop to save money to go travelling (work).

2 Mark Walker _____ Amazon.co.uk in May last year (join). Before that he _____ first as a retail bookseller and then as an editor on *Gramophone* magazine (work).

3 I _____ for B&Q as a graduate management trainee in 2008 and 2009 (work). Since then, I _____ on some smaller projects (work).

4 I was at the Doncaster office recently. I thought what they _____ looked marvellous (do). The finished project looked fantastic.

5 In pairs, use the time expressions in exercise 3 to ask questions and tell each other about your own past.

Stage 1

Work in pairs. You work for a company in the clothes industry (or an industry of your choice), and you are going to make a short introductory presentation about your company to a potential foreign distributor (choose the location). Look at the list of questions you need to think about for your presentation.

Questions to consider:
- When did your company start?
- What were some of the important developments in your company's past?
- What market does your company target (women, young people, etc.)?
- Have you changed target markets during your history?
- What age groups, gender and demographics (e.g. income group) do you target?
- Why did you decide to enter this foreign market?
- What problems have you had with other distributors before?
- What do you expect from this distributor?
- What support can you offer this distributor?
- Why is your company interesting?

Stage 2

Form groups of six people (three pairs). Each pair makes its presentation to the others, who are the distributors. After all the presentations, all six people vote for the best presentation, but each pair is not allowed to vote for itself.

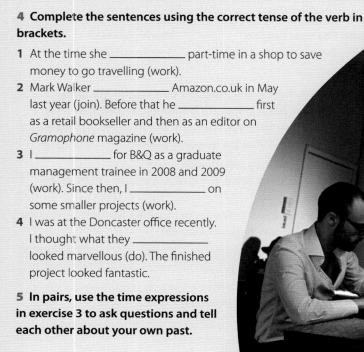

Learning outcomes

- Develop relationships with other companies.
- Create a good impression in informal business situations.
- Learn strategies for small talk.

Introduction

Business view

Peter Drucker, 'the founding father of management studies' said:

> ❝ More business decisions occur over lunch and dinner than at any other time, yet no MBA courses are given on the subject. ❞

1 Do you agree that building cooperative relationships can give you and your company a competitive edge? Why/Why not?

2 When meeting people for the first time in business, what conversation topics are suitable? Make a list. Move around the classroom and try to have as many short conversations with your classmates as you can in three minutes. Finish the conversation by saying 'Well, it's been nice talking to you, but I have to … '.

3 Which of the conversation starters below would be suitable in an informal international business situation in your culture? What would you think about the speaker if they opened the conversation with any of these sentences?

- Did you know I went to the best university in my country?
- Hi. We're really excited about our new venture together.
- I really hate my boss. Have you met her?
- My husband is out of work at the moment.
- Have you tried the local food? It's very good.

Listening 1: Pre-meeting small talk

1.05

You will hear the beginning of a logistics planning meeting between two large pharmaceutical companies. The participants are:

LHN Pharmaceuticals	**Worldpharma**
Manufacturing director (Brian)	Supply manager (Helga)
Finance manager (Eldric)	Supply manager (Gisella)

Brian is from the UK and the other participants are from Germany. The participants are working together to develop a new production facility in Germany. Listen to the recording and then answer the following questions.

1 What topic do they talk about?

2 Why do you think Brian, the director, asks so much about the meal?

3 Does this communication seem more like a business meeting or a conversation between friends?

Critical analysis

In meetings between different companies, people often 'chat' at the beginning and end of meetings.

- Why do people tend to talk about non-business related topics at these stages of meetings?
- Why could it be a problem for your business if you don't join in with these discussions?
- Would this be the same in your first language?

Language focus 1: Making your feelings understood

 1.06

It's not just the things we say but the way we say them that is important. When talking socially it is important to sound interested and friendly, so the way you speak can be very important.

1 Listen to a speaker say *The hotel was fine* five times, all with different meanings. Match the recording with the choices below.

a a worried question about the hotel	_____
b the speaker is amused	_____
c the speaker is bored	_____
d the speaker is angry	_____
e the speaker is relieved	_____

2 In pairs, take turns to ask *How was the flight?* and to reply *It was OK*. When answering the question, use one of the emotions above.

3 The way we say things can also show what is important information and what is not. In the above example, is the word 'flight' emphasised?

4 Listen to the answer: *Well, the flight was OK, but the hotel was terrible.* Which words are stressed and why?

 1.07

5 Now practise doing the same with these answers, giving feedback to your partner.

- Well, the food was OK, but the service was terrible.
- The flight was OK, but the taxi from the airport wasn't.

Language focus 2: Sounding friendly in informal situations

Sometimes we leave words out of a sentence because the meaning can be understood from the situation. This is much more usual in informal situations.

1 Which of the sentences below have some words missing? What are the missing words?

1 Nice place?
2 I haven't been there.
3 Little bit jealous, actually.
4 I had a bowl of cereal.

2 Make these responses shorter and friendlier by taking words out.

1 I've just been to the café.
2 Have you read the report?
3 Can I have a glass of water, please?

3 Missing out words like this is known as *ellipsis*. It makes the communication more direct and informal. Would it be appropriate to use ellipsis with your boss? What about with a very important, powerful client?

Listening 2: Judging emotions

1.05

Listen to the recording of the meeting again and answer these questions.

1 What do you notice about Brian (the first speaker)? Does he seem: friendly? aggressive? bored? interested?

2 Does Brian often use ellipsis? Look at the audio script on pages 147–8 and underline all the examples of ellipsis. Does this make him seem friendly?

3 When using ellipsis, why is intonation especially important? Think about the grammar.

4 How successful does this conversation seem as small talk?

Output: Developing the relationship

Work in groups of four, with two hosts and two visitors.

Stage 1: Hosts
You work for a company that supplies materials to manufacturers, and you are going to have a meeting with a new client. You want to develop a good relationship with the client. Make a list of ways you can develop the relationship and also list some topics that you can discuss at the beginning of the meeting. Discuss with your partner the type of impression you want to create, and how you can do it. Try to use some of the strategies from the lesson.

Stage 1: Visitors
You are going to have a first meeting with your new supplier. You are keen to develop a good relationship with the supplier, and you want to make sure you can trust them. Your previous supplier proved very untrustworthy, and you do not want to make the same mistake again! Discuss with your partner what questions and topics you can talk about with the supplier before you begin the first meeting.

Stage 2
The hosts should welcome the visitors, and start the meeting.

Stage 3
When you have finished, discuss these questions in your groups:

- How well did you help to build a relationship?
- Do you have any advice about what the group could do better?
- What would you do differently next time?

2 Future uncertainty

2.1 Theory: STEEP analysis

Learning outcomes
- Understand how business deals with future uncertainty.
- Learn language of future certainty and uncertainty.
- Prepare a macro-environmental STEEP analysis.

Introduction

66 Nothing can be certain except death and taxes. 99

Benjamin Franklin, scientist and one of the founding fathers of the USA

1 Are you optimistic or pessimistic about the future of your country? Give some examples.

2 Imagine that the following changes happen in your country over the next five to ten years. Which of them might affect your future career or your company the most? Explain why.

1 A law is passed to reduce the average working week to 30 hours.
2 Friends see each other far less, online friendship is the norm.
3 Immigration increases dramatically.
4 Bank interest rates go down 50 percent.
5 The price of oil rises 100 percent.
6 Your government refuses to sign international agreements to limit carbon emissions.
7 The cost of using internet-enabled mobile phones falls to almost nothing.
8 Clouds of volcanic dust regularly stop all air travel.
9 Your country joins/leaves an international trading bloc (EU, ASEAN, NAFTA, etc.).
10 Higher broadband speeds lead to a big increase in online distance-learning courses.

3 How much do you think individuals and companies are able to control their own future?

Reading: STEEP analysis

A STEEP analysis is a commonly used tool in business that companies and organisations use to make sense of their wider macro-environment. The theory is widely taught in business schools.

1 Read the first part of a text on STEEP analysis from learn marketing.net on page 19, and find words which have the same meaning as these:

1 influence (*verb*) _____
2 buy _____
3 very large _____
4 natural foods grown without chemicals _____
5 on the other hand _____
6 insufficient supplies _____
7 thinking again _____

2 Answer the following questions according to the text.

1 Why are people joining health clubs and buying organic food?
2 What factor will lead to increased competition?
3 What are the two results of a rising world population?

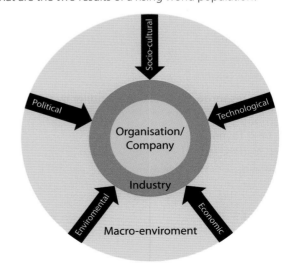

A STEEP analysis is used to identify the external forces affecting how individual companies compete within their industry sector. These external forces within the wider macro-environment consist of Socio-cultural, Technological,
5 Economic, Environmental and Political factors.

Socio-cultural

This aspect focuses its attention on forces within society such as family, friends, colleagues, neighbours and the media. Social forces affect our attitudes, interests and
10 opinions. These forces shape who we are as people, the way we behave and ultimately what we purchase. For example, in many countries in the world, people's attitudes are changing towards their diet and health. As a result, these countries are seeing an increase in the number of people joining fitness
15 clubs and a massive growth in the demand for organic food.

Population changes also have a direct impact on organisations. Changes in the structure of a population will affect the supply and demand of goods and services within an economy. Falling birth rates will result in decreased demand
20 and greater competition as the number of consumers fall in developed countries. Conversely, an increase in the global population is currently leading to calls for greater investment in food production. Due to food shortages African countries, such as Uganda, are now reconsidering their rejection of
25 genetically modified foods.

3 Work in groups of four.

- Student A will read about technological factors – see page 137.
- Student B will read about economic factors – see page 142.
- Student C will read about environmental factors – see page 145.
- Student D will read about political factors – see page 146.

After reading the text carefully, close your books and tell each other about what you have read.

4 As a group, categorise the changes in exercise 2 of the Introduction into the relevant STEEP factor.

Example: 1 Political

Listening 1: STEEP factors

 1.08

Business view

Dr Hans-Martin Beyer is Professor and Associate Dean at ESB Business School Reutlingen University, Germany and former project manager for New Business Development at the Ford Motor Corporation (Europe).

1 Listen to Dr Hans-Martin Beyer describe five long-term trends in the macro-environment that he believes will have an impact on business in the future. Write the STEEP factors 1–5 in the table below in the order you hear them.

	STEEP factor	Notes
1		
2		
3		
4		
5		

2 Listen again and note down some of the details mentioned for each of these factors.

3 How might some of these factors impact directly or indirectly on an industry such as the global automotive or computer industry? Are they opportunities or threats for the industry?

4 What other trends do you think will be important for these two industries? Will they present new opportunities or be a threat?

Listening 2: How industries plan for the future

 1.09

Listen to the second part of the interview with Dr Hans-Martin Beyer, in which he talks about how industries plan for the future. Answer the following questions.

1 How long does it take to develop a new car?
2 What do manufacturers of 'complex products' need to do?
3 In what way was Bill Gates right about the future?
4 How does Apple manage to get the future right?
5 In what way have some automotive companies 'not made the right decisions' about the future?
6 Where are the decisions made 'at the end of the day'?
7 How important are the methods used by companies to forecast the future?

Critical analysis

1 Do you think Apple and Microsoft are still 'getting it right' about the future? Why/Why not?
2 Which car manufacturers do you think are 'getting it right'? Which ones aren't? Why?

Language focus: Future certainty and uncertainty

1 Look at the following sentences from Listening 1 and place them on the scale below.

1 I think people will be more mobile …
2 We will need to look to Asia …
3 We may even see Russia join the EU …
4 It'll probably be the dominating subject …

Uncertain ◄───────────────────► Certain

1.10

2 Listen to the following pairs of predictions from meetings. Which prediction in each pair (A or B) seems the most certain? Why? Think about the words and the intonation.

1 A I guess they may come back to me.
   B We may subcontract that to a partner.
2 A Noel will stop on Thursday as well, won't he?
   B Things will change.
3 A We will definitely sign the contract.
   B We might well find a solution during the meeting.
4 A You're going to need a firewall.
   B I suppose it's how many you think you might need in Ireland.

1.11

3 Listen to 1B again. This time the intonation is very different. Which word is stressed in the less certain version? Practise saying this.

4 Look at the predictions in exercise 2 and underline the verbs that are used to talk about the future.

5 Put the following words and phrases in the table below:

| could   looks probable that   is highly unlikely that   must |

possible	probable	certain

Now add the words you underlined in exercise 2 in the table above.

6 Which of the following companies and industries might benefit or lose the most, if the changes in the Introduction came true? Explain why.

Example: *Leisure industries such as cinemas and theatres might well benefit from a shorter working week as people would have more leisure time.*

- leisure industries, e.g. cinemas and theatres
- companies with high debts
- tourism
- publishers of educational textbooks
- pizza home-delivery companies
- online advertising industry
- global car manufacturers
- e-marketing consultancies

Output: Conduct an industry sector STEEP analysis

You are going to conduct a brief STEEP analysis of different segments of the automotive industry and then report your findings to another group.

Stage 1
In small groups, think about the following types of car which represent market segments. Future sales of these cars will depend on STEEP factors.

luxury cars
sports cars
family cars
small city cars
low-priced budget cars
SUVs
people carriers
electric cars
hybrid cars

Example: *A rising middle class in emerging economies, especially in Asia, will really push the demand for budget cars as people sell their motorcycles and trade up to their first car.*

Think about the situation in your country and then globally over the next five to ten years. Discuss the questions below in your group and make notes.

- Which segment do you think will grow fastest/slowest?
- Do you predict that sales might decline for certain segments? Why/Why not?
- Which STEEP factors are pushing sales up or down?
- How are they doing this?

Stage 2
Present your findings to another group and discuss together how these changes might affect competition within the industry both globally and in your own countries.

2.2 Practice: Global consumer goods industry

Learning outcomes
- Understand the scope and future trends of the consumer goods industry.
- Use speed-reading techniques.
- Present the launch of a consumer product in a new country market.

Profile: The global consumer goods industry

The global consumer goods industry is a huge industry consisting of manufacturers and retailers of different industry sectors covering a vast range of products from milk to washing machines. The biggest of these sectors is FMCG (Fast Moving Consumer Goods) which itself takes in massive sectors, such as food and drink, homecare, and health and beauty. These products are generally of low value and sold on a daily basis, very quickly in large quantities. A large number of sales of these products in many countries in the world are made through large supermarket chains.

ी, पनीर आणि चीज

Introduction

1 Do you tend to shop in small shops or supermarkets? What are the advantages and disadvantages of both?

2 What changes have happened during your lifetime in the way people shop for food?

3 Products such as mobile phones and washing machines are also now sold in large supermarkets in many countries in the world. In the past, these types of product were considered 'consumer durables', which customers kept for a long time and were not available in supermarkets. Why do you think this has now changed?

1 Look at the table and match the companies to the industry sectors and sub-sectors they are most associated with.

Example: Tesco, Walmart, Carrefour, Metro → 4 supermarket retail → f most (or all) of the above product sectors

Multinational companies	Industry sector	Sub-sector
Procter & Gamble	1 food and drink	a kitchen care, laundry care, bathroom care
Tesco, Walmart, Carrefour, Metro	2 consumer electronics	b hair care, skin care, cosmetics, dental care, fragrance
Johnson & Johnson	3 home care	c small electrical appliances, small kitchen appliances, large kitchen appliances
Sony, Samsung, LG, Philips	4 supermarket retail	d mobile phones, computing, TV and audio
Nestlé, Kraft	5 health and beauty / personal care	e bakery, frozen, dairy, confectionery
Whirlpool, Bosch, Electrolux	6 home electrical	f most (or all) of the above product sectors

2 Brainstorm examples of as many products as possible for these sub-sectors within a time limit of 3 minutes. Try to identify at least two products per sub-sector.

3 In which countries do the companies in the table have their headquarters? Have you ever used any of their products? Which ones?

Transferable skill: Speed-reading

Speed-reading enables you to increase your speed and improve your comprehension. Read through the four phases of this process and answer the questions about the text which follows. Compare your answers with a partner after each phase.

Phase 1: Text orientation and prediction (time limit – 2 minutes)
1 Check the source of the article → How will this affect how the text is written and will it favour a particular point of view?

2 Read the title carefully → What do you think this text will be about?

3 Read the first paragraph carefully. It often contains the key to the organisation of the text → How will the text be structured?

Phase 2: Skim-reading (time limit – 3 minutes)
1 Read the text quickly (don't read every word) → Were the predictions that you made in phase 1 correct or not?

2 Build a 'map of the text' by skim-reading it again to understand better the structure of the text so you know where blocks of information are located. How many blocks (or sections) does the text contain?

3 Put the following section titles in the text to divide it correctly into four sections.
a A rise in incomes and consumption
b Urbanisation
c Serving the needs of low-income consumers
d The ageing population

After this phase you should have a reasonably good *general* understanding of what the text is about.

Phase 3: Scan-reading (time limit – 2 minutes)
Scan a section of the text looking for *specific* information to answer a question. We are *not* concerned at this stage with what the answer is, we want to know *where* it is.

Without looking at the text, read the following questions. What section will you find the answers in?

1 What kind of flavours will older people be demanding from food producers?
2 What partners does the global consumer goods industry need to work with to reach the poorest people in Asia?
3 How many people will migrate to the cities over the next few decades in Asia?
4 What has been the result of higher incomes in India?

Phase 4: Detailed reading (time limit – 3 minutes)
Finally, read only the section of the text you identified in phase 3 to answer the questions (1–4) above.

1 Urbanisation and a growing elderly population are clear global trends. These two demographic swings are also apparent across most Asian countries, along with the polarisation between the new middle class and the poor.

2 Projections indicate that more than 500,000,000 Asians will move to cities in the next 25 years – almost 2,000,000 people per month. This movement is placing a huge strain on already inadequate transport, electricity, water and sanitation systems.

3 Improved health care is resulting in the elderly living longer. The increase in the elderly population is particularly significant in Japan, where more than 20% of the population is over 65.

4 In Japan, unlike many other markets including much of the West, Japanese pensioners have economic security and considerable buying power. They also command a great deal of respect from society.

5 This growing demographic group presents unique physical and emotional needs and requires different product design, packaging, marketing and retail distribution. Over the next ten years this group will trigger a surge in products that focus on the elderly, from preserving health and wellness to spicier foods to stimulate aged palates. But these Japanese senior citizens of the future will also be spending money on their grand- and great-grandchildren, creating a market for premium children's products.

6 In most Asian countries, average household incomes are increasing significantly. This is particularly so in cities: urban households in China have over three times more disposable income than rural households, according to the National Bureau of Statistics of China.

7 India, in particular, has experienced dramatic income growth for a large segment of the population in the last two decades. This prosperity has revolutionised consumer aspirations.

8 At the same time as average income is rising, there is still a vast segment of Asian households that live on very low incomes, particularly in India but also in rural China too. This income disparity has implications for the grocery industry, which needs to rise to the challenge of serving the needs of low-income consumers. To deliver this, our industry will need to work together and with governments and communities to develop innovative products and services.

Source: GCI (Global Commerce Initiative), Global Consumer Goods Industry Association Industry Report (Spotlight on Asia)

In what other ways do you think that urbanisation, a rising middle class, continuing poverty and ageing population could impact on the consumer goods industry in Asia?

You are going to launch new consumer products on the Japanese market. Your target market is the over-50s. Read the information below. Work in four groups, and look at page 137.

Target market

You are launching a new product on the Japanese market. Your target market is the over-50s, who are increasing in number and who have a high amount of disposable income. Before you market your product, look at the following factors which are all of importance to the target group.

- Raw materials in Japan are scarce. The main agricultural products are rice, vegetables, fruit, dairy products, eggs and fish.
- Increased worries about the environment, global warming and product safety are prime concerns.
- Known as 'silver surfers', the vast majority of the over-50s have access to the Internet.

Task

You should design a 3-minute pitch that you will then give to the other groups.

When you have heard all the presentations, choose which product you will invest in. You cannot choose your own product.

2.3 Skills: Presenting a case at a meeting

Learning outcomes
- Present the benefits and stages of a future change.
- Use discourse markers to organise and clarify your arguments.
- Analyse differences in presentation styles across cultures.

Introduction

1 What are the main differences between a meeting and a presentation?

2 Have you ever had to give a formal presentation in class or at work? How did you feel?

3 Would you prefer to give a formal presentation or lead a Q&A (question and answer) session where you have to provide the answers?

4 Complete the table below comparing formal presentations and Q&A sessions in meetings. The first has been done for you.

	Formal presentation	Q&A session
Turn-taking	Not usually	Yes
Spontaneous speech		
Communication is one-way		
Questions and answers		
Rhetorical questions (asked for effect, not for an answer)		
Active listening (responses, e.g. *yes, uh-huh*)		
Immediate responses		

5 Which requires more preparation, a presentation or a Q&A session? Can you prepare for a Q&A session?

6 Choose one of the following:
- Your company has launched a new product, e.g. food, clothing, media. Think of what the product might be. It is not selling well and your boss wants to know why. Think of a course of action, and present it.
- Think about how you could market a product that sells well in your domestic market to an international audience. Think of ways of making this product popular abroad, and present it.

Listening 1: Upgrading the operating system

🎧 1.12

When making a presentation at a meeting, the speaker usually presents the case first, and a discussion or Q&A session then follows. You are going to listen to a presentation at the Tokyo office of a multinational bank's IT department. The presenter, Alison, is describing the upgrading of a new operating system.

1 Before you listen, think of two reasons why installing an up-to-date operating system (OS) is important for a company.

2 The presentation has the following stages. Put them into a logical order. Then listen to the presentation and see if you were correct.

A Giving background information
B Outlining the problem and the risk
C Outlining how the solution will be achieved in practice
D Starting the presentation
E Stating the proposed change

Intercultural analysis: Presentation styles

Presentation styles are different in different cultures. For example, in the USA the main point of the presentation is usually made at the start. In some countries, like Japan, people often give the background and state the main point near the end. The presentation at the meeting you have listened to is from an American bank in Japan.

Which style do you think is preferred in the workplace in the Listening? Which style do you prefer? What are the advantages and disadvantages of each?

Language focus: Discourse markers

Discourse markers link segments of talk to one another and show how speakers organise, manage and feel about the information. They do not contain information. Common markers include: *So, I mean, right, on the other hand, it's time to, then*. A presentation that contains many discourse markers is easier to follow.

1 Here are some sentences from the presentation you heard in Listening 1. Underline the discourse markers.

1 OK, we may as well start.
2 So, our Windows operating system. We've been using our present OS in Japan for at least four years and it's time to upgrade.
3 It's more a question of what will happen if we don't upgrade … Obviously, this creates a business risk for us because … The longer we wait, the greater this risk becomes.
4 So, how do we start? Well, I've already done this.
5 So, just to give you a bit of background. Mainstream support for the present system expired …

2 Match the sentences with the five stages in Listening 1 exercise 2.

Listening 2: Q&A session

1.13

Following the presentation, there is a Q&A session. One person in the audience, Nigel, asks about the global implementation of the new operating system (OS). He wants to know if any departments have implemented this system in all of their worldwide offices. Listen to the recording.

1 What answer does the presenter give to the question?

2 The answer given by the speaker is not very clear. What are some possible reasons for this?

3 When answering questions, the following format is useful:
Showing you will rephrase, e.g. *So you mean …*
Rephrasing, e.g. *You want to know …*
Checking the response is sufficient, e.g. *Does that answer your question?*

Listen again and see if the speaker follows this format.

4 Practise this format in pairs by asking each other a question.

Output: Presenting a case

Stage 1

Look back at Listening 1 and the five stages in a presentation. Work in pairs. Prepare a 3-minute presentation on one of these topics:

- The problem of motivating lazy workers/students
- The introduction of new working hours at your workplace / place of study

Use the five stages to put your presentation in a logical order, and make sure you use discourse markers to organise your presentation. Remember to note some key language from the audio script (page 149). Make your solutions as imaginative as you like. Then try to predict two or three questions that you might be asked in a Q&A session. Practise answering them following the steps in Listening 2.

Stage 2

Make your presentation to another pair, and encourage questions afterwards. Listen to the other pair's presentation, and ask some follow-up questions.

▶◀ **Watch Sequence 1 on the DVD to find out more about Business environment.**

Writing 1: Preparing presentation slides

Learning outcomes

- Summarise information into concise bullet points.
- Discuss dos and don'ts of slide-writing techniques.
- Create presentation slides with strong visual impact.

Slide 1

Introduction

Business view

❝ A picture tells a thousand words. **❞**

Fred R. Barnard, advertising executive

1 Do you agree with the quote? Why/Why not?

2 Look at some other units in the book. Can you find two images which you think work very well with the unit title? Why do you think the images you have found are suitable for the unit title?

3 Can you think of any presentations or lectures that you have been to where the slides were particularly good or bad? In what way were they good or bad?

Writing skill: Creating a strong visual impact

The following slides are taken from a 10-slide presentation by the management consultancy company, Capgemini, with the title 'Eight trends and the industry opportunities for the global consumer goods industry'. Supermarket chains and food and drink producers form a large part of this industry.

1 Look at the four images in slide 1 above. What do you think the presenter will talk about when this slide is on the screen?

2 Match the following headings to the four images on slide 1 and label them. The headings are examples of micro-bullet points.

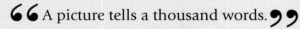

Low income   Urbanisation   Ageing population
New middle class

3 Do you like the style of slide 1 or would you prefer to see more information included on the slide?

4 Which of the four bullet points on slide 2 below does the cartoon refer to?

Rising cost (and scarcity) of raw material

- Continuing rise in cost of energy and raw material
- Population spikes put pressure on water and food supplies
- Increasingly volatile climate, affecting production and the supply chain
- Effects of political instability

50 AIN'T ENOUGH – OIL PRICES WENT UP SINCE YESTERDAY!

4 DROPS OF PETROL, PLEASE ...

GOLD LABEL

Slide 2

5 How could you change the four standard bullet points on slide 2 into four strong visual images?

Intercultural analysis

Discuss the following questions.

- Are you surprised to see humour used in a serious presentation as on slide 2?
- How useful do you think the humour is in communicating the information on the slide?
- How acceptable would it be to use humour in a presentation in your organisation or country?
- Would you personally use humour in a presentation?

The two slides in the Writing skill section show two techniques for presenting information.

Slide 1: Writing high-impact **micro-bullet points** (maximum three words)

Slide 2: Writing in **standard bullet points** (NOT in full sentences)

1 Change the four standard bullet points in slide 2 into four micro-bullet points (three words maximum each).

2 Complete the sentences below to change the four standard bullet points from slide 2 into full sentences.

1 There _____ (be) a continuing rise in _____ cost of energy and raw material.
2 Population spikes _____ (put) pressure on water and food supplies.
3 _____ increasingly volatile climate _____ (affect) production and the supply chain.
4 Rising costs _____ (lead) to political instability. What will be the effects of that instability on the _____ _____ industry?

3 The trends below are full sentence descriptions of the four micro-bullets in slide 1. Change them into four standard bullet points.

1 Rapid urbanisation across the developing world is expected to increase even faster.
2 There will still be a very large segment of the world's population living on very low incomes.
3 Ageing populations are going to create challenges as well as opportunities.
4 There will be a big increase in the number of middle-class consumers, particularly in Asia.

4 The headings of slides are often written as statements, although they often pose a question. Change the micro-bullet points for slide 1 into full sentence questions.

Critical analysis

1 There are some presentation slide guidelines at the back of the book. Student A should read about how **not** to write presentation slides on pages 137–8, while Student B should read about how to write them on pages 142–3.
2 Look at two pairs of slides (slides 3A and 3B, 4A and 4B) and decide which slide in each pair you prefer. Explain your reasons to your partner with reference to the guidelines you have just read.

Slide 3A

Slide 3B

Slide 4A

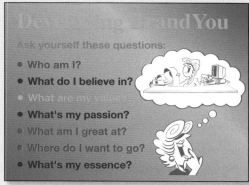

Slide 4B

Output: Designing effective presentation slides

In pairs, sketch out two slides in the same format as slides 1 and 2 on page 26 on the topic 'The future'. Decide whether to take a personal, company, industry or global focus. After finishing your slides, present the information to another pair.

3 Rewarding performance

3.1 Theory: Employee reward strategies

Learning outcomes
- Learn about the pros and cons of different types of reward system.
- Learn word partnerships with *incentive* and *pay*.
- Construct an appropriate reward package for your boss or teacher.

Introduction

1 John Wesley Hardin was a dangerous Texas gunfighter in the 19th century who killed over 30 people. Why do you think the authorities had to pay a reward to capture him? What would have happened if they had increased or decreased the reward they were offering?

2 The word **reward** can be used as a compound noun and as a verb in relation to executive pay, as in the statements below. Read the statements and decide to what extent you agree with them. Circle the number that reflects your opinion.

1 = strongly agree   7 = strongly disagree

1	Rewarding people with a higher salary is the best way of motivating them.	1	2	3	4	5	6	7
2	Most senior executive reward packages are far too generous.	1	2	3	4	5	6	7
3	Managers should be rewarded for their performance at work.	1	2	3	4	5	6	7
4	It's impossible to create a reward system that truly aligns managers' pay to their company's success.	1	2	3	4	5	6	7

Compare your answers in pairs and give reasons for your opinions.

3 What are the similarities and differences between a bounty hunter in the 19th century who got paid a reward to capture a wanted man and how senior business executives are rewarded today?

4 The nouns in the table below are all synonyms to describe earnings, but they have slightly different meanings. Match each word to its definition.

1 pay	**a** a technical word often seen in recruitment adverts for senior positions
2 reward	**b** a generic word to describe workers' earnings
3 salary	**c** used generally but also specifically to describe office workers' earnings, usually paid monthly by bank transfer
4 wage	**d** used generally but also specifically to describe company earnings
5 remuneration	**e** a semi-technical word emphasising payment linked to performance
6 income	**f** used generally but also specifically to describe factory workers' earnings, traditionally paid weekly in cash

Listening 1: The role and function of pay

Business view

Professor Stan Siebert, Professor of Labour Economics at the University of Birmingham Business School, is a specialist in the study of company reward strategies.

🔊 **1.14**

Listen to the first part of the interview with Professor Stan Siebert and answer the following questions.

1 What are the two main functions of pay?
2 What are the two main types of reward system?
3 What are the different ways you can pay a company chief executive, an apple picker and a coal miner?

Listening 2: Advantages and disadvantages of different reward systems

🔊 **1.15**

1 Listen to the second part of the interview and complete the gaps in the table. Use no more than three words in each gap.

	Disadvantages
Payment by time	1 There is a cost in terms of _____ .
Payment by output	2 You need to find a _____ that is in the best interests of the company.
	Advantages
Payment by time	3 It is _____ .
Payment by output	4 People put in _____ .

2 Listen again and answer the following questions.

1 What are some of the risks of paying chief executives according to share prices?
2 What reward system is used to calculate Professor Stan Siebert's pay?

Listening 3: Fair pay and motivation

🔊 **1.16**

Listen to the final part of the interview. Answer the following questions by choosing the best answer (A–C).

1 What does Professor Stan Siebert say about the Theory X and Theory Y view of people?
   A Theory X views people as mainly motivated by money.
   B Theory Y views people as mainly motivated by money.
   C Theory X and Y are confusing.
2 According to Professor Stan Siebert, how big a factor is pay in motivating people?
   A It's probably an enormous factor.
   B It's probably a small factor.
   C It's probably a changeable factor.
3 What is Professor Stan Siebert's view on fair pay?
   A People are right to be worried about fair pay.
   B The idea of fair pay is in both companies' and workers' interests.
   C He is not very concerned about fair pay.
4 What does Professor Stan Siebert say about his own salary?
   A It wasn't enough 30 years ago.
   B It's not enough now.
   C It's appropriate.

Critical analysis

1 How important do you think fair pay is in general? What about groups of workers, notably women, who are consistently paid less than their male counterparts?
2 Professor Stan Siebert mentioned how apple pickers and chief executives can twist incentives for their own personal benefit. How can the owner of the apple farm or the directors of companies stop this happening? Are there alternative reward systems that can produce better results for the farmer or the shareholders?

Language focus: Word partnerships with *incentive* and *pay*

1 Complete the gaps in the *Cambridge Advanced Learner's Dictionary* definitions of *incentive* and *pay*.

1 **incentive** /ɪnˈsentɪv/ *noun* something which _____ someone to do something
2 **incentivise** /ɪnˈsentɪvaɪz/ *verb* to _____ someone want to do something
3 **pay** /peɪ/ *verb* (paid, paid) – to give money to someone for _____ which they have done
4 **pay** /peɪ/ *noun* the money you receive for doing a _____

2 The words *pay* (uncountable noun) and *payment* (countable noun) can be confused. *Payment* refers to the amount of money paid for goods or services provided, while *pay* is a synonym for salary or wage. Complete the following sentences using *pay* or *payment(s)*.

1 It's an interesting job, but the _____ is really bad.
2 We need a deposit of £165 plus monthly _____ of £60.
3 Executive _____ is increasing at an alarming rate.
4 Usually we ask for _____ on receipt of the goods.

3 The following groups of words often collocate with *incentive*, *incentivise* and *pay*. Circle the word or phrase in each group that does not make a collocation with the target word.

1 provide a(n) / give a(n) / big / bright / financial / less / little / long-term / no / strong – **incentive**
2 **incentive** – bonus / plan / package / pay / programme / scheme / finance
3 difficult to / designed to / forecast to / the best way to / want to – **incentivise**
4 **incentivise** – investment in / management to / inflation to / staff to / sales force to
5 high / low / average / strong / basic / performance-related / annual / executive – **pay** *(noun)*
6 **pay** *(noun)* – rate / package / cut / terms / scale / rise

4 Complete the gaps using the correct collocation listed above.

1 Supermarkets have a big _____ incentive to sell ethnic food as Hispanic shoppers spend more per annum.
2 CEO W.J. Sanders earns an incentive _____ equal to 0.6% of operating profits.
3 Winsor complains that Network Rail is _____ incentivise due to the absence of shareholders.
4 The government finds it difficult to incentivise _____ renewable energy from private capital.
5 The company's policy on _____ pay for sales staff means they get paid by how much they sell.
6 He had to take a pay _____ when he decided to go part-time.

5 Write a list of points on the topic below. Each point should include a collocation from exercise 3.

Topic: What are the best ways to motivate people at work?
Example: Companies should incentivise staff to keep fit by offering to cover 50% of the cost of gym membership.

Compare your points with other students and agree on a shortlist of the best points.

In small groups, decide on an appropriate reward package for your boss or teacher.

Stage 1
In your discussions you should reach agreement on at least five outputs you are going to measure (e.g. how much homework he/she marks). Remember that he/she might find ways to use your incentive scheme to personal advantage (e.g. he/she might not mark the homework properly if there is a lot to mark). Make notes and complete the table below.

Output to be measured	Comments
1	
2	
3	
4	
5	

Stage 2
Discuss and agree on the individual weighting (percentage) for each of these five factors. For example, if your group thinks that each of the five weightings is equally important, then each factor will be weighted at 20%. Complete the table below.

Output to be measured	Weighting (%)	Reasons
1		
2		
3		
4		
5		

Stage 3
Decide what proportion of your boss or teacher's reward package should be linked to time spent working and how much to the total outputs of their work. Draw a pie chart to reflect your decision. For example, if your group thinks that three-quarters of the pay package should be linked to outputs, it will look similar to the one below.

Are there any other factors which you think should be included? If so, note them down and include them in your pie chart.

Stage 4
Present your plans to another group.

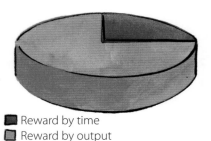

■ Reward by time
■ Reward by output

3.2 Practice: Performance-Related Pay (PRP) in practice

Learning outcomes
- Understand how and why PRP is used.
- Distinguish main ideas from supporting information.
- Learn how to form compound nouns.

Profile: Nokia Corporation

Nokia was formed in 1865 and started life as a paper mill. It took its name from the Nokianvirta river in Finland, on which the mill was situated. In 1960 it started its first electronics department after becoming one of the major players in the paper industry. In 1967 Nokia merged with Finnish Rubber Works and Finnish Cable to create Nokia Corporation. The new company began to concentrate on mobile communications. It is now one of the best-known and most successful manufacturers of mobile phones in the world.

Introduction

1 Which of the following motivates you the most in choosing a job: money, holidays, job security, job satisfaction, comfortable working conditions, a good social side to the job? How about motivating you to keep working? Are the factors the same?

2 Which of the following jobs do you think should use some form of performance-related pay (payment by results not just time): investment bankers, elementary school teachers, professional sports players, salespeople, cleaners, doctors, actors, others? Which of these jobs do you think should be the most highly paid? Why?

Language focus: Compound nouns

1 Match the following phrases with their meanings on the right.

1	compensation programme	a	the percentage of customers that stay loyal for the long term
2	stretch goals / stretch targets	b	cash generated from operating activities
3	comparison companies	c	system of payment and rewards for employees
4	annual base salary	d	company earnings before interest and taxes
5	short-term cash incentives	e	stock given to employees as rewards
6	increased shareholder value	f	better returns for shareholders / maximisation of share value
7	operating profit	g	strategic objectives that are extremely difficult to achieve
8	operating cash flow	h	bonuses to encourage better performance
9	equity-based awards	i	income generated from recently released products
10	new product revenue	j	yearly salary, excluding bonuses, pensions, etc.
11	customer-retention rates	k	competitors

2 The phrases on the left above are all compound nouns. Which of the patterns below do they follow? Do any of them not follow these patterns?

- adjective + noun
- noun + noun
- adjective + adjective or noun + noun

3 Do you think compound nouns are more common in spoken or written business English?

1 What would a company like Nokia hope to achieve by using PRP?

2 Read through the first part of Nokia's report on executive compensation. Why do you think Nokia considers each objective important? Which objective do you think is the most important?

> ### The objectives of Nokia's executive compensation programmes are to:
>
> - attract and retain outstanding executive talent;
> - deliver a significant amount of performance-related variable compensation for the achievement of both short- and long-term stretch goals;
> - appropriately balance rewards between both Nokia's and an individual's performance; and
> - align the interests of the executive officers with those of the shareholders through long-term incentives in the form of equity-based awards.

3 The personnel committee considers the factors below in its review when determining the compensation of Nokia's executives. Which of the following factors do you think the executives can directly control?

1 The compensation levels for similar positions in relevant comparison companies.
2 The performance demonstrated by the executive officer during the last year.
3 The size and impact of the role on Nokia's overall performance and strategic direction.
4 The internal comparison to the compensation levels of the other executive officers of Nokia.
5 Past experience and time in role.

4 Which of the above factors do you think is the most important for maintaining motivation within the company? Which are important for encouraging executives to stay with Nokia? Can you think of any other factors that should be considered?

1 Read through the next part of Nokia's report. Are the following statements true or false?

1 Shares are given as short-term incentives.
2 Cash incentives can be considerable amounts of money.
3 Financial objectives are based on goals that are easy to achieve.
4 The company's and individual's targets are assessed by the personnel committee.
5 The president and the CEO are responsible for entry into new markets.

> ### Components of executive compensation
>
> Our compensation programme for executive officers includes annual cash compensation in the form of a base salary, short-term cash incentives and long-term equity-based incentive awards in the form of stock options and shares.
>
> ### Annual cash compensation: short-term cash incentives
>
> Short-term cash incentives are tied directly to performance and represent a significant portion of an executive officer's total annual cash compensation. Measurement criteria for the short-term cash incentive plan include those financial objectives that are considered important measures of Nokia's success in driving increased shareholder value. Financial objectives are established which are based on a number of factors and are intended to be stretch targets that, when achieved, Nokia believes, will result in performance that will exceed that of Nokia's key competitors in the high technology, telecommunications and internet services industries.
>
> The incentive payout is based on performance relative to targets set for each measurement criterion listed: (a) a comparison of Nokia's actual performance to pre-established targets for net sales, operating profit and operating cash flow and (b) a comparison of each executive officer's individual performance to his/her pre-defined individual strategic objectives and targets. Individual strategic objectives include market share, quality, technology innovation, new product revenue, customer-retention rates, environmental achievements and other objectives of key strategic importance which require a discretionary assessment of performance by the personnel committee. In the case of the president and CEO, the annual incentive award is also partly based on his performance compared against strategic leadership objectives, including entry into new markets and services and executive development.
>
> Source: Nokia report on Corporate Governance

2 Discuss the following questions in small groups.

1 Do you think that people in similar positions in different organisations should receive approximately the same pay? Why/Why not?

2 Do you think people working for the same organisation in the same position in different countries should receive the same pay? Why/Why not?

3 What do you think about pay being linked to experience? Should pay be based more on merit, or experience, or time spent with the company?

Critical analysis

In some companies, the CEO may receive 20 times the pay of the average worker, or possibly much more. Do you think this is fair?

Transferable skill: Distinguishing main ideas from supporting information

1 We can separate main ideas from supporting information through our use of language. What is the main idea and what is the supporting information in the following sentence? What language helps to separate the ideas?

> Our compensation programme for executive officers includes annual cash compensation in the form of a base salary, short-term cash incentives and long-term equity-based incentive awards in the form of stock options and shares.

2 What are the main ideas of the texts in Reading 1 and Reading 2? Summarise the main points in less than 50 words.

Output: Boardroom PRP decisions

Work in small groups. You are the board of directors for a large telecommunications company, and you have to make decisions on the following situations.

Stage 1

You have to develop a new benefits package for your executives. Several of your executives have recently left the company and moved to your competitors. Traditionally, your company pays the average salary for the industry, with substantial equity-based awards. Up until now, only the CEO has received substantial bonuses. Make the reward package as detailed as possible.

Stage 2

Over the past six months your company has not entered any new markets or developed any new services. These key objectives are the responsibility of your (new) CEO. Decide what size bonus, if any, you will give him/her. The previous CEO was very strong in these areas, but left last year for one of your competitors.

Stage 3

Maria Rodriguez, the sales director for Asia and Africa, has worked for the company for five years longer than Geoff Mutton, the director of sales for Europe. Maria's first four years were successful, but last year she performed badly due to a cancelled contract in South Africa. Geoff has only worked for the company for one year and has increased sales due to a big contract in Italy. Decide who should receive a bigger bonus.

Stage 4

Compare your decisions with another group.

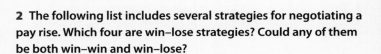

3.3 Skills: Negotiating a pay rise

Learning outcomes
- Negotiate a pay rise.
- Use vague language to negotiate.
- Learn and use strategies to negotiate.

Introduction

Business view

6 6 The purpose of business negotiations is to solve problems of conflicting interests. 9 9

Professor Anne Marie Bulow, Department of Culture and Communication, Copenhagen Business School

1 Which people are usually involved in pay negotiations in a company (e.g. during a performance review), and what are some of the possible 'problems' and 'conflicting interests'?

2 If you were a boss deciding on an employee's pay rise, what factors would you consider? With a partner, make a list of five factors (e.g. relations with colleagues) and put them in order of importance.

3 Find another pair with a different list of priorities, and negotiate with them to come to an agreement about the two or three most important factors.

Listening 1: Performance review

🎧 1.17

Listen to a performance appraisal between a trainee business adviser (Sophie) and her boss (Leroy) at a business consultancy company.

- Is Sophie, the trainee, for or against having PRP (Performance-Related Pay), and why?

Listening 2: Negotiating for more money

🎧 1.18

1 Negotiations are often described as win–win (where both the employee and the company can have a positive result), or win–lose (where one side takes a risk to get what they want). For example, threatening to leave the company unless your demands are met is a win–lose strategy. Which do you think is better for pay negotiations? A win–lose approach or a win–win approach?

2 The following list includes several strategies for negotiating a pay rise. Which four are win–lose strategies? Could any of them be both win–win and win–lose?

1 Threaten to leave the company.
2 Say you'd like to be considered for promotion in the future.
3 Say you've had to give up your second job.
4 Mention you've been offered another post somewhere else.
5 State the salary is insufficient for your needs.
6 Say that you're disappointed with previous pay rises.
7 Say that you're thinking about leaving the company.
8 Say that you're not considering leaving the company.
9 Say how much you love this job.
10 Say how challenging this job is.

3 Listen to the second part of the conversation between the trainee and the manager. Which strategies from the above list does Sophie, the trainee, use?

4 Do you think that this negotiation is more of a win–win or win–lose negotiation?

3 Vagueness can sometimes lead to misunderstanding, so if someone says something vague you should try to clarify the meaning. Match these clarifications with the sentences above.

a So you mean she may not like it?
b So by 'other things' you mean pay?
c By 'all that stuff' you mean the routes and weights?
d How sure of that are you?
e So you mean cities on or near the coast in China? How about Hangzhou?
f So you mean there's not a very good chance of it happening, is that right?

4 How can you make the following statements vaguer?

1 Your sales results are the lowest in the company.
2 I want a pay increase of 15%.
3 If I don't get a pay rise, I will definitely leave the company within the next month.
4 We will consider your pay situation in six months.

5 In pairs, practise saying the sentences above and asking clarifying questions.

6 Read through the audio script about negotiating for more money on pages 150–1, and find the following phrases. Are they are collaborative or competitive in style?

1 and all that kind of thing
2 probably more than double
3 I would be able to get a job as a business advisor
4 It's not a huge issue, but it may become one
5 allowances and everything else
6 and that kind of thing

Language focus: Vague language

1 Being deliberately vague can be very useful in a negotiation, both as a way of showing you share understanding (collaborative strategy), and as a bargaining technique (competitive strategy).

A *Showing shared knowledge (collaborative strategy)*
- You know, like having to be approachable and flexible and having to meet clients earlier in the morning or having to meet them after the working day or having to work through lunch **and all that kind of thing**.
- We talked about budgets and pricing **and things like that**.

B *Not showing your true position (competitive strategy)*
- We **might** be able to do it.
- It will **probably** cost **about** $40 a unit.

2 Are the following sentences examples of A or B?

1 I would have to consider other options.
2 Let's review the logistical implications and all that stuff.
3 I don't know how my boss will react to that.
4 I don't know exactly but I think it's about four thousand.
5 We're thinking about Beijing, Shanghai, and places like that.
6 I could do that if other things are good.

Output: Negotiating a pay rise

Work in pairs.

Stage 1
Do you think the following advice for somebody who is negotiating a pay rise is good or not?

- Ask your friends in different types of job about their salary.
- Find out the salary of people in jobs similar to yours.
- Think about your experience before you negotiate.
- Tell your boss how much cash you need.
- Tell your boss how much cash you deserve.

Stage 2
Student A: look at page 138 and read the instructions.
Student B: look at page 143 and read the instructions.

4 Fostering creativity

4.1 Theory: Creative thinking and creative management

Learning outcomes
- Understand principles and thinking behind creative management.
- Learn and use word formations connected to creativity.
- Take part in a creative problem-solving process.

Introduction

1 What does the image tell you about creativity?

2 What do the quotes mean? Do you agree with them?

❝ Creative thinking is not a talent, it is a skill that can be learnt. ❞

Edward de Bono, champion of 'lateral thinking'

❝ A business has to be evolving, it has to be fun and it has to exercise your creative instincts. ❞

Richard Branson, successful entrepreneur and founder of Virgin

Language focus: Word formations connected with creativity

1 Match the following nouns connected to creative management with the correct definition.

1 imagination	**a** production of original and unusual ideas
2 creativity	**b** use of a new idea
3 invention	**c** the ability to visualise new ideas
4 interaction	**d** putting a plan into action
5 implementation	**e** movement of ideas and opinions to the same point (they become similar)
6 innovation	**f** movement of ideas and opinions away from each other (they become more different)
7 convergence	**g** something which has never been made before
8 divergence	**h** when two or more people or things communicate with each other

2 The majority of these nouns are formed with -tion. How are adjectives generally formed? Change the nouns in the table above into adjectives (where possible).

3 Write down the verb equivalent for the nouns above.

4 Who do you think is more creative, an inventor or an innovator? Why?

Business view

Dr Jane Henry is senior lecturer in Applied Psychology at the Open University Business School and a writer on creativity.

1 Read the Introduction to an extract from *Creative Management* by Dr Jane Henry. Then predict what the rest of the text will be about by looking at the table.

Creative people	Creative processes
a You need creative people, innovators and _____ _____	**e** Traditional creative thinking is about _____ _____
b Creative people should not be _____ _____	**f** Convergent thinking enables you to _____ _____

Creative places	Creative products
c Creativity happens where people are not _____	**g** In the West new product development _____ _____
d The organisational structure should be _____ _____	**h** In Japan new product development _____ _____

Making sense of creativity

Introduction

Creativity is about the quality of originality that leads to new ways of seeing and new ideas. It is a thinking process associated with imagination, invention and innovation. However, creativity is not just about an idea that is new and different: for an idea to be truly creative it must also be appropriate and useful.

A number of commentators have found it convenient to distinguish between creative people, creative processes, creative places and creative products.

2 Work in pairs. Student A should read the sections about People and Place and Student B should read about Process and Product. When you have finished, cover the text and tell each other what you have read.

People

Considerable energy and research has gone into trying to work out the characteristics of creative individuals. Three broad types of individuals have been identified: creative people, innovators and entrepreneurs. Creative people are usually seen as people who generate ideas, innovators as those who take an idea and develop it into something real (such as a product or service or business process) and entrepreneurs as those who take the product to market or implement the process and make it a commercial success. Entrepreneurs in large organisations are referred to as intrapreneurs.

Studies of creative people show characteristics such as independent thinking, not being affected by peer pressure, good verbal communication skills, imagination and a reasonable but not outstanding level of intelligence. Creative people are said to be better at asking the right questions. They also appear comfortable with risk-taking and are open to new ideas.

Place

These days a good deal of management thinking argues that the society we live in and the organisational climate, culture and structure have a major impact on creative output. The suggestion is that creative ideas flow where new ideas and challenges are welcomed and where people are encouraged to play rather than controlled and threatened. It follows then that organisations that want to promote creativity might need to look at creating a flatter organisational structure (removing levels of hierarchy) in an attempt to reduce bureaucracy and speed up the creative processes.

Process

The creative thinking process is traditionally linked to imaginative thinking which is expansive and divergent in nature (such as brainstorming and lateral thinking) as opposed to evaluative thinking which is convergent in character. Divergent thinking helps people to generate a large number and variety of ideas and approach problems from different angles. The emphasis here is on quantity where an 'anything goes' attitude is encouraged. Convergent thinking on the other hand, is needed to narrow down the output from the divergent phase. The focus here is on quality – making one or two selections from a huge number of possibilities. In practice, the creative process requires a framework which allows for alternating phases between divergent and convergent thinking.

Product

Creative products may arise from a radical breakthrough or a series of small incremental steps. Management methods in the West have emphasised radical breakthroughs, while Japan has built much of its success on small incremental steps. The task of the manager is to encourage and coordinate multi-disciplinary teams working on product development and drive these processes along.

3 After you have read your sections of the text, complete the table with your partner.

4 Read the statements below and decide in which section you would expect to find the answer: Person, Place, Process or Product. Are the following statements true or false?

1 Research shows you need to be very intelligent to be creative.
2 A playful culture at work helps the creative process.
3 Convergent thinking plays no part in the creative thinking process.
4 The product development manager's role is to create new products.
5 Intrapreneurs are focused on making profits.
6 At all stages of creative thinking you need to choose carefully the ideas you put forward.

5 Would you make a good creative manager? Why/Why not?

---

1 Read about the following two creative techniques. How useful are they? Could you use any of them in your work, studies or personal life?

5Ws and 1H

Ask questions: Why …?, What …?, Where …?, Who …?, When …?, How …?

This is a standard brainstorming technique to explore different angles to a core problem.

Example: *I don't have enough money to go on holiday.*
- *Why don't you have enough money to go on holiday?*
- *What did you spend your money on?*
- *Where do you want to go on holiday?*
- *Who could you ask for money?*
- *When would be a cheaper time to go?*
- *How could you save money?*

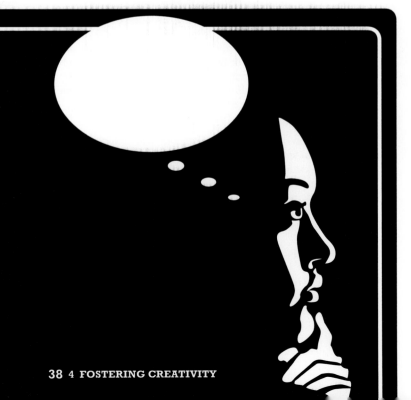

Reverse thinking

This is a lateral thinking technique: you reframe the problem and look at it from the opposite perspective.

Example: *We don't have enough money to develop this new product.*
What do we have enough money to develop?

2 Work with a partner to discuss this problem: *I never have enough time.* Use the 5Ws and 1H and reverse-thinking techniques to think about how you would help a person with this problem.

Example: *'When do you feel the problem is most intense?' (5Ws and 1H)*
*'What activities do you **have** time for?' (Reverse thinking)*

Stage 1
In small groups, brainstorm a list of problems that you personally have in your professional lives or with your studies, such as 'I always feel tired', 'I find it nearly impossible to meet deadlines', etc. This is the expansive, divergent phase of thinking where 'anything goes'. Don't judge if the problem is a 'good one' or not at this stage – simply write the problems down in a list with the name of the person who has this problem. Focus on the quantity of ideas and keep the atmosphere playful and fun.

Stage 2
Select one problem from the list that you as a group would like to focus on. This is the convergent evaluative phase of the process. Ask practical questions such as: 'How interesting is the problem?' and 'How useful is solving the problem for the whole of the group?'

Stage 3
Using the techniques you have learnt, explore the problem more deeply by asking the 'problem holder' questions (divergent phase). One person in the group should take notes.

Stage 4
Discuss how helpful the techniques were in solving the problems. Which one do you think is more useful, 5Ws and 1H or reverse thinking?

Learning outcomes

- Understand how innovation works in practice.
- Use modals to criticise past actions and explore alternative solutions.
- Discuss and present stages of innovative product development.

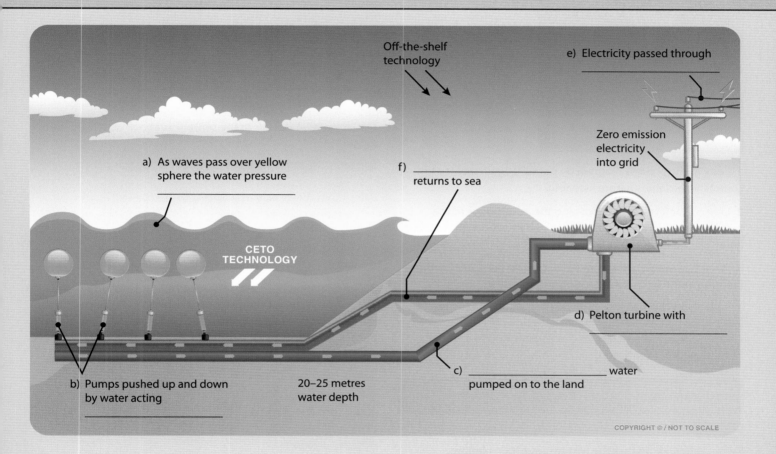

a) As waves pass over yellow sphere the water pressure _____

b) Pumps pushed up and down by water acting _____

20–25 metres water depth

CETO TECHNOLOGY

Off-the-shelf technology

f) _____ returns to sea

c) _____ water pumped on to the land

d) Pelton turbine with _____

e) Electricity passed through _____

Zero emission electricity into grid

COPYRIGHT © / NOT TO SCALE

Profile: Carnegie Wave Energy

Carnegie Wave Energy is a small to medium-sized Australian company based in Perth that invests in and develops clean energy projects. Its most important project is a wave energy technology known as CETO. Most competitor wave technologies have generally been located on the surface of the water where the energy levels are very high and where there is a high risk of destruction by stormy seas. What is different about the CETO technology is that it is below the rough water level, where the risks of damage are much lower.

Introduction

1 Read the profile of Carnegie Wave Energy. What is the advantage of CETO wave energy technology compared to its competitor wave technologies?

2 Put these energy sources in two groups: renewable and non-renewable.

nuclear   gas   solar   coal   wind   wave   oil

3 What are some of the advantages and disadvantages of the above energy sources?

4 Work in pairs. Look at the CETO process diagram above. How do you think the technology might work?

1.19

Business view

Jeff Harding is an entrepreneur and Non-Executive Director of Carnegie Wave Energy.

1 Look at the process diagram on page 39 again and try to complete the labels before listening.

2 Listen to Jeff Harding describing the advantages of the technology and how it works. While you listen, complete the labels on the diagram.

3 What two advantages from the list below does Jeff Harding mention at the end of this part of the interview?

a It produces electricity on land.
b It uses all new technology.
c It uses a mix of new and old technologies.
d It's protected in the ocean.

 1.20

Before listening, discuss the first two questions below.

1 Which of the experiences below might have helped the inventor come up with the idea of CETO?

a He was in a boat doing some work.
b He was lying in the bath playing with a rubber duck.
c He was swimming in the sea watching the fish.

2 What does an organisation like Carnegie need, in order to develop and commercialise an innovative technology such as CETO? Choose from the list below and mark the factors as follows:
C = Commercialisation   D = Development   N = Not needed

1 clear rules and guidelines
2 distribution skills*
3 joint venture with a large company
4 recruit new people
5 culture of openness
6 money
7 good team-working
8 accept crazy ideas

* knowing how to get the product to the customer

3 Listen to the next part of the interview and answer the questions in 1 and 2 above with the answers Jeff Harding gives.

Language focus: Past modals

1 Past modals in English are often formed like this: verb + *have* + past participle. The past modals are underlined in the sentences below.

1 Sven <u>could have been</u> in Claudio's job now, but he didn't apply for it.
2 You <u>should have told</u> him that you planned to be late today, he wouldn't be angry now.
3 Caterina <u>might have finished</u> the report by now. I know she was working until late.
4 They <u>can't have forgotten</u> about the appointment. I emailed them a reminder yesterday.
5 We <u>shouldn't have hired</u> her – she doesn't have enough experience to do the job properly.
6 Manuel <u>must have been disappointed</u> not to get promotion.

Match the past modals in the sentences above with their use below.

a It's possible that this happened, but the speaker is not completely sure.
b It's impossible or very unlikely that this happened.
c The speaker is sure that this is the result of something that happened.
d A past possibility, which did not come true.
e Something that was advisable in the past. (*two answers*)

2 The following is a list of reasons why innovations can fail. Use modal verbs to make sentences which offer advice, criticise the problems, or suggest different outcomes. There are several possibilities.

Example: The leadership should have been better. / Better leadership might have led to success.

a bad leadership
b bad communication
c badly defined goals
d bad teamwork

3 What mistakes have you and your colleagues made at work or at college over the last two or three months? How could you have dealt with the situation any better? Discuss in pairs, using past modal verbs.

4 Some 'crazy ideas' lead to very serious products, and some don't. In groups, explain how the US patented invention shown on page 41 could or should have worked and what the inventor could or should have done to improve it.

Dog Rides Comfortably in Sack on Running Board

Your dog will ride safely in this sack, which is quickly attached or removed

HOLE FOR HEAD

GROMMETS

LARGE CANVAS SACK

SEWED

When you take your dog along for a ride, but prefer not having it inside the car, it can ride safely and comfortably in this sack, which is carried on the running board. The bottom of the sack is clamped to the running board and the top is fastened to the lower part of an open window, with hooks covered with small rubber tubing to prevent marring the car.

US Patent – Detachable dog sack

Output: Making a product into a commercial success

Some 'crazy ideas' are patented into innovative, fun and profitable products.

Work in small groups (A and B). Look at the following information.

Group A

Stage 1

Birth and development stage

Study the product from Phonefingers.com on page 138, a small company based in Austria. It was designed to stop you leaving fingerprints all over your phones or computer. Discuss how this idea might have been born and some of the problems the company might have had during the development stages.

Group B

Stage 1

Birth and development stage

Study the product from Kittywigs.com on page 143, a small company based in Canada. It was designed for people to have fun with their cats. Discuss how this idea might have been born and some of the problems the company might have had during the development stages.

Groups A and B

Stage 2

Commercialisation stage

Brainstorm a marketing strategy for your company. At the end of your discussion, take notes and prepare to present the product and your marketing strategy to the other group. When deciding on the marketing strategy, you will need to discuss the following points:

- Who is the target market for this product?
- How is the product best distributed (direct sales on the Internet or high street shops)?
- What are the best channels to promote it?
- What message do you want to communicate in promotion and advertising?
- What price would you sell it for?
- What new innovative variations of the product could you develop?
- How might you counter objections that 'nobody would buy it'?
- Would you consider a joint venture with a larger company? Why/Why not?

Stage 3

Present your product and marketing strategy to the other group.

Learning outcomes

- Understand a decision-making process.
- Evaluate using metaphors and idioms.
- Make a decision about possible options.

a

b

c

Introduction

1 Decision-making is closely tied to problem-solving, and is often broken down into three stages. Put a, b and c in order so that they make a logical process.

a choose and implement the best option

b explore and find the exact problem

c discuss possible solutions

2 In pairs, look at the pictures above, discuss the situation, and arrange them to follow the three stages above.

3 In small groups, think about one problem you each have when studying English. Take a few minutes to discuss some solutions to each problem and choose the best solution to it, following the process above.

4 Different people are good or bad at different stages of the decision-making process. Answer the following questions (1 = strongly disagree, 5 = strongly agree), and then compare your answers with a partner. Discuss whether you are a good decision-maker.

Listening 1: Renewing a contract

🔵 1.21

You are going to listen to part of a meeting between directors from two IT companies. The sales director (Steve) and finance director (Fiona) are discussing the details of a new contract with their new client (Anabel).

1 What types of customer support would you pay extra for if you hired a company to help you with IT issues in your company?

2 Listen to Steve, the sales director, outlining the key features of the gold contract. Are the statements below true or false?

1 Twenty-four seven coverage is optional.

2 The client finds the problem and reports it to Steve's company, who then fix it.

3 A senior engineer looks after the client's server.

I am a person who ...

• enjoys thinking about things deeply	**1**	**2**	**3**	**4**	**5**
• spends a lot of time deciding what to do	**1**	**2**	**3**	**4**	**5**
• finds it easy to come up with ideas	**1**	**2**	**3**	**4**	**5**
• is good at offering advice	**1**	**2**	**3**	**4**	**5**
• is happy about the decisions I've made in my life so far	**1**	**2**	**3**	**4**	**5**
• enjoys looking at details and specific aspects of a problem	**1**	**2**	**3**	**4**	**5**

1.22

1 Why is Anabel (the client) not happy with the proposed pricing for separate incidents?

2 Which two of the options does Fiona (the finance director) suggest?

a buying a cheaper package

b negotiating the cost

c using a separate automated service

3 Discuss in pairs which stage of the decision-making process you think this meeting is concerned with. Why do you think it is this part of the meeting? If necessary, refer to the audio script on page 152.

Language focus: Evaluative metaphors and idioms

Evaluating (judging something) is used at all stages of the decision-making process. Two very common types of evaluative language found in business communication are metaphors and idioms.

1 Match up these definitions.

1 metaphors
2 idioms

a Language from another situation that describes what something is like, rather than what it literally is.
Example: *They took their eye off the ball and lost the contract.*

b A group of words whose meaning is different from the individual words themselves.
Example: *day in day out*

In real communication it is often difficult to distinguish between idioms and metaphors. The important point is that they are both used to evaluate.

2 Read these four examples of idioms and metaphors from the listening extracts and match them to the definitions. Do they evaluate the situation positively or negatively?

1 have most issue with

2 sticks in the throat

3 a serious cost on top

4 a pair of the right hands

a something you are very unhappy about agreeing to

b a good level of support

c something you strongly disagree with

d an extra, very big increase

3 Read through the audio scripts on pages 151–2 and find four more examples of metaphors and idioms. What do the idioms and metaphors you have found mean?

4 Evaluations often happen towards the end of each stage of the decision-making process. Do these examples evaluate positively or negatively?

1 Looking good …

2 (the plans were) completely unreal …

3 (the rent is) stupid …

4 That's absolute madness …

5 (That's) a good way forward …

6 It eats into the time …

7 (These are) solid plans …

8 I would really welcome that.

5 Managers use metaphors and idioms more than subordinates. Why do you think this is? Why might it be a problem for a subordinate to use a lot of evaluative language with a manager?

Output: Deciding which contract suits you

Work in pairs. Imagine that you are the executives of an IT sales company, and have to make a decision about whether to renew your contract with the company that looks after your internet server (see the audio scripts on pages 151–2).

Stage 1

1 What are the advantages of staying with the same company? What are the risks of changing company?

2 Summarise the benefits and problems with the gold level of service. Think about: support time, attractiveness of the option to your customers, the degree of support, the level and understanding of the engineer and the flat-rate cost.

3 Evaluate the options and make a decision about whether to:

a agree to the contract as proposed

b agree to the contract but negotiate some aspects, such as the cost

c decide to find a new company.

Stage 2

Join another group and discuss the option that you have chosen.

▶◀ **Watch Sequence 2 on the DVD to find out more about Managing people.**

Writing 2: Describing a process

Learning outcomes
- Describe a process.
- Review passive forms.
- Use linkers of sequencing, structuring and providing reasons.

Introduction

Discuss the following questions.

1 What do you think this diagram is about?

2 How does the visual impact of the diagram help you understand the process better?

3 Diagrams of processes are very common. Are the following processes industrial, technical, business, natural or intellectual processes or two of these processes combined?

1 global warming
2 client software support assistance
3 steel production
4 online shopping
5 converting solar energy into electricity
6 learning Business English

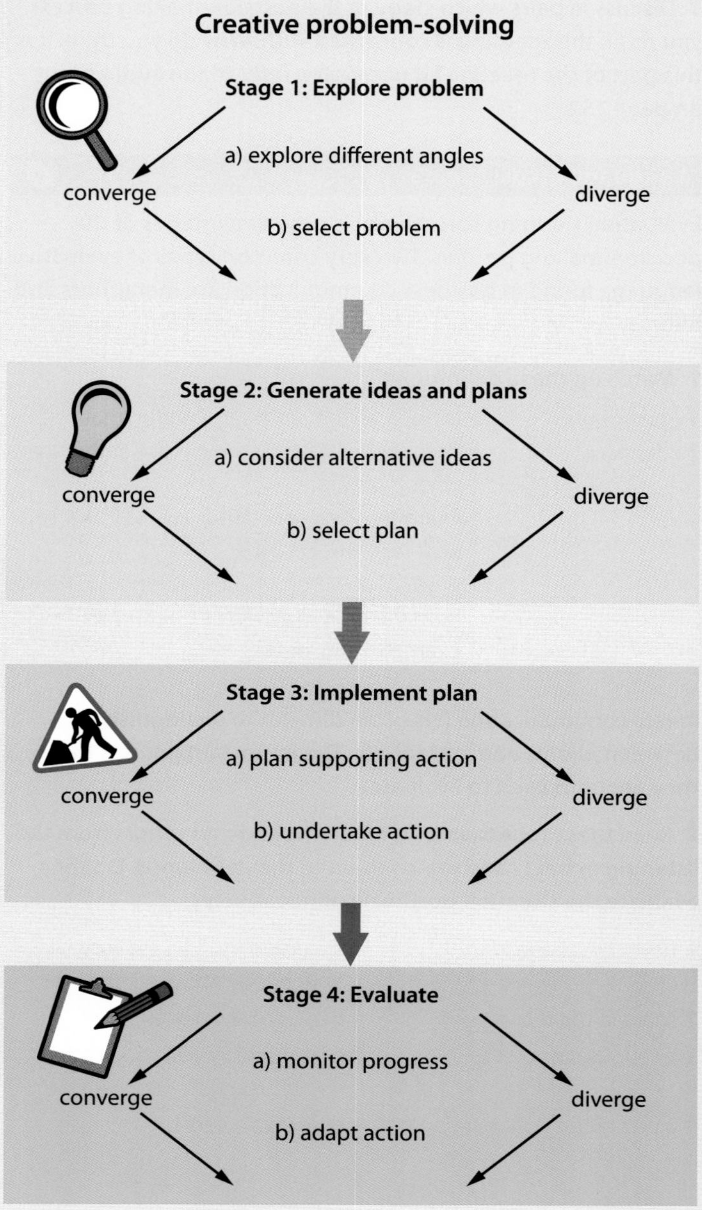

Writing skill: Describe a creative problem-solving process

1 Read the following description of the diagram and complete the gaps using the words below. The diagram shows the creative problem-solving process which is taught on MBA programmes and is widely used in business.

main   splitting   initial   third   since   overall   phase
stages   followed

Creative problem-solving works by 1 _____ the thinking about a problem into a number of different 2 _____ .
Many authorities talk in terms of three 3 _____ stages: an 4 _____ exploratory phase where the problem to work on is identified and considered from different angles; a second 5 _____ when alternative ways of dealing with the problem are considered; and a 6 _____ phase where the detailed implementation of a chosen way forward is worked out. Within each of these phases it is common to encourage an imaginative phase where different acts and possibilities are considered, 7 _____ by an evaluative phase where these possibilities are considered and a way forward is chosen. 8 _____ the whole process is itself experimental, it needs its own 9 _____ evaluation phase as well – in effect a fourth stage.

Source: Open University MBA Programme

Creative problem-solving

Stage 1: Explore problem
a) explore different angles
converge   diverge
b) select problem

Stage 2: Generate ideas and plans
a) consider alternative ideas
converge   diverge
b) select plan

Stage 3: Implement plan
a) plan supporting action
converge   diverge
b) undertake action

Stage 4: Evaluate
a) monitor progress
converge   diverge
b) adapt action

2 What is the function of the colon (:) and semi-colons (;) in the description?

3 What tense and voice (active or passive) is used to describe this process? Why?

Language focus 1: Review of tenses in passive form

1 Read the following sentences about processes. Are the sentences in the active or passive or mixed (both active and passive)?

Example: Sentence 1 is in the present simple passive.

1 More than a year is needed before that essential part of the process is undertaken.
2 Staff have worked too hard to rush the process now.
3 The Chief Executive said: 'The whole process has been badly planned from the beginning.'
4 Have we started the recruitment process yet?
5 His shares were in the process of being transferred into a pension plan.

2 Identify the tenses used in each sentence above.

3 Match the following definitions, which describe how the active and passive forms can be used, to the sentences above (1–5).

a It clarifies who is doing the action.
b It is used when you decide not to name someone.
c It emphasises the process rather than the agent/doer.

4 Why do you think the Chief Executive in sentence 3 decided not to use the active form?

Language focus 2: Linkers of sequencing, structuring and providing reasons

1 Look at the list of words needed to complete the text in Writing skill exercise 1. These words will help you sequence, structure and provide reasons in your writing or when giving a formal talk. Categorise the words into these three groups.

Sequence	Structure	Provide reasons
initial		

2 Look at the groups of words below and decide which word or phrase is not part of each group. Circle one word or phrase in each group.

1 main   core   key   principle   principal
2 stage   phase   platform   part   section
3 since   while   because   as   considering
4 an initial   an opening   firstly   an introductory   a beginning
5 splitting   breaking down   dividing   separating   breaking up
6 followed by   leading to   preceded by   after which comes

3 The following jumbled sentences are about business process management. Put them into the correct order.

1 the initial phase of the project / followed rapidly by a technology-based approach / The emphasis on / was market-driven
2 better than the competition / you need to undertake / Firstly / the needs of the customer / a redefinition of the product to satisfy
3 and difficult to follow / the real data and model / I have not used / since it is more complex

Output: Writing a short description of a business process

Stage 1
Work in two groups. One group should look at the diagram of an ordering process on page 138. The other group should look at the diagram about dealing with software technical support queries on page 143.

Stage 2
In groups, discuss your diagram.

Stage 3
Work on your own and write a description of your diagram.

Stage 4
Read out your description to a partner from the other group. They should try and draw the diagram from your description. When you have finished, change roles.

5 Organisational cultures

5.1 Theory: Understanding organisations

Learning outcomes
- Understand types of organisational culture.
- Learn vocabulary to describe organisational cultures.
- Discuss what cultures suit different organisations.

Introduction

1 Complete the following questionnaire about yourself by choosing one answer (A–D) for each of the questions.

What organisational culture suits you?

1 I like working in places that have:
- **A** a clear set of rules and methods to follow.
- **B** flexible ways of working.
- **C** no rules whatsoever.
- **D** few rules, but these are made by the boss.

2 I think that key decision-making in the workplace is best taken:
- **A** by my line manager.
- **B** in a group where everyone has an equal say.
- **C** by myself.
- **D** by a strong leader.

3 I prefer organisations that communicate:
- **A** through official means of communication.
- **B** through a direct exchange of views.
- **C** the minimum possible.
- **D** through personal relationships.

4 I dislike working in organisations that:
- **A** have no clear idea of what they want from you.
- **B** place limits on your freedom to do the job.
- **C** ask too much from you.
- **D** treat you as a number and don't recognise your individuality.

5 Which of these words best describe you?
- **A** loyal and trustworthy
- **B** creative
- **C** independent
- **D** a winner

6 I think bosses should:
- **A** do their job.
- **B** provide me with the resources to do my job.
- **C** be invisible.
- **D** be respected and followed.

2 Now turn to pages 138–9 to see which type of organisational culture you are best suited to working in.

3 Do you agree with the result of the questionnaire? Why/Why not?

Language focus: Vocabulary to talk about organisations

1 Look at the table below and match the target vocabulary to the examples. All the target words appear in the reading text which follows.

Target vocabulary	Examples
1 personality	**a** advertising, travel, stationery, product development
2 reward systems	**b** outgoing, quiet, amusing
3 dress code	**c** relaxed, playful, serious, stressful
4 expense accounts	**d** 'work hard, play hard'; 'winning is everything'; 'people before profit'
5 organisational structures	**e** fixed monthly salary, payment by results
6 values	**f** smart, casual, smart-casual, dress-down Friday
7 norms	**g** no smoking, flying business class only permitted on intercontinental flights
8 atmosphere at work	**h** Purchasing, Production, R&D
9 rules	**i** for dealing with customer enquiries, for emergencies
10 procedures	**j** hierarchical, centralised, decentralised
11 departments	**k** nobody leaves work before the boss at the end of the day; staff socialise together on Friday evenings
12 budgets	**l** corporate entertainment, travel costs, business lunches

2 Can you think of any more examples of these target words? Add to the list with a partner.

Business view

Professor Charles Handy is a business guru, writer and academic, specialising in organisational management.

1 Read the following extract from Professor Charles Handy's book *Understanding Organizations*. Are these statements true or false according to the text?

1 There is a lot of similarity in how different organisations behave.
2 There are more differences between organisations than between nations and societies.
3 The structures and systems of an organisation create the organisational culture.
4 One organisation generally has more than one organisational culture.

Anyone who has spent time with any variety of organizations will have been struck by the different atmospheres, the different ways of doing things, the different levels of energy, of individual freedoms, of kinds of personality. For organizations are as different and varied as the nations and societies of the world. They have different cultures – sets of values and norms and beliefs, which lead to different structures and systems.

In organizations there are deep-set beliefs about the way work should be organized, the way authority should be exercised, people rewarded, people controlled. Do work hours or dress codes matter? What about expense accounts, secretaries, stock options? These are all parts of the culture of an organization. Even within organizations cultures will differ. The R&D laboratory in the fields of the countryside will have a different atmosphere to the director's floor in the central office, creating different departmental cultures.

2 Have you noticed whether dress codes, attitudes, personalities and energy levels vary from organisation to organisation?

1 Work in pairs. Student A will read about Task culture below and Student B about Role culture on page 48. After reading your text, complete the notes on the diagrams.

2 Explain the diagrams to each other and tell your partner about the culture you have read about.

Student A: Task culture

Task culture is job- or project-orientated. It is a team culture, characterized by high levels of cooperation and fast decision-making. Its structure can be best illustrated as a net. This clearly shows communication across departments (the horizontal lines), not just within departments (the vertical lines). Some of the strands of the net are thicker and stronger than others, showing that some communication lines have more influence. This influence is based more on expert power than on job position or personal power. Much of the power and influence lies at the intersections of the net, at the knots. Task culture is very adaptable and focuses on achieving results above all else. It works best when given enough resources to do the job. If there is too much pressure on time and money then the cooperative nature of the task culture starts to disappear and other cultures take its place.

Task culture

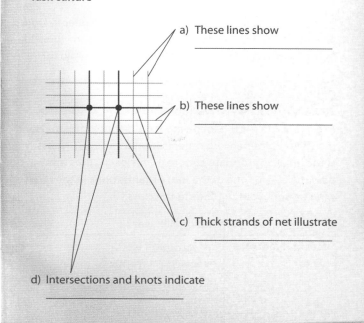

a) These lines show
_____

b) These lines show
_____

c) Thick strands of net illustrate
_____

d) Intersections and knots indicate
_____

Student B: Role culture

Role culture can be pictured as a Greek temple. Role culture places its strengths in its columns. These columns represent the different departments, e.g. the finance department and the purchasing department. The work of the columns and the interaction between the columns is controlled by procedures which describe in detail what each department does and what each person does in their job by means of a job description. This structure is highly suited to stable environments or environments where the organization has a lot of market power, such as monopolies. The columns are coordinated at the top by a narrow band of senior management. An organization with a role culture is generally believed to be very stable but poor at implementing change and adapting to a fast-changing macro-environment.

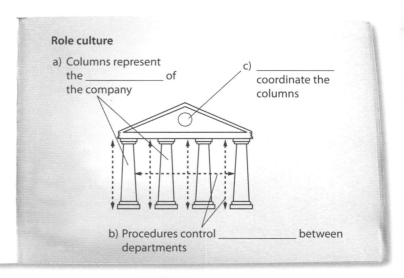

Role culture

a) Columns represent the _____ of the company

c) _____ coordinate the columns

b) Procedures control _____ between departments

3 In pairs, identify the strengths and weaknesses of these two organisational cultures by circling the correct answer, Task or Role.

Strengths

1 Flexible and focused on objectives   Task / Role
2 Works well in environments that it can control   Task / Role

Weaknesses

3 Inflexible and slow to change   Task / Role
4 Breaks down where budgets and deadlines are tight   Task / Role

4 In which organisational culture would you prefer to work? Why? Is this the same type of organisation that the questionnaire in the Introduction suggested you were most suited to?

Output: Deciding on an appropriate culture for an organisation

In groups, look at the following factors that Professor Handy identifies as influencing organisational culture. Discuss what is the most appropriate culture or mix of cultures (power/task/person/role) for one of the four organisations in the chart and then present your findings to the class.

	National Power	Eco-Energy	Polyglot	Global-Me
Size and industry sector	Large national electricity-generating company	Medium-sized renewable energy company	Small online translation agency with branches in 3 countries	Large global NFP (Not For Profit organisation) working in disaster relief
Age	40 years	3 years	1 year (start-up)	5 years
Technology	Expensive technology	Highly specialist technology	Online but low-tech	Low-tech
Goals and objectives	Mixed. Range of stakeholders (from customers and shareholders to community and government)	Grow the company; aim to sell company in 3 years	Maximise profits	Save lives and serve the international community
Environment	Stable but complex	Complex and fast-changing	Stable	Alternating stable and fast-changing environments

5.2 Practice: Creating a successful culture

Learning outcomes
- Understand the organisation and culture of a company.
- Predict content when listening.
- Allocate budgets for different departments.

a

b

d

Profile: Mundipharma International Limited

Mundipharma International Limited (MINT) is a family-owned, international pharmaceutical company with several associate companies, and annual turnover of around $4 billion. It regularly scores very highly in surveys of 'best places to work', and is credited as having an excellent workplace culture.

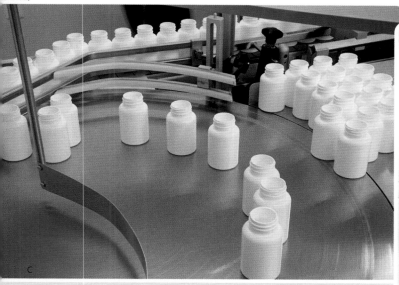
c

Introduction

1 Match the pictures above to the following departments:

| Finance | Research and Development (R&D) | Production | Sales |

2 Discuss the following questions in pairs.
- What do you think it is like to work in each of these departments?
- What do you think the atmosphere is like?
- Which department would you most like and least like to belong to?

3 Cultural differences in business relationships can arise at the following levels:

1 National (e.g. Germany and Thailand)
2 Professional (e.g. accounting and marketing, in the same company)
3 Institutional (e.g. IBM and Toyota)

What are some of the possible problems that cultural differences can lead to? What opportunities can they lead to?

4 Match the following situations with one of the examples of cultural differences in exercise 3. Are they problems or opportunities?

1 The R&D (Research and Development) department in your company keeps rejecting the sales department's requests for changes to the product.
2 You are upset with your foreign distributor because they never give you a straight answer.
3 Your overseas office has come up with a great solution to your domestic marketing problem.
4 You think you can apply the same manufacturing process that your main competitor has recently introduced.

Transferable skill: Predicting context and content when listening

In our first languages, we automatically predict language and content. It is important to develop these skills when learning a foreign language. Prediction involves two key stages:

- making a prediction based on the context
- listening and deciding whether your prediction was correct, partly correct, or wrong.

Even if your predictions are wrong, predicting still helps you understand, if you are willing to change your mind.

Look at the titles of Listening 1, 2, 3, 4 and 5 based on an interview with a director at Mundipharma and try to predict two things you would expect to hear in each one.

Listening 1: Company and culture

 1.23

Business view

Ake Wikström is the regional director of Mundipharma International Ltd.

1 Ake Wikström talks about the size of Mundipharma and its culture. Before you listen, think about what you already know about the interview. For example, what do you know about the company (see Profile), the speaker, this type of interview, the title of this lesson, and this listening exercise? Predict answers to the questions below and give reasons for your predictions.

1 Has the company grown or shrunk in recent years?
2 Has the culture got better or worse since Ake Wikström joined the company?
3 Does Ake Wikström criticise other companies?

2 After listening, check your answers to the questions above and summarise what Ake Wikström said about Mundipharma in terms of growth, the ownership of the company, its turnover and its culture.

Listening 2: Company departments

 1.24

1 Ake Wikström mentions five different departments in Mundipharma in the UK. In pairs, predict which departments he will mention from this list:

Sales Logistics Internal complaints Production R&D
Marketing Administration Sports injuries Construction

Give reasons why you think he will mention these departments.

2 Listen to the recording and see if your predictions were correct.

Listening 3: Department cultures

1.25

1 Ake Wikström compares Marketing and Production. Before you listen, think about what these departments do. Look at the comments below and circle which department – Marketing (M), or Production (P) – you think they refer to:

'They have fun …'	M / P
'They love to work together'	M / P
'Nothing seems to stand in their way'	M / P
'They work three shifts a day and they don't travel'	M / P

2 Ake Wikström states what he thinks is the most important factor in the success of a department. Predict his answer.

3 Listen to the recording and see if your predictions were correct.

Listening 4: Creating a successful culture

1.26

1 Ake Wikström talks about the use of employee surveys in creating a successful corporate culture. Why do you think Mundipharma use such surveys?

- to evaluate staff and check their progress
- to find out what engages staff

2 Predict what Ake Wikström says about industry benchmarks (measurable standards) and employee satisfaction surveys. Complete the gaps.

1 Employee satisfaction surveys show what makes employees _____ and willing to contribute to an _____ .
2 We started at 6 or 7% _____ industry benchmarks, now we are running 7 or 8% above.

Listen to the recording and see if you were correct.

Listening 5: Managers and the surveys

🔊 1.27

1 What do you think Ake Wikström thinks is the most important feature of the survey process?

2 How do you think the attitude of managers has changed towards the surveys?

Now listen to the recording to see if you were correct.

Language focus: Asking questions effectively

In spoken communication, asking the right type of question at the right time in the right way often makes the difference between successful and unsuccessful communication.

Questions in spoken communication have two basic purposes: to get a response of some kind, and to comment on what somebody has already said.

1 Look at these two exchanges from meetings, and decide which question requires a response, and which one shows the listener's surprise.

1 **Manager:** Which Saab model is it?
 Salesperson: I don't know which Saab model it is.

2 **Salesperson:** I can't really see the point of contacting Dominic.
 Manager: Really?

2 **Spoken questions have many different functions. Below are some of the most important functions. In pairs, think of a question you could ask to do the following:**

1 ask somebody to do something
 Could you pick me up at 8 o'clock?
2 check understanding or seek agreement
3 show surprise or interest
4 show politeness
5 make a suggestion
6 criticise somebody or show dissatisfaction

3 **Which questions above do you think are more often used by more senior people in business? Which ones can have a negative effect on a relationship?**

4 **Look at the questions below and match them with the functions in exercise 2 above.**

a Can you change my email password?
b It's all right, isn't it?
c Why haven't you met your targets?
d Can I ask you to do something for me?
e A: I've got a contact there. B: Have you?
f Why don't we take one product this afternoon?

Intercultural analysis

Intercultural can describe communication between professional cultures, not only national cultures.

1 Match the following departments in a typical company to their main activities. The first has been done for you.

Sales — testing of products
Sales — promoting the product
R&D — developing/maintaining client relationships
R&D — researching the market
Marketing — hitting sales targets
Marketing — creative thinking

2 Discuss how the different purposes may affect the priorities of each department, e.g. for Sales, the priority is selling as many products as often as possible, and probably not the internal design of the product.

Output: Working in a cross-departmental team

You are part of a cross-departmental team, working on developing, marketing and selling a new pharmaceutical product. You are discussing how to allocate the $10,000,000 budget for the next financial year and there are considerable differences of opinion concerning where funds should be allocated.

Stage 1

Work in small groups. One group is the R&D department, one group is Sales, one is Marketing, and another is from Finance (the Chair). Look at page 139 and prepare for the meeting.

1 **Prepare your arguments for why your department needs more money.**

2 **Think about the arguments the other departments are likely to have, and how you can respond to them.**

3 **If you are the Chair, think about some questions you want to ask each department to find out why they need money.**

Stage 2

Separate into new groups, with one person from each department and one group leader. Have the meeting, and try to come to a decision that all members agree with.

5.3 Skills: Dealing with problems across departments

Learning outcomes

- Understand different attitudes within different company departments.
- Use strategic summaries to support your argument.
- Confront and negotiate problems with colleagues from different departments.

Introduction

1 Look at the photo and discuss these questions.

- What is the problem, and how would you deal with it if you were in this situation?
- If you were the manager, what would you do?

2 The extracts below are all from meetings where a director of one department is criticising the staff of another. Discuss with a partner what the extracts mean, and what some of the problems might be.

a They should think, 'Hang on, the customer's my salary.'
b People should take problem ownership …
c They've got to be very customer facing …
d They have got to be proactive rather than reactive …
e Good morning, this is your salary talking …
f That's a mindset change …
g They're very much, 'I know what's best …'

Critical analysis

1 In many companies, the relationship between different departments can be difficult. For example, technical staff may not want to be involved in sales issues, and sales may think that the finance department does not appreciate their efforts. Why do you think this is?

2 What are the benefits for a company if the technical team takes an interest in sales and the sales team takes an interest in the technical side?

Listening 1: Introducing the problem

 1.28

You are going to listen to three separate stages of an inter-departmental meeting in an IT company, between the finance director (Laura) and the technical director (Doz). The company expects the technical team to become more 'project management focused' in dealing with installations, which means they will have to communicate more with the customers.

Listen to the first part of the meeting.

1 According to Laura, what is the technical staff's attitude?
2 How does their attitude need to change?
3 What does Doz say about the technical team's attitude?

Listening 2: Specific issues

 1.29

Listen to the recording and answer the questions.

1 What does Doz think the problem is?

2 What recommendation does Laura make about calling customers?

Listening 3: Reaching agreement

 1.30

Listen to the recording and answer the questions.

1 According to Laura, what type of technical person is ideal?

2 What happens at the moment when Doz asks his staff to call a customer? Why do you think this is a problem?

Intercultural analysis

Read through the audio scripts on pages 153–4 and discuss in small groups whether the finance director is an effective negotiator. Do you think she would be a successful negotiator in your culture? What, if anything, would you do differently?

Language focus: Strategically summarising a position

When negotiating, speakers often 'strategically summarise' the discussion at different points of the conversation. This means that they summarise the points to suit their argument. This also allows them to show they agree with the other person before they argue the point.

Example: But **all I'm saying is** that the attitude has got to slightly change.

1 Which of these expressions could be used as strategic summaries?

You're/We're/I'm saying …
You're/We're/I'm talking about …
And then …
My point is …
What I mean is …
I think, to be honest with you …
What do you mean …?
So this means that …
I don't understand, to be honest …

2 Find other examples in the audio scripts on pages 153–4. How do the phrases help Laura to try and persuade Doz to agree with her point?

3 You can also use strategic summaries to clarify what you mean by stating what you don't mean.

Example: **I'm not saying that**. I think they're fabulous with customers. **What I'm saying is** that if the customer doesn't ring them back in ten minutes' time they've got to ring them again.

Clarify your position on each of the following in the same way, using summarising language.

1 Your colleagues are not lazy, but they could work longer hours.
2 We don't disagree with the proposal, but we need some more time to think about it.
3 Your staff think about sales, but they could think more.
4 Your staff know something about technical issues. However, more understanding would benefit the company.

Output: Improving communication across departments

Imagine you work for a company which manufactures electronic books. However, communication between the R&D (research and development) department and the sales department is very bad. A meeting has been called between the senior staff of the two departments to see what the problems are and how they can be improved. In groups of four, one pair should read the sales staff card on page 139, and the other pair should read the R&D card on page 143.

Stage 1
Prepare for the meeting with your partner and decide what you want to say. Plan how you can use strategic summaries to support each other and your arguments in the discussion.

Stage 2
Have the full meeting and decide on a set of 'action points' that will improve the situation.

6 Working across cultures

6.1 Theory: Culture and individual strategies in business

Learning outcomes
- Use 'rapport management' to develop good business relationships.
- Use direct and indirect reported speech with questions.
- Distinguish fact from opinion.

Introduction

> ❝ If you have to work and particularly do something significant in a country it is much easier if somehow you [are] connected with the country and you like the country and you respect the people and you are curious about the culture. ❞

Carlos Ghosn, CEO and President of Renault-Nissan

> ❝ Well over 10% of business can be lost because of cultural barriers. ❞

Professor Stephen Hagen, author of *Business Communication Across Borders*

> ❝ In order to sell a product or a service, a company must establish a relationship with the consumer. It must build trust and rapport. ❞

Jay Levinson, advertising expert and author of *Guerrilla Marketing*

In this lesson we will look at rapport management and concepts of politeness to see how they can improve working relationships across cultures.

1 Discuss the following questions.
- What are the main points of the three quotes above?
- Are they facts or opinions?
- Are you surprised by any of the information?
- Do you agree with the opinions?

2 How would you feel and what would you do in the following situations?
- You don't get promoted, and somebody less qualified and experienced than you gets the job.
- You are in a meeting and the foreign guests disagree with everything you say.
- You don't feel your boss and/or your colleagues give you respect at work.
- You are unhappy about the level of cooperation in your team/ department.

Listening 1: What is rapport management?

🔘 1.31

Business view

Professor Helen Spencer-Oatey is director of Global People and author of *Culturally Speaking: Culture, Communication and Politeness*. She is also director of applied linguistics at the University of Warwick.

Listen to Professor Helen Spencer-Oatey introduce her theory of 'rapport management', and answer the following questions.

1 What is rapport management?

2 In what situations is it important?

Listening 2: Face, rights and problems

 1.32

Listen to the second part of the interview with Professor Helen Spencer-Oatey, and answer the following questions.

1 What is the meaning of the concept of 'face'?

A How you want others to see you
B How others actually see you

2 What can happen if someone challenges our self-image? Tick the following that apply.

A It's embarrassing.
B It's expected.
C It impacts negatively on rapport.
D You feel your right to be treated in a certain way has not been respected.

3 What types of problems can affect rapport?

4 Read through the following short extract from an article by Professor Helen Spencer-Oatey. Underline the nouns that describe the following:

a face
b sociality rights

> '… rapport management involves two main components: the management of face and the management of sociality rights … face is associated with personal/social value, and is concerned with people's sense of worth, credibility, dignity, honour, reputation, competence and so on. Sociality rights, on the other hand, are concerned with personal/social entitlements, and reflect people's concerns over fairness, consideration, social inclusion/exclusion and so on.'

5 Do the following relate to face or sociality rights, or both? How might each situation affect your future relationship with the person concerned?

1 Someone in your group cheats and gets a higher score than you.
2 Your boss gives you a compliment about your performance.
3 Your boss threatens to fire you in front of your colleagues.
4 Your boss asks you to work seven days a week for no extra pay (but with lots of compliments).

Language focus 1: Vocabulary related to culture

1 Match the words on the left with the definitions on the right.

1 face		**a**	the distinct personality of an individual
2 sociality rights		**b**	the positive self-image we have
3 rapport		**c**	the access we have to social networks and services in society
4 social inclusion			
5 dignity		**d**	how well you are getting on with someone
6 competence		**e**	being worthy of respect
7 identity		**f**	our ability in a given field
		g	what members of society expect they are entitled to

2 The words in exercise 1 are important words from the lesson. Can you think of any other words that could be added to this list?

3 Look again at the first situation in exercise 2 in the Introduction on page 54 (*You don't get promoted, and somebody less qualified and experienced than you gets the job*). Which of the concepts from the list of words in exercise 1 are relevant to this situation?

Critical analysis

Look at the audio script for Listening 2 on page 154 and find what Professor Helen Spencer-Oatey says about multiple identities. Discuss the following questions with a partner.

- Do you have different identities when you are with different people?
- Do you think it is useful to be able to behave differently towards other people in different situations?
- How can this be useful for intercultural communication?

Listening 3: Email anecdote

 1.33

Listen to the third part of the interview with Professor Helen Spencer-Oatey and answer the following questions.

1 Which countries were involved in the eChina project?

2 Why was the Chinese leader upset?

3 Which was affected, his face or his rights?

Intercultural analysis

According to Professor Helen Spencer-Oatey, the Chinese leader of the project expected a separate email addressed specifically to him because of his status, whereas in Britain the leader would be included in all emails. Discuss these questions in small groups.

- In your culture, which style do you think would be appropriate?
- What does the difference suggest about power differences and status in the two university cultures?
- Such differences may be reflected in other ways, for example in the use of names and titles (Professor or Helen or Professor Spencer-Oatey). How do you address your boss or teacher?
- How do the concepts of face and rights help explain such issues in intercultural professional communication?

Language focus 2: Reporting verbs

There are several verbs that are commonly used when reporting speech, such as *thank* and *promise*.

1 Match sentences 1–8 below with the verbs a–h to show what each sentence is illustrating.

a thank	**b** encourage	**c** deny	**d** promise	**e** apologise
f refuse	**g** offer	**h** agree		

1 'Yes, good idea, let's do it.'
2 'There's no way we are going there. The Liverpool site is a terrible site.'
3 'I'm ever so sorry, Carla, you know I didn't even realise.'
4 'I can help you.'
5 'We can make sure that those 64 operating companies get a copy of the magazine.'
6 'Thank you for cleaning up the website – it looks much better.'
7 'I've never mentioned a price to him, Robert.'
8 'You should apply for the job, you know you have all the skills.'

2 Put the verbs from exercise 1 into the following categories. You can use a dictionary to help you. The first one has been done as an example.

Verb + *to* + infinitive	Verb + obj. + *for* + *-ing*
	thank
Verb + *-ing*	**Verb + *for* + *-ing***

3 Use verbs a–h to report sentences 1–8 in exercise 1 above.

Example: 'Yes, good idea, let's do it.'
→ She agreed to do it.

Output: Dealing with face and rights

Stage 1

In pairs, act out each of these situations.

Scenario 1

A: You are the boss. You need your employee to work overtime again this week.

B: You have worked late every night this week, and you want to spend more time with your family.

Scenario 2

A: You have just bought a house and your children have just started at a new school. You like your job very much.

B: You are the boss. You need employee A to transfer to Shanghai because he/she is the best person for the job.

Scenario 3

A: You are the boss. You need to make employee B redundant because of falling sales, even though he/she has a good record.

B: You consider yourself the best salesperson in the team. You are expecting a pay rise.

Scenario 4

A: You want to complain about a client because the client is very rude every time you visit the company.

B: You are the boss. Employee A has received a very serious complaint because he/she has missed several meetings with the client.

Stage 2

Report back to another pair about what you said, and ask the other pair about their discussion. You should discuss how face and rights were affected in the situation, and whether the concerns and outcomes might be different in different cultures.

6.2 Practice: Multicultural mergers

Learning outcomes

- Use cultural differences as an advantage in business.
- Overcome cultural problems in an intercultural alliance.
- Identify different genres, and use nouns to make positive and negative judgements.

CEO Carlos Ghosn with the Leaf, Renault–Nissan's first all-electric car

Profile: Renault–Nissan

The Renault–Nissan alliance was established in 1999 and was the first industrial and commercial partnership involving French and Japanese companies. At the start of the alliance, many commentators thought the partnership would not be a success, as both companies had been performing badly. However, the alliance has gone from strength to strength and is one of the few success stories of the car industry over the last few years.

Introduction

1 Read the profile above. Discuss the following questions briefly in pairs.

- Would you rather work for a domestic or foreign company? Why/Why not?
- Would you like to work for your whole career in your own country, or would you like to work abroad as well?
- Which companies in your country do a lot of international business? Would you like to work for such a company? Why/Why not?
- Would you rather work for a boss of the same nationality as yourself? Why/Why not?
- What qualities do you think a boss in a multicultural team needs?

2 Do you know of any successful or unsuccessful relationships between companies from different countries? Many cross-cultural mergers and alliances fail. What types of problem might companies from different cultures have when they work together?

Transferable skill: Recognising genres

1 Different texts are written for different purposes. What is the purpose of an academic journal article, and what is the purpose of a company report for shareholders?

2 Read through the following two short extracts. Which is from the Nissan company website, and which is from an academic article? What language helped you decide?

Extract 1

Nissan's employees, both men and women, are of many nationalities and boast a wide variety of experiences. All members of the globally active Nissan family build strong relationships of trust with one another by understanding the viewpoints of and listening to opinions from their counterparts around the world. The synergies created by bringing this diverse group together drive sustainable growth for Nissan.

Extract 2

Conflicting national and organisational cultures are blamed for the failure of international alliances. However, the Renault-Nissan experience provides strong evidence that where these differences are explicitly recognised and accepted, and where appropriate processes and structures are put in place, national and organisational culture obstacles can be overcome. ... In order to create synergy between the two companies that values and uses difference, management must employ an intercultural communication framework.

3 Although the two extracts are from very different texts, they both suggest the cultural differences don't have to be a problem. What steps do they recommend for achieving success?

Critical analysis

Both extracts refer to the idea of 'synergy'.

> **synergy** the combined power of a group of things when they are working together which is greater than the total power achieved by each working separately

How does this idea of synergy motivate intercultural alliances? According to Geert Hofstede, founder of the Institute for Research on International Cooperation, 'Cultural differences are a nuisance at best and often a disaster.'

In your opinion, do you think intercultural business communication is an opportunity for synergy, or a potential disaster?

Reading 1: How can cultural differences be reconciled?

1 The following text is from the Renault–Nissan report on sustainability. Read paragraph 1. What are the three approaches for reconciling cultural differences?

Paragraph 1

Reconciliation of cultural differences can be approached in a number of different ways. The most common one is to adopt one partner's culture as dominant. The other alternative is to separate or limit the activities of the partners so as to minimise cultural interaction and hence the likelihood of cultural clashes. These not only limit the prospect of cultural conflicts but also reduce the potential of the partners learning and benefiting from each other's culture and business experience. The most integrative approach remains to face up to, manage cultural differences by involving partners at all levels, and participate in cross-cultural development programmes.

---

2 Before reading paragraph 2, discuss in pairs what might be the benefits and drawbacks of the three approaches in paragraph 1.

3 Discuss in pairs which approach you think Renault-Nissan used. Read paragraph 2 to find out if your predictions were correct.

Paragraph 2

More recent research has claimed that it is not the initial cultural clashes that create problems, but the different organisations having different beliefs and values which give rise to problematic situations. ... Strong and efficient cultures are typically characteristic of Japanese firms such as Nissan Motor Co. Renault culture is also seen as very efficient, but both companies were used to different management styles. They both needed to be aware that a successful enterprise would only grow if they acknowledged and respected each other's respective cultures and were committed to cooperating and working closely together.

---

4 According to the paragraphs, what gives rise to problems and what is the solution?

Reading 2: The alliance's principles

1 The alliance between Nissan and Renault was based on trust and fairness. In pairs, decide which of the principles below about partnership structures relate to trust and which to fairness.

Principles for partnership structures

1 They should be simple and understandable by both companies.
2 They should be trans-national.
3 They should facilitate confidence and transparency.
4 They should be based on the spirit of a win–win scenario.
5 No party should lose its cultural identities and/or brand.
6 Continuous dialogues and communication, despite geographical distance, should be encouraged to promote a spirit of partnership at all times.

---

2 Look at the problems below, and decide which of the alliance's principles above are being broken.

a We don't understand what this means.
b We think this favours the other side.
c We think that the other side has lied about this.
d We don't think this is relevant for our market.
e All of the decisions are made on a local level.
f The distance between the offices is too far to have frequent meetings.

Language focus: Nouns to make positive and negative judgements

In both written and spoken business communication, people use nouns to evaluate past, present and future relationships and situations positively or negatively. Examples are: *synergy/synergies, opportunity/opportunities, chance(s), conflict(s), problem(s), transparency/transparencies.*

1 Which of the above nouns are positive and which are negative?

2 Work with a partner. Which of these nouns do you think are more typical in written business and which are more typical in spoken business communication? Can you see any similarities between the nouns that are more typically written?

3 Match the nouns above with the verbs and prepositions that go with them to make collocations.

  Example: *create synergies between*

Verbs
seize   explore   lack   resolve   exploit   have   get give   stand   create   seek   avoid   inhibit   enhance   raise solve   cause

Prepositions
between   of   with   to   for   in   among

4 In pairs, think of a problem relationship you have had (with either an individual or an institution) and use some of these expressions to describe the situation.

Output: Managing an alliance

Two sports shoe companies from different countries are in an international alliance together. The alliance has been successful in the past, but recently there have been differences of view between the two companies. Work in groups of four and discuss how these differences can be reconciled.

Stage 1

Now divide into pairs. You work for sports shoe companies in the international alliance. Pair A work for a company in South America and Pair B work for a company in Asia. Pair A should look at page 139 and Pair B at page 144. Read the information about your negotiation positions.

Stage 2

Prepare your arguments and then have a meeting with the other pair to make four key decisions.

Stage 3

After the meeting, look back at Renault–Nissan's principles. Do you think the decisions you made would fit in with these principles? Explain your findings to another group or the rest of the class.

Learning outcomes

- Understand issues and stages in international team-building.
- Show progress through metaphors.
- Deal with problems and develop guidelines for international teams.

Introduction

1 People from different countries who work together may have different expectations about the best way to behave in certain situations. The following is a list of areas that can cause problems in international work teams. In small groups, decide whether international teams should make guidelines for any of these areas (you don't need to decide what the guidelines are at this stage).

- Dress at work
- Time-keeping at work
- Physical contact at work (touching, kissing, shaking hands, etc.)
- Direct/indirect communication at work
- Problem-solving and decision-making
- Communication between genders
- Socialising outside the workplace
- Other?

2 Work in small groups. Imagine someone from overseas is going to work in your country for one year. What advice would you give him or her in some of these areas? How might the type of job affect your advice (e.g. banker, teacher, cleaner)? Briefly outline your suggestions to another group.

Listening 1: The stages of building a team

 1.34

1 Team-building is often described as having the following four consecutive stages: *forming, storming, norming* and *performing*. In pairs, discuss briefly what you think each stage is about.

2 Now listen to Tim Rabone, co-founder of IGB Network, the management and organisational consultancy firm, talking about multicultural team-building.

1 What advice does he give to people setting guidelines for multicultural teams?

2 How long, according to Tim Rabone, does it take to reach the performing stage?

Listening 2: An international team meeting

1.35

Listen to the recording of an international business meeting about the issue of quality control, and answer the following questions.

1 How often does the chair (Mark) think checking should occur?

2 What stage of the relationship do you think this team is at, storming or performing?

Language focus: Metaphors of movement

A metaphor involves using one idea or expression to talk about something else. In business, metaphors are very common; for example, if we want to improve a damaged relationship we might say we want *to fix broken fences*. Metaphors of movement to describe progress are also very common in business. Look at the following examples:

So things are <u>moving forward</u> now ... but it was obvious that things were <u>going nowhere</u> at one particular stage.

1 What do the underlined expressions mean in this context?

2 Metaphors are often used in business situations to increase understanding between speakers. Are the following statements about metaphor true or false?

1 They rely on shared knowledge.
2 They are often indirect.
3 They evaluate the situation.
4 They are not literal.

3 Many metaphors in business are used to show progress or movement. Look at the following metaphors. Do they show progress, a lack of progress, or a desire for progress?

1 Can we move on?
2 I'm completely lost.
3 I haven't got anywhere with them.
4 Moving forward, …
5 The first step … / the next step …
6 … go backwards.

4 Read through the audio script for Listening 2 on pages 154–5 and find the five metaphors the chair (Mark) uses. What do they mean?

5 Can you think of any other metaphors like the ones above that involve progress? Are the same metaphors used in your first language?

Critical analysis

According to Carlos Ghosn, CEO of Renault–Nissan, 'When you have a very diverse team – people of different backgrounds, different culture, different gender, different age, you are going to get a more creative team, [and will] probably [be] getting better solutions.'

What do you think he means? Do you agree or not? Are there any negative aspects of multicultural teams?

Output: Developing guidelines for an international team

For each stage, work in groups of four. Appoint a chair who is responsible for 'moving the meeting along'.

Stage 1
You are in charge of developing guidelines for a multicultural team that is going to work together and meet socially for one year (you are at the forming stage). Write guidelines about the following points. Remember that the guidelines should be reasonably flexible at this stage.

- What should people wear to work?
- How should staff behave when they disagree with each other? What about if they disagree with their manager?
- How punctual should staff be for work and meetings? Can start and finish times be flexible?
- What guidelines should there be concerning physical contact in the workplace, for example touching people or kissing?
- Do you think men should speak to women in the same way they do to each other? Should there be any differences in the way men and women speak to each other?
- What guidelines, if any, should there be for social events? For example, should everyone attend, should certain topics be taboo, should there be guidelines for dress?

Stage 2
Discuss the following questions.

- Could any of the guidelines you have written cause any problems?
- How do you think people from cultures other than your own would feel about these guidelines?

Have a storming meeting where you alter the guidelines. Imagine your team has been applying the guidelines discussed in stage 1 for two months and has experienced some problems. Try to use metaphors to express these concerns and suggestions, for example those that show progress being blocked or slowed down such as 'We can't move forward with this because … '.

▶◀ **Watch Sequence 3 on the DVD to find out more about Managing cultures.**

Writing 3: Argument-led writing

Introduction

1 Read the statements below and circle the number which best reflects your opinion.

1 = strongly disagree 2 = disagree 3 = no opinion 4 = agree
5 = strongly agree

1 Roads and bridges are public services and so should be free.	1	2	3	4	5
2 The more privatisation the better.	1	2	3	4	5
3 Governments should raise funds by selling services to private companies.	1	2	3	4	5
4 Governments consider the least well-off, private companies do not.	1	2	3	4	5
5 Lower taxes are better than free roads and bridges.	1	2	3	4	5

2 Work in pairs and discuss your opinions about the statements above.

3 When writing about arguments for and against something, you need to consider both sides of the argument. Look at the opinions above and decide whether they are for or against the privatisation of roads.

Writing skill: Arguments for and against

Read the text below about privatising roads and bridges, and note the points under the following headings.

Arguments for privatisation   **Arguments against privatisation**

There are some advantages to private control of roads, utilities, lotteries, parking garages, water systems, airports, and other properties. To pay for their upkeep, private firms can raise rates at the tollbooth without fear of being penalised in the voting booth. Private sector operators are also freer to experiment with ideas like peak pricing, a market-based approach to relieving traffic jams. And governments are making use of the cash they're pulling in – balancing budgets, decreasing debt, investing in social programmes, etc.

But are investors getting an even better deal? It's a question with major policy implications as governments sell major public assets for years to come. Some public interest groups complain that the revenue from the higher tolls which all citizens have to pay will benefit only a handful of private investors, not society in general. The aggressive toll hikes embedded in deals all but guarantee pain for lower-income citizens – and enormous profits for the buyers.

There's also reason to worry about the quality of service on deals that can span 100 years. The newly private toll roads are being managed well now, but owners could sell them to other parties that might not operate them as capably in the future. Already, the experience outside of toll roads has been mixed. The Atlanta city water system, for example, was so poorly managed by private owners that the government had to take it back into public ownership. ■

Source: *BusinessWeek*

1 Do the following sentences present reasons, state results or make contrasts?

1 To pay for their upkeep, private firms can raise rates at the tollbooth.

2 The newly private toll roads are being managed well now, but owners could sell them to other parties that might not operate them as capably in the future.

3 The Atlanta city water system, for example, was so poorly managed by private owners that the government had to take it back into public ownership.

4 The aggressive toll hikes embedded in deals all but guarantee pain for lower-income citizens – and enormous profits for the buyers.

2 There are also several words and phrases that can be used to present reasons, state results and make a contrast.

Present reasons: because; since; for; in that; seeing as …; for the reason that …

State results: so; so that; as a result; therefore

Make a contrast: but; while; whilst; even though; although; however

Use some of the words and phrases above to make three sentences about your opinions regarding the statements in the Introduction.

Critical analysis

One of the possible results of privatisation in the text on page 62 is 'pain for lower-income citizens – and enormous profits for the buyers'. Do you think these are desirable, unavoidable or unacceptable results of privatisation in general?

If you were involved in managing the privatisation of your country's public services or utilities, would you recommend any measures to counter these effects? What would you do?

Stage 1

Take a maximum of 5 minutes to write notes for a brief outline for a one-page report on the topic of 'pros and cons of private ownership of roads (or another sector) in my country'. Follow this pattern:

Introduction: introduce the topic; give background information
Main body
Paragraph 1: outline and analyse pros
Paragraph 2: outline and analyse cons
Conclusion
Summarise key points
State your conclusion

Stage 2

Write the main body paragraphs, under the heading 'Pros and cons of private ownership of roads (or another sector) in my country'. Make sure you use the functions practised in the activities.

Stage 3

Compare your paragraphs with your partner's, and give feedback to each other.

7 Change management

7.1 Theory: DICE theory

Learning outcomes
- Understand the DICE theory of successful change management.
- Learn idioms and the language of cohesion and referencing.
- Plan and evaluate change using the DICE formula.

> **" A leopard doesn't change his spots. "**
> Anon.

Who says you can't change?

Introduction

1 How have you changed over the past five years? Which changes have been for the better? How did you make the changes?

2 What would you like to change about your job/study environment? What factors or people are stopping you making these changes?

3 What would you like to change about yourself in the future? Make a list of three things you want to change, and discuss the best way to achieve your goals.

Language focus 1: Idiomatic language

1 The following idioms and metaphors are underlined in the reading text which follows. Try to guess their meaning by matching them to their definitions. The first one has been done as an example.

Idiom
1 peter out
2 windows of opportunity
3 crave the limelight

4 take root
5 at the coal face
6 gut-wrenching
7 tackle the thorny issues
8 run into trouble

Definition
a feel very uncomfortable
b deal with difficult problems
c the place where the hardest work is done
d start to have problems
e want to be the focus of attention
f start to become established
g chances/possibilities
h slow down to a stop

2 Complete the following sentences using four of the idioms in exercise 1.

1 People in direct sales are working _____ . It is a really difficult job.
2 The rise in unemployment might mean that the economic recovery is starting to _____ .
3 He loves all the attention. He really does
_____ .
4 Airline mergers traditionally _____ with pilots' unions.

Reading: DICE theory – the hard side of change management

Business view

The article which follows is by Harold L. Sirkin, Perry Keenan and Alan Jackson, senior management consultants at The Boston Consulting Group.

1 The article says that two out of three initiatives to bring about change within an organisation fail. Why do you think this is? Before you read the article, predict which four of the factors from the list below you think are most relevant.

1 Staff are not fully consulted.
2 Senior managers do not communicate clearly.
3 Staff are frightened of change.
4 The change process is not reviewed regularly.
5 Change is forced upon staff.
6 The change project team lacks good enough people.
7 Top managers aren't fully committed.
8 Staff need to make too much effort to make the changes.

Now read the first three paragraphs of the article (lines 1 to 17). Which are the four factors the authors describe in the text? Do they match your predictions?

2 Working in groups of four, read one section each of the main text (Student A: Duration, Student B: Integrity, Student C: Commitment, Student D: Effort). Then close your books and tell each other about what you have read, using some of the idioms underlined.

3 Now read the whole article. Are the following statements true or false?

1 Companies' assumptions about long projects are correct. (Duration)

2 Well-liked managers make good team leaders. (Integrity)

3 The most influential people are not always the most senior managers. (Commitment)

4 Change projects will probably fail if there is any increase in existing day-to-day workloads. (Effort)

The hard side of change management

When French novelist Jean-Baptiste Karr (1808–1890) wrote 'Plus ça change, plus c'est la même chose' ('The more things change, the more they stay the same'), he could have been writing about change management, as studies show that in most organisations, two out of
5 three transformation initiatives fail.

Managing change is tough, but part of the problem is that there is little agreement on what factors most influence transformation initiatives. Ask five executives to name the one factor critical for the success of these programs, and you'll probably get five different answers.

10 We researched change programs in a study of 225 companies and found a consistent link between the outcomes (success or failure) of change programs and four hard factors: project duration, particularly the time between project reviews; performance integrity, or the capabilities of project teams; the commitment of both senior executives and the staff
15 whom the change will affect the most; and the additional effort that employees must make to cope with the change. We called these variables the DICE factors because we could load them in favor of projects' success.

Duration

Companies make the mistake of worrying mostly about the time it will
20 take to implement change programs. They assume that the longer an initiative carries on, the more likely it is to fail – the early momentum will <u>peter out</u>, <u>windows of opportunity</u> will close, objectives will be forgotten, key supporters will leave or lose their enthusiasm, and problems will accumulate. However, contrary to popular perception,
25 our studies show that a long project that is reviewed frequently is more likely to succeed than a short project that isn't reviewed frequently.
1 _____

_____

Integrity

30 By performance integrity, we mean the extent to which companies can rely on teams of managers, supervisors, and staff to execute change projects successfully. As the success of change programs depends on the quality of teams, companies must free up the best staff while making sure that day-to-day operations keep going.

35 Since project teams handle a wide range of activities, resources, pressures and unforeseen obstacles, they must be cohesive and well led. It's not enough for senior executives to ask people at the watercooler if a project team is doing well; they must clarify members' roles, commitments and accountability. They must choose the team
40 leader and, most important, work out the team's composition.
2 _____

_____

Executives often make the mistake of assuming that because someone is a good, well-liked manager, he or she will also make a decent team
45 leader. 3 _____

_____

Usually, good team leaders have problem-solving skills, are results oriented, are methodical in their approach but tolerate ambiguity, are willing to accept responsibility for decisions, and while being highly
50 motivated, don't <u>crave the limelight</u>.

Commitment

Companies must boost the commitment of two different groups of people if they want change projects to <u>take root</u>. They must get visible backing from the most influential executives (what we call C1), who are not
55 necessarily those with the top titles. And they must take into account the enthusiasm – or often, lack of it – of the people who must deal with the new systems, processes, or ways of working (C2).

Top-level commitment is vital to increasing commitment from those <u>at the coal face</u>. 4 _____
60 _____

In one financial services firm, top management's commitment to a program that would reduce errors and slash costs was low because it meant people would lose their jobs. Senior executives found it <u>gut-wrenching</u> to talk about layoffs in an organisation that had prided itself
65 on being a place where good people could find lifetime employment. However, the CEO realised that he needed to <u>tackle the thorny issues</u> around the layoffs to get the project implemented on schedule. He asked a senior company veteran to organise a series of speeches and meetings in order to provide consistent explanations for the
70 layoffs, the timing, the consequences for job security, and so on. He also appointed a well-respected general manager to lead the change program. 5 _____

_____

Effort

75 When companies launch transformation efforts, they frequently don't realise, or don't know how to deal with the fact, that employees are already busy with their day-to-day responsibilities. According to staffing tables, people in many businesses work 80-plus-hour weeks. If, on top of existing responsibilities, line managers and staff have to deal with changes to their
80 work or to the systems they use, they will resist.

Project teams must calculate how much work employees will have to do beyond their existing responsibilities to change over to new processes. Ideally,
85 no one's workload should increase more than 10%. Go beyond that, and the initiative will probably <u>run into trouble</u>. Resources will become overstretched and compromise either the change program
90 or normal operations. 6 _____

_____

Source: *Harvard Business Review*

Critical analysis

1 The term 'hard factors' refers to factors that you can measure or quantify. The DICE factors are seen by the authors as 'hard factors', but how easy do you think it really is to measure these four factors?

2 'Soft factors' refer to factors such as organisational cultures, leadership and motivation, and are generally seen as being very important for successful change management but very difficult to measure. How do you think it might be possible to measure them?

Language focus 2: Cohesion and referencing

Using cohesive and referencing words helps you produce language (written and spoken) that is properly joined together. Understanding the significance of these words helps you improve your reading and listening skills.

1 Match the two parts of the following sentences to explain how different cohesive and referencing words and phrases from the Reading article are used.

1 If you read the word *thus*, then	a the information will follow that names and contrasts these two groups.
2 If you read the phrase *that sounds reasonable, but*, then	b you know that named people's opinions were stated previously.
3 If you read the words *those actions*, then	c it will be followed by a consequence relating to the information mentioned previously.
4 If you read the words *they assume*, then	d the information that follows will contrast with the information mentioned before.
5 If you read the words *two different groups of people*, then	e you would expect to read something that contrasts with the valid point mentioned before.
6 If a sentence or clause starts with *however*, then	f you know the actions were mentioned before.

2 Look at the Reading text again and choose the best sentences below to fill the gaps 1–6 in the article. Use the information in the table to help you decide your answers.

a If employees don't see that the company's leadership is backing a project, they're unlikely to change.

b That sounds reasonable, but effective managers of the status quo aren't necessarily good at changing organisations.

c Senior executives should personally interview people for the project team so that they can construct the right portfolio of skills, knowledge, and social networks.

d Thus, the time between reviews is more critical for success than a project's lifespan.

e Those actions reassured employees that the organisation would tackle the layoffs in a professional and humane fashion.

f Employee morale will fall, and conflict may arise between teams and line staff.

3 Complete the following sentences about change management.

1 Change which involves laying off staff will always be resisted. Thus …

2 There are two different types of factor which change managers can focus on: …

3 A company that refuses to change will die. That sounds reasonable, but …

Output: Planning and evaluating change using DICE theory

In small groups, choose one of the following:

- At college or university – introduce a new form of course assessment *or* a new study timetable.
- At work – introduce a new form of job assessment *or* system of working hours.

Stage 1

You are course directors or senior managers for your organisation. Agree what you need to do to make sure your change project is successful by discussing the questions in the table on pages 139–40. Make notes when you answer the questions.

Stage 2

Present your change plans to another team. One team presents while the other team evaluates their chances of success by completing the table for the five factors indicated.

Use the following marking scale to judge how good the project team's plan is for each of the five factors:

1 = Excellent   2 = Good   3 = Satisfactory   4 = Unsatisfactory

Stage 3

As a group, compare your marks for the five factors in the table and agree on your evaluation for the other team. Then calculate their DICE score using the following formula:

DICE score = D + (2 x I) + (2 x C1) + C2 + E

Tell the other team the DICE score you have agreed on. Then look at page 140 to see whether your change plan is likely to be successful or not.

7.2 Practice: Implementing change

Learning outcomes
- Understand how change can be implemented in a company.
- Persuade staff of the need to change.
- Use and contrast the present perfect and present perfect continuous.

Profile: Laird Technologies Beijing

Laird Technologies Beijing is a subsidiary of the UK multinational Laird PLC, one of the world's largest manufacturers of mobile phone parts. For example, every day it produces one million phone antennae. Its largest customer is Nokia. After starting production in Beijing in 2001 with just four people, it now has a factory in Beijing employing 4,000 people, which accounts for 23% of the parent company's total sales revenue.

Introduction

1 What have been the biggest changes in your lifetime in your country?

2 Being open to and ready to implement change is seen as one of the key qualities of a successful manager. Why is this? What types of change might be required?

3 You are going to listen to an interview in which Charlie Peppiatt of Laird PLC discusses five steps for successful change management. Which of the steps below do you think is not one of these five?

- Develop a blame-free culture.
- Maintain the respect and self-confidence of others.
- Focus on team-working.
- Punish those workers who make mistakes.
- Reward people who get things done.
- Managers should set the right example.

4 Choose one step from the list above that you think is very important. Why do you think it is so important?

Listening 1: An overview of the interview

Business view

Charlie Peppiatt was General Manager of Laird Technologies Beijing from 2006 to 2009. He has managed operations and change in Europe, the US and China, and he is now Vice-President of Global Operations of Laird PLC.

🎧 1.36

Listen to four extracts (A–D) from the interview about managing change with Charlie Peppiatt. Match these summaries to the four extracts.

1 Importance of change from a manager's viewpoint ☐

2 Resistance to change within the company ☐

3 Successfully overcoming resistance to change ☐

4 Different cultural attitudes to change ☐

Listening 2: Dealing with resistors to change

 1.37

Listen to the recording and answer the questions.

1 According to Charlie Peppiatt, how should an organisation approach the problem of resistance to change?

2 How many people in a well-managed company will be resistant to change?

Listening 3: Successfully implementing change

 1.38

Listen to the recording and answer the questions.

1 What does Charlie Peppiatt say about customers?

2 How did he establish some basic principles in the Laird Beijing factory?

Transferable skill: Non-verbal communication

Charlie Peppiatt says that, when in international meetings, 'You need to be far more observant of people's body language, almost of what they're not saying as well as what they are saying.'

1 What types of non-verbal communication (NVC) can you think of?

2 Why do you think it is important to be aware of different forms of non-verbal communication in different cultures?

3 Look at the pictures. What do you think the orang-utans are communicating? Are you sure? One of the biggest problems in intercultural communication is that the speaker's intended meaning may not be interpreted as intended by the listener. Why is this a problem, and why do you think it often happens with NVC?

4 In pairs, count all the different facial gestures you use in your first language(s). Compare with another pair, and discuss any different facial gestures that you know are used in other cultures.

5 Look at this list of different types of NVC:

facial expressions	hand gestures	head movements
body movements	eye contact	distance between speakers
touching	kissing	bowing	shaking hands

Think of an example of each one that conveys meaning. Then, in pairs, try to communicate a message to your partner without saying anything, using as many types of NVC from the list as you can. Next, ask your partner an open question (where the answer is not yes or no), which they have to answer using NVC.

6 Are any types of NVC taboo in your culture? Do you know of any NVC taboos in other cultures? Why is such information important in international business?

Critical analysis

Charlie Peppiatt says in the interview that managers should be 'hard on the issue, fair on the person'. In what circumstances do you think managers should be 'hard on the person'? What would this mean in practice? Have you ever had to be 'hard on a person', either at work or in a school or university team or group?

Language focus: Present perfect simple and present perfect continuous

1 Look at these two sentences. The first sentence uses the present perfect simple and the second uses the present perfect continuous.

- Charlie Peppiatt **has managed** operations and change in Europe, the US and China.
- The Board **has been working** on establishing a set of core values for the group.

Both of these tenses can refer to events and situations in the past that have results in the present. However, there are differences. Which tense cannot be used about a single action? Which tense is used to focus on a result?

2 Look at the following points. Are they applicable to one or both tenses?

a Used to talk about past time
b Usually used to talk about the length of time
c To emphasise completion of an action
d To emphasise the situation is continuing now
e To show that the past action is still relevant
f Usually used to ask about amount (not time)

3 Match the points in exercise 2 with these sentences. Some of the points can be applied to more than one sentence.

1 They have been looking for a new location for the factory for ages.
2 How many spaces have we booked?
3 She's given me her mobile number, so I can call her.
4 I would prefer Dell because I've worked with Dell.
5 He's been working on the project for six weeks.
6 I've finished writing the report.

4 Look at the sentence below. Which tense refers to a single action, and which refers to a repeated action?

- They've been buying cranes from us for five years and have never ever paid a carriage charge.

5 Make similar sentences to the example above using these prompts.

1 come here / years … no problem
2 shop there / 2009 … manager / once
3 buy products / child … single complaint

6 How could you say the following using either the present perfect simple or present perfect continuous?

1 ask the length of time of an employee's career in a company
2 ask the number of items produced by an employee since last week
3 say the employee received three complaints since last month
4 ask the number of sick days taken by the employee in the past six months
5 say the company started losing money last year, and it still is

Imagine you work for a company where the team productivity levels have been low, and you have also had the following problems:

- Staff have taken a high number of sick days over the last year.
- There has been a high turnover of staff for the past two years.
- Productivity is low on Monday mornings and Friday afternoons.
- The quality of the product is inconsistent and high numbers of faults have been found.
- Staff do not greet customers in a friendly way.

Stage 1
Work in small groups. Brainstorm possible reasons for these problems and possible solutions.

Stage 2
Half of each group are the production team and half are the managers of the team. Have a meeting to discuss why some of these problems have happened, and how changes can be made to solve them.

Stage 3
After one month, the senior management reports that the changes have not happened. Discuss what the managers should do to improve the situation.

Laird Technologies Beijing

7.3 Skills: External negotiating

Learning outcomes
- Negotiate with people from other companies.
- Structure spoken language in face-to-face negotiations and meetings.
- Discuss complaints at work.

Introduction

1 Would you describe yourself as someone who complains a lot or very little? What or who do you often complain about? Who do you complain to?

2 Look at the following list of customer complaints. In pairs, put them in order in terms of the size of the problem. Then discuss what you think the company should do about each one.

a Customers have complained that several of your sales staff are rude to them.

b Many customers say your products are not as fashionable as they used to be.

c One manager was seen sleeping at his desk by a customer.

d You receive many complaints about the high price of your products.

e Customers have said your shops open too late in the morning.

f A group of customers is taking your company to court about product reliability.

3 In pairs, choose one of the above situations and have a mini-role play: Student A is the customer and Student B is a concerned and apologetic manager.

Intercultural analysis

Whether people apologise or not can vary according to culture, as well as personality. In your culture, do you think people would apologise in the following situations? Why/Why not?

- You crash your car, but it isn't clear whose fault it is.
- You accidentally bang into someone on a crowded train.
- You are late for work because the train was delayed.
- You lose a client at work because you made a mistake.

Listening 1: Complaints

🔘 1.39

You are going to listen to a negotiation between two multinational pharmaceutical companies (First Pharma, based in Germany, and ABC Pharmaceuticals, from the UK). First Pharma will start to produce and distribute ABC's products from this year. They are talking about the issue of complaints, and how responsibility for complaints is recorded in reports. The participants are Ada from First Pharma and Giles and Helen from ABC Pharmaceuticals.

Listen to the first part of the meeting and answer the following questions.

1 How many complaints have been made?

2 What is a 'stock out'?

Listening 2: Discussing the complaints procedure

🔘 1.40

Listen to the next part of the meeting and answer the following questions.

1 Does Ada from First Pharma agree or disagree with the way 'stock out' complaints are described in the report?

2 What is Giles's reaction?

Listening 3: Compliance complaints

🎧 1.41

Listen to the final part of the meeting and answer the following questions.

1 Does Ada from First Pharma agree or disagree with the way the compliance complaints are described in the report?

2 Why do you think Giles agrees with Ada here?

Language focus: Organising spoken language – head, body, tail

Spoken language and written language are different: writers make sentences, but speakers take turns. The structure of sentences and turns can also be different.

1 Look at the examples of spoken language below and divide each sentence into three parts.

- But the figures are already in a database anyway, aren't they?
- So, the document will have a final review before it's sent, you mean?

2 This pattern can be called HBT (head, body, tail). Not all spoken English follows this HBT structure, but it is good to be prepared to use it in face-to-face communication in meetings, negotiations and general conversation. In pairs, discuss how to address one of the complaints from the Introduction using the language in this table.

Head	Body	Tail
Speaker 1: I think	X is an attractive option,	don't you?
Speaker 2: Well, yes, I see	X is interesting, but Y may be possible too,	do you see what I mean?
Speaker 1: I see what you mean, but	Y is/has _____ ,	doesn't it?

3 Are the following words and expressions heads or tails? They can be one or both.

> Right   You know   Well   I see what you mean but
> I mean   you know what I mean   do you see what I mean
> OK   As far as I'm concerned   But   So   Yeah
> I'm sorry to trouble you   Erm   Basically   In my opinion

4 Are the following statements true or false?

1 Heads allow you to develop a relationship with the previous speaker.
2 Heads allow you to link your talk to the previous speaker.
3 Bodies contain the main information of your message.
4 Heads contain no new information.
5 Tails contain the key information.

5 Read through the audio script for Listening 1 on page 156, and find the turns that start with heads. Notice how more than one head can be used at the beginning of a turn.

Critical analysis

Do you use heads and tails in your first language? Many people who learn only written English at school sometimes have difficulty using heads and tails. What are some of the problems with speaking in a very 'written' style?

Output: Joint venture difficulties

Two mobile phone companies (one local and one multinational) have set up a separate joint venture company in the local company's home country market. This joint venture is owned 50/50 between the two companies.

The multinational company is responsible for the technology and design of the mobile phone as well as providing the manufacturing know-how and expertise. The local company is responsible for the marketing and sales. Their expertise lies in their understanding of the local market and what local consumers really need and want.

The joint venture has been established for one year and both companies are keen to maintain the good relationships that have developed between them. However, there have been several problems and they need to agree who is responsible and propose solutions.

Stage 1
Divide into small groups, with some groups taking the role of the local mobile phone manufacturer and other groups taking the role of the multinational mobile phone manufacturer, and prepare for the negotiation with the other company. Who was responsible for the mistakes listed below and how can the problems be resolved?

- There have been several delays in production, especially in the first half of the year.
- The manufacturing equipment (plant) was not totally suitable, as it was originally used for landline phones.
- The cost of the phones was initially set too high for the market.
- Customers complained that the product quality was not consistent.
- Customers have said the phones are too big.

Stage 2
Now work with a group from the other company and have the negotiation meeting.

8 Project management

Learning outcomes

- Understand the principles of project management.
- Learn the language of project management.
- Take part in a project planning meeting.

Introduction

1 Read the following definition of 'project'. Which words in the definition mean the same as *deadline*, *budget* and *quality objective*?

> A project is a task or set of tasks undertaken within specific timescales and cost constraints in order to achieve a particular benefit.

Business – The Ultimate Resource

2 On a corporate level, projects can range in scale from organising a stand at a trade show, developing a new product or service or building a giant sports stadium. Projects are also something individuals do in their own lives. Note down the time, cost and quality objectives of a project that you have completed in the last few years such as:

- organising a party
- making a career change
- arranging a holiday
- moving house

3 There is always conflict between the three variables of time, cost and quality. What might happen to the costs and quality objectives in the project you described above if you had half the time available? What would happen to your deadline and quality objectives if the budget was suddenly cut by 50%?

4 There are similarities in approach to many projects. Work in pairs and look at the photos above. Choose one of the following projects and consider the preparation needed:

- a climbing expedition up Mount Everest
- a scheme to reduce traffic in a city centre
- the launch of an exciting new product

Language focus 1: Project stages

1 Look at the six-stage model of project management. Match the words in the box with the words with similar meanings underlined in the sentences.

Stage 1   Proposal – identify the idea or need.

Stage 2   [1]Initial investigation – a [2]brief [3]overview of the possible [4]requirements and solutions.

Stage 3   Detailed investigation – [5]undertake a feasibility study of the options and define the chosen solution.

Stage 4   Development and testing – build the solution.

Stage 5   Trial – [6]pilot the solution with real people.

Stage 6   Operation and closure – [7]put it into practice and close the project.

a first   b short   c needs   d do   e general view
f implement   g test something new

2 Why do you think the early stages of project management are considered to be the most important?

Transferable skill: Engaging with the text

One of the best ways to improve your understanding of a text is to engage with it actively and not simply passively take in information.

1 Read the following opinions about project management and mark which ones you agree or disagree with or don't know about.

1 Projects need to be directed by a group of people, not one single individual.

2 You should always make a detailed plan of the whole project before you begin.

3 Different projects require very different processes and approaches.

4 The early stage of a project (planning, testing, investigating) takes 75% of the total time.

5 Making changes to the project once it is in full operation is very costly.

6 Everybody involved in the project or affected by the project should be engaged in the project.

7 Frequent meetings make teams work more closely together.

8 It's almost impossible to communicate with your team if you have no plan.

9 Having a good plan, combined with the right controls and processes, can help to eliminate risk.

10 All good projects should come to an end.

2 Now read the text which follows and decide whether the author agrees or disagrees with each of the above opinions. Compare your answers with a partner and explain why you agree or disagree with the text.

Reading: The principles of project management

1 Read the following extract from *The Project Workout* by Robert Buttrick.

1 Make sure your projects are driven by benefits that support your strategy.
You should be able to demonstrate explicitly how each project you undertake fits your business strategy. It is essential to screen out unwanted projects as soon as possible. The less clear the strategy, the more likely unsuitable projects are to pass the screening.

Each project should have a single project sponsor who is accountable for directing the project and ensuring that the expected benefits fit the strategy and are likely to be realised.

2 Use a consistent staged approach to manage your project.
It is rarely possible to plan a project from start to finish. However, you should be able to plan the next stage in detail and to the end of the project in outline. As you progress through the project you gather information, reduce uncertainty and increase confidence.

3 Use a typical staged project framework.
You should use the same generic stages for all types of project. This makes the use and understanding of the process familiar and easier, avoiding the need to learn different processes for various types of project. This generic framework should then be tailored to take into account the content of each project, the level of activity, the nature of the activity, the resources required and the stakeholders and decision-makers needed.

4 Place high emphasis on the early stages of the project.
High emphasis might mean that between 30% and 50% of the project's lifecycle is devoted to investigative stages. Studies clearly show that placing a heavy emphasis on

research decreases the time of completion. Good investigative work means clearer objectives and plans. In the early stages, creative solutions can slash delivery times by half and cut costs dramatically. Once development is under way, changes can be very costly.

5 Engage your stakeholders and understand their current and future needs.
A stakeholder is any person involved in or affected by a project. The involvement of stakeholders such as users and customers adds considerable value at all stages of the project. Engaging the stakeholders is a powerful mover for change, while ignoring them can lead to failure. When viewed from a stakeholder perspective, your project might be just one more problem they have to cope with. If their consent is required to make things happen, it is unwise to ignore them.

6 Encourage teamwork and commitment.
The more closely people from different disciplines work and the more open the management style, the better they perform. Although this is not always practical, closeness can be achieved by frequent meetings and good communication.

7 Monitor against the plan.
Good planning and control are essential for effective project management. If you have no definition of the project and no plan, you're unlikely to be successful. It will be virtually impossible to communicate your intentions to the project team and stakeholders. If there is no plan, terms such as 'early', 'late' and 'within budget' have no meaning.

Risk management is key: using a staged approach is itself a risk management technique, with each stage acting as a formal review point at which risk is put in the context of the business benefits and costs of delivery. Projects are risky. It is essential to analyse the project, determine which are the inherently risky parts, and take action to reduce, avoid, or, in some cases, insure against those risks.

Despite all this foresight and care, things will not always go smoothly. Unforeseen issues do arise that, if not resolved, threaten the success of the project. Monitoring against the agreed plan is a discipline that ensures events do not take those involved in the project by surprise.

8 Manage the project control cycle.
Monitoring should focus more on the future than on what has actually been completed. The project manager should continually check that the plan is still fit for purpose and likely to deliver the business benefits on time.

Many projects are late or never even get completed. One of the reasons for this is 'scope creep': more and more ideas are incorporated into the project, resulting in higher costs and late delivery.

9 Formally close the project.
Finally, every project must be closed, either because it has completed its work, or because it has been terminated early. By explicitly closing a project you make sure that all work ceases, lessons are learned, and any remaining assets, funding or resources can be released for other purposes.

2 With a partner, write down six comprehension questions on a separate piece of paper that you can ask another pair of students. Complete the two half-written questions below about Parts 1 and 3 of the text, and then write four more questions about the rest of the text on page 73 (Parts 4–9). Write answers to your six questions on the back of the piece of paper.

1 When is the best time to … ? (Part 1)
2 Why is it a good idea to … ? (Part 3)

Exchange your questions with another pair of students.

Language focus 2: Verb/noun combinations for project planning

1 Without looking at the text, make collocations by completing the following table with the words below.

information   the stakeholders   costs   delivery times
unwanted projects   confidence   teamwork

Part 1	screen out	unwanted projects
Part 2	gather	
Part 2	increase	
Part 4	slash	
Part 4	cut	
Part 5	engaging	
Part 6	encourage	

Now look at the text to check your answers.

Output: Scheduling a project

You are at the early stage of a proposed project to improve traffic flow in your local city centre. Your task is to hold a meeting and appropriately plan the different stages of this two-year project.

2 Complete these sentences using some of the verb/noun combinations from exercise 1.

1 We are going to have to _____ if we want to get the project finished on time.
2 Strong individuals may like taking control, but a good project manager will _____ .
3 Successful project managers will have no problems in _____ inside and outside the organisation.
4 Unfortunately, we are going to have to _____ if we want to get the project finished on budget.
5 It's important that we _____ and know exactly what we need to do before we start the project.
6 After the last project failed, we need to _____ amongst the shareholders if we want to attract investment.

Critical analysis

1 The Reading text places a strong emphasis on planning, yet what might be some of the dangers of too much planning?
2 Many people might disagree that having frequent meetings means that people will work well together. What other ways are there of building strong teams?

Stage 1
In small groups, look at the project schedule below. Discuss what order the stages should logically be done in. Complete the column marked Stage in the table.

Stage 2
Discuss how long each stage of the project should take. Then complete the table by shading in the cells. The first stage has already been programmed over three months.

Project Stage	City Centre Traffic Management Project Schedule																									
	Stage	Year 1												Year 2												
		J	F	M	A	M	J	J	A	S	O	N	D	J	F	M	A	M	J	J	A	S	O	N	D
Survey car and van drivers coming into the city centre																									
Put together project team, initial plan and schedule	1	▓	▓	▓																					
Implement the selected traffic-flow solutions across the city																									
Propose selected solutions to key stakeholders to improve traffic flows																									
Measure car, van and bus traffic flows coming into city centre																									
Have preliminary meetings with all major stakeholders																									
Pilot and test possible solutions to improve traffic flow in one part of city																									
Monitor effectiveness of the new traffic-flow scheme																									
Visit other similar cities which use effective traffic-flow schemes																									

8.2 Practice: Russian oil industry – Sakhalin-1 Project

Learning outcomes

- Get an insider's view on one of the world's biggest projects.
- Learn future perfect and future continuous tenses.
- Plan project goals and objectives.

Profile: Russian oil industry – Sakhalin–1 Project

The Russian Federation is one of the largest oil producers and exporters in the world, with proven reserves of over 60 billion barrels of oil. Most of these reserves are located in isolated and remote areas such as Siberia and the far east of the country. Sakhalin–1 Project is a vast oil and gas project on the island of Sakhalin.

Introduction

Look at the photos and read the brief profile above. Discuss the following questions.

1 What do you imagine the living and working conditions are like for people working on projects like this?

2 What type of personality and what type of skills do you think people need to have to work in the oil industry in remote and isolated locations?

3 Do you think you personally could work in the Russian oil industry as a project manager on site? Why/Why not?

Reading: Sakhalin – the place and the project

1 Work in pairs. Student A should read the project profile and Student B should read the island profile.

Project profile

Oil port on Sakhalin

Sakhalin-1 Project in the Russian Federation is one of the biggest oil and gas projects in the world, with projected reserves estimated at 2.3 billion barrels of oil. In the first phase of the project, engineers had to design and drill highly complex offshore wells from an onshore rig using extended drilling for record-breaking distances of over ten kilometres, build oil terminals for storage and construct a pipeline to transport the oil. In the second phase of the project, an offshore platform was built. The operator of the project is Exxon Neftegas Limited, which is an affiliate of the Exxon Mobil Corporation in the USA. Other participants in the Sakhalin-1 Project include Russian, Indian and Japanese oil companies. Other stakeholders include the Russian government, the local government and the population in Sakhalin. At the height of the project there were over 8,000 people from all over the world working there.

Island profile

Sakhalin

The island of Sakhalin is about 950 kilometres long. It is a very remote and isolated place in the far east of the Russian Federation, situated in an earthquake and typhoon zone. It is a nine-hour flight from Moscow, with a seven-hour time difference. Temperatures reach minus 40°C and much of the island is covered in snow, ice and freezing fog for six months of the year, with huge sheets of moving ice in the surrounding sea. This sea is also home to the endangered grey whale. Mountains and forests cover most of the island, and bears and reindeer roam wild. There are over 60,000 rivers and streams, many of them breeding grounds for wild salmon. The local population is under one million inhabitants – the main economic activity is fishing.

Without looking back at the text, tell your partner about what you have read.

2 What do you think are some of the main challenges and issues of this project?

3 Look at the table below and match the issues and challenges of the project with the examples, e.g. 1g.

Issues and challenges	Examples
1 Living conditions	**a** predicting the weather and the price of oil
2 Health and safety issues	**b** non-availability of off-road vehicles that go anywhere
3 Environmental concerns	**c** establishing budgets / scheduling stages of the project
4 Dealing with the unknown	**d** different working styles and attitudes in multinational teams
5 Political issues	**e** working outside at temperatures of –40°C
6 Moving around the site	**f** effect on the grey whale population
7 Working conditions	**g** nothing to do in the evening
8 Technical and engineering issues	**h** transporting material to the site
9 Logistical complexity	**i** complex negotiations between the consortium and the Russian government
10 Intercultural communication issues	**j** disagreements between different participants within the consortium and between the consortium and the local and national government in Sakhalin and Russia
11 Stakeholder conflicts	**k** long-distance drilling / building earthquake-proof structures
12 Initial project planning issues	**l** procedures to prevent accidents and injury when dealing with heavy machinery on site in isolated locations

Listening 1: Project overview

 2.02

Business view

Suleyman Narimanov is project manager for oil transportation and storage on Sakhalin-1.

1 Listen to seven short extracts, where Suleyman Narimanov speaks about working on the Sakhalin-1 Project. Match them to seven of the areas of project management in the left column of Reading exercise 3 above.

2 What do you think HSE refers to in extract 6?

3 Before you listen again, can you remember if the following statements are true or false?

1 Extract 1: They used a tractor during building and excavation works.
2 Extract 1: The Russian Niva four-wheel drive wasn't able to survive in Sakhalin.
3 Extract 2: It's very difficult to correct mistakes made in the early stages of the project.
4 Extract 3: The pipeline was constructed in the Philippines.
5 Extract 4: The airport can close for more than two weeks during bad weather.
6 Extract 4: No one responds to the office email during bad weather.
7 Extract 5: All material must be built for arctic conditions.
8 Extract 6: There were some major injuries on the project.
9 Extract 6: It was difficult to work with the HSE people.
10 Extract 7: There was only one channel on their TV.

4 Listen again. Are the statements above true or false?

5 What do you think you would find the hardest thing about living and working on Sakhalin-1?

Listening 2: Focusing on teamwork

2.03

1 When multinational teams live and work together in a remote and isolated place there can be problems. What problems, as a result of cultural differences, might occur in the following areas?

- food
- languages
- a sense of humour
- management styles
- levels of formality
- sports

2 How can project managers help multicultural teams get on well and work well together? How can the company help?

3 Listen to the second part of the interview with Suleyman Narimanov and note down what he says about the points below.

1 The problems that can occur in multinational teams
2 How the company can help people overcome cultural problems
3 The problems of having a senior manager from a different country to the rest of the team
4 The best ways to encourage good teamwork and commitment

Intercultural analysis

Different cultures can exist in different departments within the same company. Discuss the following questions.
1 Why do you think there is sometimes conflict between project managers and health and safety inspectors?
2 Who deals with the following objectives: project managers or health and safety inspectors?
  1 keep within the budget
  2 reduce risk
  3 do the job on time
  4 follow procedures

Language focus: Future perfect and future continuous

The two tenses are formed like this:

Future perfect: *will* + *have* + past participle of the verb

Future continuous: *will* + *be* + *-ing* form of the verb

1 Are the tenses in these sentences future perfect or future continuous?

1 A representative will have phoned you by the end of the week.
2 So you'll be struggling for work next year.
3 I'll have done the work you've just given me by the end of next week.
4 He'll be working on this bridge this time next year.

2 Which tense is used to do the following?

1 To talk about something in progress in the future (or expected to be in progress in the future)
2 To talk about something that is seen as already completed before a certain time

3 The future perfect is often used with phrases like *by the end of next week*, and the future continuous is often used with phrases like *this time next week*, etc.

Use the following prompts to make sentences using the future perfect or future continuous about your personal, professional or study plans.

by the end of the day	by the end of the year
this time next week	in a month's time
by the end of the month	this time next year
in a year's time	

4 Complete these sentences with the correct form of the verb in brackets, using the future perfect or future continuous.

1 We need to get on well, as we _____ together closely on this project. (work)
2 In another 10 or 15 years all the North Sea gas _____ . (go)
3 Within a month or two after graduating from this university, 98% of those seeking jobs _____ one. (find)
4 Give me the report because I _____ him some time next week. (see)
5 Fortunately, we _____ updating the server in time for the start of the new project. (finish)
6 Without more state help, local communities _____ the pain for years to come. (feel)

Output: Planning goals and objectives

You are going to take part in a meeting between project managers for a Russian oil company and independent health, safety and environmental managers hired by the company. Your aim is to agree on a project schedule that ensures the job is done in record time whilst minimising risk to the people working on site.

Stage 1
Work in small groups. Half the groups should take the role of project managers (see page 140), while the other groups should take the role of health, safety and environmental managers (see page 144). Read the project management team's schedule, the notes and your role card and prepare for the meeting.

Stage 2
Conduct the meeting and agree on the schedule.

Learning outcomes

- Discuss future arrangements with other companies.
- Maintain a good relationship with other companies by using indirect language.
- Signal differing identities and groups using 'we'.

"I'd like a 150% rise."

Introduction

1 Look at the following list. Which ideas do you think are the most important for developing a good business relationship?

> showing respect at all times   seeing the other's point of view
> reaching a compromise where there are differences
> avoiding conflict   not being too direct in requests
> showing that you are working together
> being honest and open at all times

In what ways are good relationships in business different from or similar to personal friendships?

2 We often use indirect requests to be polite. For example, if you want someone to close a window, you could say, *It's a bit cold in here, isn't it?* In pairs, discuss how you can make an indirect request for a pay rise. How many different ways can you think of to do this?

3 You will hear the following indirect request in the Listening which follows.

So I guess the best way forward is just to kind of leave you to sort of digest this. And then you know, we'll perhaps wait for you to come back to us about the next stage …

What examples of indirect language can you see? Which functions from exercise 1 might be addressed by this type of language? What would be a direct way of requesting this?

4 Directness is sometimes seen as a good thing in international business meetings. Why do you think this is?

Listening: A sales meeting between IT companies

1 Work in pairs to role play the end of a meeting between a sales manager and a client.

Sales manager: You want to tell the client you will contact them about the figures by next week and you will schedule another meeting when the client is ready. Try to develop a good relationship with the client.

Client: Try to be flexible about dates and try to develop a relationship with the sales manager.

2.04

2 Listen to the end of a meeting where the accounts manager (Charles) and the sales director (Liam) from an IT company are talking to a client (Valentina). Answer the following questions.

1 When does Liam say he can send the figures?
2 What is Valentina's response to this?
3 In your opinion, why does Liam mention the football game between the two companies?

Critical analysis

Read through the audio script of the meeting on page 79, and compare it with your role play in the Listening exercise.

1 How definite are the arrangements you made compared with those in the audio script?
2 How did the participants on the recording try to build a relationship? What about you in your role play?
3 Why do you think the speakers in the recorded meeting are so indirect?

Language focus: Signalling identities through 'we'

'We' is far more important in business than in everyday communication. This is because, in business, 'we' (and 'us') can refer to different groups of people and companies, and is used to emphasise cooperation. It can be used 'inclusively' – to talk about everyone – and 'exclusively' – to include some people (us), but not others (you/them). Some languages have different words for the inclusive and exclusive use of 'we'.

1 Look at the following two examples:

1 … **we** think you should be looking at this …

2 … so, **we** agree on that …

In these examples, is 'we' inclusive or exclusive?

2 Here is a list of some of the most common uses of 'we' in meetings between different companies. Match the uses of 'we' (1–5) to the explanations (a–e).

1 Exclusive present 'we'
2 Inclusive corporate 'we'
3 Inclusive present 'we'
4 Exclusive corporate 'we'
5 Vague 'we'

a it is unclear exactly who it refers to
b both companies
c the members of the speaker's company who are present
d all participants who are present
e the speaker's company, not the other company

3 In pairs, look at the audio script of the meeting, and highlight all the examples of 'we' and 'us'. Decide whether they are inclusive or exclusive uses.

4 'We' often emphasises cooperation. Why is it important to emphasise cooperation in business?

Intercultural analysis

Some uses of exclusive 'we' can damage a relationship. For example, if a British person says '**We** British are very polite' to somebody from another country, how might the listener feel? How could the speaker reword this?

Audio script
 2.04

Charles: … well, I mean we fully support that so it shouldn't be a problem.

Valentina: Right. OK. That might be a cheaper thing for us to do.

Charles: OK.

Valentina: Right.

Liam: So, we need to get those figures to you. We should be able to get those to you this afternoon or tomorrow.

Valentina: Whenever. There's no hurry.

Liam: No?

Valentina: No, just fit them in around what else you do. But it's just useful information for us.

Liam: OK.

Valentina: Yeah.

Charles: No problem.

Valentina: Great.

Liam: So, I guess the best way forward is just to kind of leave you to sort of digest this. And then you know, we'll perhaps wait for you to come back to us about the next stage. I'm sure you're going to have some more questions.

Valentina: Probably.

Liam: You know, really it's just about making this make sense for you and for us.

Valentina: Yes. Thank you.

Liam: And I'm sure with all this stuff there's a way of doing it where it's going to please us all. But I think next time we'll just get together and we'll work everything out then.

Valentina: Great.

Liam: OK?

Valentina: Yes. That's great. Thanks very much.

Charles: OK. Right.

Liam: And I think we've got a football match the week after next, haven't we?

Charles: Yes, I spoke to Raj.

Valentina: Is that here?

Liam: Yeah.

Output: Negotiating sensitive arrangements

Stage 1

In pairs, carry out two role plays. Student A should look at page 140, and Student B should look at page 144.

Stage 2

How effective were the meetings? What would you do differently next time?

▶◀ **Watch Sequence 4 on the DVD to find out more about Managing operations.**

Writing 4: Describing graphs

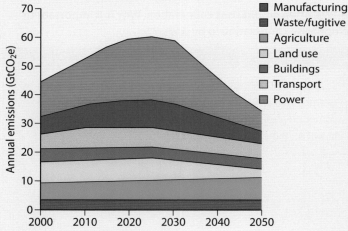

Learning outcomes

- Compare and contrast figures and trends.
- Write a report describing figures and trends in graphs.
- Understand the issue of carbon emissions across industries.

Introduction

1 Are you worried about global warming? Why/Why not?

2 Which of the possible effects of global warming below do you think is the biggest problem? Order them in terms of seriousness:

- rising sea levels
- reduced tourism
- species extinction
- water shortages
- increased disease

3 The need to reduce carbon emissions across industries to slow down global warming is often discussed. Which of the following situations do you think are most likely to happen? Which would have the greatest effect?

- Consumers change their behaviour and demand low-carbon products.
- Governments make regulations, such as a carbon tax for high-carbon industries.
- Technological advances (for example electric cars) lead to new ways to cut emissions.

4 Different industries produce different amounts of carbon. Look at the pictures above, and match them with these industries. Which one do you think produces the most carbon, and which produces the least?

a power **b** agriculture **c** manufacturing **d** transport
e waste disposal

Writing skill: Describing graphs

The graph below predicts possible carbon emissions scenarios if governments and other policy-makers follow certain regulations. Regulations could include lower speed limits for vehicles, energy efficiency standards for factories and machinery, and prohibiting the sale of certain products such as high-energy light bulbs.

Evolution of transmissions by major industrial category for Targeted regulation scenario

Annual emissions ($GtCO_2e$)

Legend:
- Manufacturing
- Waste/fugitive
- Agriculture
- Land use
- Buildings
- Transport
- Power

Source: Carbon Trust and Oxera analysis
$GtCO_2e$ = Global tonnes of CO_2 equivalent

1 Discuss these questions and make notes.

1 What does the brief description above the graph tell you?
2 What does the title of the graph tell you?
3 What do the vertical and horizontal axes show?
4 What are the general trends over the 50-year period?
5 How do emission level differences compare across differing decades? **Example:** In the 2020s ... however, in 2030 ...
6 How do certain industries differ at the same point in time? **Example:** In 2040, the manufacturing industry's emissions ...

2 Summarise the information on the graph in one sentence.

Language focus: Comparisons and contrasts

When describing graphs, two of the key functions are making comparisons and contrasts.

1 What are the mistakes in the following sentences?

- The percentage of male and female executives is particularly the same.
- The company faced a considerably low return once it didn't sell enough to break even.

2 Look at these different ways of comparing and contrasting information.

1 A is _____ bigger than B.
2 A is _____ the same as B.
3 A is _____ different from B.
4 A is _____ as big as B.
5 A is _____ the biggest.

Which of the following words can fit into each gap in 1–5 above?

considerably   virtually   exactly   somewhat   totally
completely   quite   about   slightly   a great deal
approximately   by far   not very

3 Look at the graph on page 80 and compare results from two points on the timeline using phrases from exercise 2.

Example: In 2030, the carbon emissions of the power industry are predicted to be considerably higher than in 2050.

4 Look at the mistakes below about the graph on page 80 and correct them. Some of the mistakes are language mistakes and some are about the content of the graph.

1 The considerably biggest producer of carbon is power.
2 The power industry produces exactly more CO_2 than other industries.
3 The building industry is unique in reducing its carbon emissions over the 50-year period.
4 In 2020, the power industry will have the highest CO_2 emissions. On the other hand, it will have greatly increased compared to 2000.

5 Read these incorrect comparisons of trends describing the graph on page 80, and correct them.

1 In the graph, CO_2 emissions in the waste industry rise and then fall over the 50-year period, whereas they fall steadily in the power industry.
2 Overall, CO_2 emissions gradually increase from 2000 to 2040 in both the agricultural and the power industries.
3 Both the agricultural and manufacturing industries' emissions peak at around 2025, and then decline steadily.

Output: Describing a graph

The graph below shows the predicted effects of technological advances in helping to solve the problem of carbon emissions across major industries. Such advances could include electric vehicles and cheap forms of renewable power, e.g. solar or marine power.

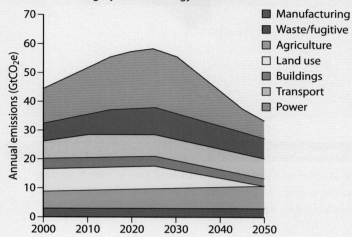

Evolution of emissions by major industrial category for Technology scenario

Source: Carbon Trust and Oxera analysis
$GtCO_2e$ = Global tonnes of CO_2 equivalent

Stage 1

Summarise the information by selecting and reporting the main features and make comparisons where relevant. You should write three paragraphs.

Paragraph 1: A general description of the graph
Paragraph 2: Explanation of what is in the graph, starting with comparisons of general trends, moving to comparisons of specific points
Paragraph 3: A one-sentence conclusion that summarises the general trend in the graph

Stage 2

In small groups, discuss whether your answers to exercise 3 in the Introduction have changed.

9 E-marketing

9.1 Theory: The 4Cs of marketing and e-marketing

Learning outcomes

- Understand marketing theory of the 4Cs applied to e-marketing.
- Learn marketing and e-marketing terms and concepts.
- Propose ideas for making retailers better e-retailers.

Can I help?

Question

Introduction

1 What does *shopping* mean to you? Tick (✓) the following reasons why you personally go shopping. Then discuss your answers with a partner.

to get the best price

to have an enjoyable experience

to buy quality products

to get what I need

to try the latest products

to make me feel good

to get something straight away

to pass the time

to spend time with friends

2 Discuss with a partner if you think you are more likely to satisfy these needs by shopping on the high street or online.

3 How do you think the high street and online shopping experience will change over the next ten years?

4 Look at the image of the virtual assistant. She has been designed for a railway company to answer customers' questions. Virtual assistants like this are said to have a 90% success rate. Discuss the advantages and disadvantages, from the point of view of both the company and the customer, of using a virtual assistant.

> **Example:** From the company's perspective, the advantage of the assistant is that the company can log all enquiries and then analyse them with software to understand customer needs better.

Language focus 1: Marketing terms

1 Put the marketing words for *shop* below into the following groups:

- online store
- high street store
- combined online and high street store

retail outlet   e-retail shop   e-tailer   bricks retailer
dot.com   multi-channel retailer   virtual store
bricks and clicks operation   physical store

2 Read the definition of *marketing* below and complete the gaps with these words and phrases:

product   price   target customers   promotion   place
marketing mix

Marketing is about having the right 1 _____ available in the right 2 _____ at the right time at a 3 _____ that people are willing to pay and that is communicated with the most attractive 4 _____ message for this group of 5 _____ . All these elements, combined together, are known as the 6 _____ or the 4Ps.

3 Read the text below comparing the 4Ps of marketing with the 4Cs and complete the gaps using the following phrases. The first has been done for you.

convenience to the customer   customer wants and needs
customer's perspective   cost to the customer
producer's perspective   communication with the customer

The 4C framework of marketing is a recent marketing theory which is considered highly relevant for retailers selling direct to the consumer via virtual or high street stores. The framework is designed to help companies view marketing from the 1 <u>customer's perspective</u> and is critical of the 4Ps, which is seen to be a framework which analyses marketing too much from the 2 _____ . While the 4P marketing managers will look at what price their company should charge for their products or services, the 4C managers look at what the 3 _____ will be. The 4P managers will focus on selling the product, yet the 4C managers will look instead at satisfying 4 _____ . In a similar fashion, advocates of the 4Ps look at the promotion of their products, whilst the 4C managers will prefer to focus on 5 _____ . Finally, in the world of 4P marketing, managers will be preoccupied with how to place their products in their customers' hands, whereas the 4C marketeers will be working out how to locate their stores both virtually and physically to provide maximum 6 _____ and make them easy to find.

Critical analysis

Some people view the 4Cs as being basically the same as the 4Ps approach. Others, however, see the customer focus of the 4Cs model as providing a more relevant and up-to-date model for today's business. Who do you agree with?

Reading: The 4Cs of e-retail and retail

Business view

You are going to read an article by Senior Marketing Lecturer Dr Charles Dennis from Brunel Business School, Brunel University London, UK, and marketing and e-marketing experts Dr Tino Fenec and Professor Bill Merrilees of Griffith University, Gold Coast, Australia.

1 Look at the section headings (C1–C4) in the text and decide where you will find the answers to the questions in exercise 2 below.

2 Now answer the questions, scanning only the section of text (C1–C4) where the answer is located.

1 How can e-tailers project a positive mood on their website?
2 What do customers think about prices online compared to the high street?
3 Which type of retail operation is more successful: e-tail or multi-channel?
4 What do customers buy instead of 'products'?
5 How are retailers different from producers in their relationship with the customer?
6 How are location decisions different for a high street retailer and a purely online one?
7 Why do some customers start their purchase online, but don't complete it?
8 Who can offer a better range of products, an e-tailer or a retailer?

C1 Convenience for the customer

'Place' (from the 4Ps), rather than implying managements' methods of placing products where they want them to be, can be thought of as 'Convenience for the customer', recognising the customers' choices for buying in ways convenient to them. For the bricks retailer, 'Place' incorporates what can be the most critical decisions concerning 'location', reflecting shoppers' preferences for short travel journeys, easy access, parking and so on. For the e-retailer, this is also important, as many customers prefer a multi-channel approach: browse on the web, buy instore or vice versa – or buy on the web and then return

to the store for a refund! This perhaps goes some way towards explaining the success of high street and multi-channel retailers in e-retail, compared to the dot.com 'pure plays'. 'Location' for the e-retailer also means virtual location and the ease of finding the website. This entails registration with search engines, location in e-malls and links from associates. 'Convenience' also includes key aspects of website design such as navigation, layout and ease of purchase.

C2 Customer wants and needs

'Product', rather than being something that a company has to sell, can be thought of as 'Customer wants and needs' – meaning the bundle of services and satisfaction wanted by customers. People do not buy 'products' as such, but rather good feelings or solutions to problems. An essential task of retail and e-retail is selecting the range of products offered for sale – assembled for target markets from diverse sources. The wide and deep range that can be offered is one of the areas where the 'clicks' e-retailer can score relative to the 'bricks' retailer. The lowest price does not always result in the highest sales, as many shoppers may value aspects such as style, design and fashion, for example.

C3 Cost to the customer

'Price' may be what companies decide to charge for their products, but 'Cost to the customer' represents the real cost that customers will pay, including, for example, in the case of 'bricks' retail, their own transport costs. For 'clicks' e-retail, there are also the costs of carriage and perhaps taxes to be added to the quoted prices. High carriage charges may be one reason for the high rate of carts abandoned at the checkout. Consumers have a perception that prices should be lower online than instore, and this can cause problems when customers buying via other channels realise that they are paying more than online customers.

C4 Communication with the customer

'Promotion' suggests ways in which companies persuade people to buy, whereas 'Communication' is a two-way process also involving feedback from customers to suppliers. Retailers are closer to the customer than manufacturers are and have more access to customer feedback. 'Communication' is not just advertising, though, but all the ways in which retailers communicate with their customers, including, for example, direct mail, marketing database and loyalty schemes. In addition to solving problems there is another reason for customers buying products – to get good feelings. This is a particularly difficult area for e-retailers. E-retailers can create a 'web atmosphere' using, for example, music and visuals such as 3D displays and downloadable video clips. Such enhancements must always be a compromise, on account of the need to avoid long download times.

Source: *International Journal of Retail & Distribution Management*

Read the following definition of 'critical thinking' from the Critical Thinking Foundation (a non-profit-making organisation that aims to promote educational change through developing critical thinking ideas) and answer the following questions about the text using the method below:

66 Critical thinking is the art of analysing and evaluating thinking with a view to improving it. **99**

1 Identify point of view: What position does the writer take, pro 4Cs or pro 4Ps? What do the authors imply about the 4Ps?

2 Identify and challenge assumptions: The fourth C, 'Communication with the customer', assumes that customers want a two-way communication with the company and are open to having an on-going relationship. Are these assumptions valid?

3 Consider the issue from an alternative perspective: How might a supporter of the 4Ps framework criticise the 4Cs?

4 Engage personally: What is your personal view? Are you more influenced by the 4Cs or the 4Ps? How can you relate this to your own personal experience of shopping or doing business?

Language focus 2: E-marketing terms

1 Look at the following list of e-marketing tools and techniques and match each of them to the two most relevant of the 4Cs.

1 *Database marketing* enables companies to analyse such things as online customer feedback and enquiries with powerful software which helps them understand their customers better.

2 *Smart card loyalty schemes* are an example of customer relationship marketing, whereby retailers can deepen their relationships with customers by giving them valuable information to offer personalised products and services which they hope will keep their customers loyal.

3 *Web optimisation* is all about how companies can best design their website by making it fast and easy to navigate, a pleasant place to browse, and above all, easy to find via search engines (known as search engine optimisation).

4 *Social media marketing* helps companies create new media campaigns using blogs and social network sites to interact in a two-way process with their customers.

2 Can you think of some more examples or applications of each of the e-marketing practices?

3 How have you experienced some of these practices as a customer?

Output: Improving a company's e-retailing operation

Stage 1

Work in groups. You are going to make a proposal to the Marketing Director on how you can improve your company's e-retail operation. Choose one of the following companies:

Group A – KidZ Books
Group B – KarlZ Koffee
Group C – Carla's Cakes
Group D – Metropolitan Railways

Stage 2

Look at these pages and follow the instructions:

Group A – pages 140–1
Group B – page 145
Group C – page 146
Group D – page 146

Stage 3

When you are ready, give the presentation to the rest of the class. Make sure that everybody in your group speaks.

9.2 Practice: The benefits of selling on- and offline

Learning outcomes
- Learn about Dell Computers' e-marketing strategy.
- Learn mixed conditionals and review standard conditionals.
- Conduct e-marketing research.

Profile: Dell Computers

Dell was founded by Michael Dell in 1984, with only $1,000 in start-up capital, and was the first company to sell computers directly to the customer, bypassing any intermediary. It is now one of the largest providers of PCs in the world and for a number of years has been the No. 1 PC supplier to small and medium-sized businesses in the US. In 1996 the company launched www.dell.com and now a huge number of their total sales are made on the Internet. Until recently it was not possible to buy their computers in retail shops on the high street. This strategy has now changed in a number of countries.

Introduction

Read the company profile and discuss the following questions with a partner.

1 What do you think are the advantages to you as a customer in buying a computer direct from the manufacturer over the Internet?
2 What might be the advantages for Dell of this business model?
3 What disadvantages might there be for the customer and the company?
4 Why do you think Dell changed its strategy and is now also selling through shops?
5 What does this change of strategy say about the limits of e-marketing?

Listening 1: A definition of e-marketing

Business view

Alastair Brown, Chief Operating Officer of Bizantra, London, and former Marketing Director of Dell, Asia

Read the summary below of the first part of the interview with Alastair Brown and try to predict the words he uses.

E-marketing is about using electronic media for marketing purposes – not just the Internet, but also 1 e_____ and 2 m_____ marketing. In one sense, e-marketing is very different to marketing because it means you can have a closer 3 r_____ with the customer. On the other hand, e-marketing is simply an extension of marketing. You use the same 4 a _____ but use them through different 5 c_____ .

Now listen and check your answers.

🔘 2.05

Listening 2: Online communication and sales channels

🔘 2.06

Listen to the second part of the interview and answer the questions below.

1 Which advantages of e-marketing does Alastair Brown mention?

1 You can communicate your message quickly.
2 You can interact with your customers.
3 You can grow your business and make money.
4 You can easily measure how successful your communications are.

2 Are the statements below about Dell's sales channels true or false?

1 Traditional marketing communication channels have no place in Dell's business model.
2 All Dell's sales made directly to the customer are done online.
3 Until recently the only place you could buy a Dell computer was from Dell.

 Listening 3: The benefits of online selling

🎧 2.07

Listen to the third part of the interview with Alastair Brown and complete the notes below with what he says.

Benefits to company	Benefits to customer
1 Dell can know _____	2 Dell can design and build computers to order. For example, customers can order a computer with _____ if they do graphics or play games.
3 Dell doesn't have to hold _____	
4 Online selling means Dell can cut out _____	

Listening 4: Problems with online sales channels

🎧 2.08

1 Listen to the final part of the interview and answer the questions below.

1 Which type of companies does Dell target first when it enters a new market?
2 Which type of companies does Dell target next?
3 How do these two customer groups prefer to buy?
4 Why do these customer groups prefer to buy in this way?
5 Why are individual consumers different from companies?

2 After listening, discuss with a partner whether you agree with this analysis of consumer buying behaviour. How do you prefer to buy computer equipment and other electronic goods?

Language focus 1: Review standard conditionals

1 Complete the following table about conditionals with the information below. The first one has been done for you.

Type of conditional	Grammar	Use
Zero	If + present simple in both clauses	To talk about a general truth
First		
Second		
Third		

Grammar

If + past simple / would + infinitive
If + present simple / will + infinitive
If + past perfect / would + have + past participle
If + present simple in both clauses

Use

The past conditional – to talk about the hypothetical unreal past
To talk about a likely result in the future
To talk about a general truth
The hypothetical conditional – to talk about a result if the present or future was different

2 Are the conditionals in the following sentences examples of the zero, first, second or third conditional?

1 Market research shows that, if their favourite star moves, many football fans across Asia will transfer their support to a different club.
2 If you get a big marketing campaign, you're able to reach a lot of people.
3 You would have avoided paying interest if you had known about the charges earlier.
4 How would the company's shareholders feel, if they knew its marketing strategy was influenced by corporate entertainment?

Language focus 2: Mixed conditionals

Mixed conditionals are also common, especially in spoken English. Look at the following examples.

If you had looked at the financial commentary … ⟶ … you would see that 45% of our work is for regional railways.
(past hypothetical condition) (present hypothetical result)

If I were paid that much … ⟶ … I wouldn't have minded paying the tax.
(present hypothetical condition) (past hypothetical result)

1 Complete the following sentences to show present (hypothetical) results of these past conditions for Dell and its marketing strategy. (The first has been done for you as a suggested possible answer.)

1 If Dell had focused more on the consumer market in the beginning, _they wouldn't be changing their business strategy now._
2 If Dell hadn't started selling its PCs through high street shops, _____
3 If there hadn't been high levels of broadband in South Korea, _____
4 If Dell had never adopted a business model based on selling direct, _____

2 Complete the following sentences to show past hypothetical results of these present hypothetical conditions for Dell and its marketing strategy. (The first has been done for you as a suggested possible answer.)

1 If Dell didn't use traditional marketing media such as newspaper ads, _they wouldn't have had the same levels of success._
2 If Dell used exclusively online sales channels, _____
3 If individual consumers behaved like companies, _____
4 If Dell held limited stock of pre-assembled computers, _____

Output: E-market research

A major computer company is reviewing its strategy and e-marketing, and needs information before it can make major decisions.

Stage 1

In pairs, conduct a short market research survey to collect information. Student A should look at page 141 and Student B at page 145.

Stage 2

Compare your answers with another pair. How might your results impact on the strategy and e-marketing policy of the computer company?

Stage 3

Report the findings of your survey and how you think they could have an impact on the computer company's future strategy and e-marketing to the rest of the class.

Learning outcomes

- Structure a presentation in a logical order.
- Introduce and link slides.
- Prepare and deliver an e-presentation.

Introduction

1 It is often said that, with presentations, it's not *what* you say but *how* you say it that counts. Do you agree? Discuss with a partner whether style is more important than content for presentations.

2 Do the following presentation guidelines refer to *content* (C) or *style* (S)?

1 keep the message simple
2 show enthusiasm
3 use slides with strong visual images
4 keep eye contact with audience
5 present information logically
6 use appropriate body language
7 speak slower than normal speech
8 make sure to keep to the time limit

In pairs, discuss which guidelines are the most important for content and for style. Are there any other guidelines you can think of?

Listening 1: Beginning an e-presentation

🔘 2.09

Business view

Philip Weiss is Managing Director of ZN, a specialist e-marketing agency.

1	Introduction to ZN

2	Let's get started

In this presentation:

- About ZN
- HQ challenges
- How we can help you

3	

E-marketing for European HQs

A 5-minute online presentation

4	Introduction to ZN

- HQs
- 10 years
- E-marketing

Before listening to the first part of Philip Weiss's presentation, look at the first four presentation slides above (from a total of nine) and answer the following questions.

1 What is the correct order of the slides?
2 Who is the presentation aimed at?
3 What does 'HQs' refer to?

Listen to the first part of Philip Weiss's presentation on his company's website and check your answers.

Listening 2: Developing an e-presentation

🔘 2.10

1 Look at the table below, which outlines the structure of the whole presentation (slides 1–9). Try to guess the content of the remaining five slides by making a rough drawing of each one.

Slide	Information communicated
1	Make personal introduction / open presentation
2	Summarise what the presentation will be about
3/4	Introduce the company
5/6	Outline challenges facing prospective clients
7/8	Propose solutions for clients
9	Request client makes contact / close presentation

Turn to page 141 to see the last five slides.

2 Listen to the final part of Philip Weiss's presentation and put the remaining slides on page 141 into the correct order. Complete the missing information on the slides using one or two words.

Critical analysis

1 Do you think this is a good presentation? Why/Why not? Use the guidelines on *style* and *content* in the Introduction to assess this. Mark each guideline as either: *Excellent, Good, Average* or *Below average*. Which guidelines are impossible to assess as this is an e-presentation online and not face-to-face?

2 Here are some features of e-presentations:
- You can build a relationship with your audience online.
- Customers can replay sections of your presentation at will.
- You can reach a worldwide audience 24/7.
- You can track who watches your presentation.

Do you agree that these are advantages of e-presentations? What are some of the disadvantages?

Language focus: Introducing and linking slides

1 **Put these introductions to each slide in the correct order by numbering each slide. The first one is done for you.**

Slide	Introduction to slides
	a If you're interested in pursuing this conversation, we look forward …
	b … and we focus specifically on …
	c The way we start our work is to focus first on …
	d Over the next five minutes I'll give you a brief introduction of …
	e We're an e-marketing agency based in …
1	**f** Hi, my name is Philip Weiss, and I'm …
	g Well, we've seen a big change in the role a headquarters had over …
	h So what are the main challenges facing HQs … ?
	i So how can we help … ?

2 **After you have checked your answers, try to complete the introductory sentence to each slide with a partner.**

Example: Hi, my name's Philip Weiss, and I'm Managing Director of ZN.

When you have finished, you can check your answers with the audio script on pages 158–9 or listen to the recordings again.

3 **Rhetorical questions (asking and answering your own questions as in slide 5) are a good way to introduce slides as they create a sense of dialogue with the audience and help presenters structure their talk more easily. Make rhetorical questions to introduce the information on the following four slides. Practise saying them.**

Example: Slide 1: 'Who are the customers of tomorrow?'

1 customers of tomorrow
2 statistics and graphs forecasting company sales over the next two years
3 detailed analysis of sales figures for principal country markets
4 reasons for failure to break into markets in Asia last year

4 **Phrases such as *Now let's look at …* are also very common when introducing and linking slides. Similar phrases are: *Now let's turn to … / Moving on now to … / Now, I'd like to talk about …* . Practise in pairs and try to introduce some of the above information using these phrases.**

Output: Preparing and delivering an e-presentation

In small groups, prepare and deliver an e-presentation to introduce a company or organisation.

Stage 1
Write a maximum of eight slides to do the following:

1 Open your presentation and introduce yourself.
2 Summarise what your presentation will be about.
3 Introduce the company.
4 Describe present market conditions and customer needs.
5 Show how your company can meet these needs.
6 Close the presentation.

Write each slide on a single piece of paper using a large font or use presentation software if you have access to it.

Stage 2
Deliver the e-presentation to the class. One student should hold up the slide at the front of the class (or use a computer), whilst another student provides the voiceover.

10 Branding

10.1 Theory: What is branding?

Learning outcomes
- Understand the main ideas of branding.
- Use a range of vocabulary associated with branding.
- Argue for and against different approaches to branding.

Introduction

66 If Coca-Cola were to lose all of its production-related assets in a disaster, the company would survive. By contrast, if all consumers were to have a sudden lapse of memory and forget everything related to Coca-Cola, the company would go out of business. **99**

1 Look at the quote above from an unnamed Coca-Cola executive. In pairs, discuss what they mean. Why do people regularly buy this drink?

2 Look at the pictures above. Which brands do you associate with products like these?

3 Look at the characteristics of brands listed below. How well do the brands you identified in exercise 2 match these characteristics?

Brands …
- should be familiar to us.
- represent more than just the product.
- help develop a relationship with the customer.
- are relatively expensive.
- have a personality.

Language focus: Branding expressions

1 The following words all go before or after the word *brand*. Put the words in the correct position below. The first two have been done for you.

image licensed awareness equity extension manufacturer's own positioning repositioning luxury

licensed   **brand**   *image*

2 Match each branding expression from exercise 1 with the following definitions:

1 A measurement of the number of people who know the brand.
2 The public perception of the brand.
3 The value investors put on a brand.
4 The use of an established brand name with a different product.
5 A brand that is used by the company that developed and produced the product.
6 A brand that is used by the distributor or shop selling the product, not the manufacturer.
7 A brand that is leased to a manufacturer, who then makes the product under that name.
8 The location of a particular brand in relation to the competition.
9 A high-priced product aimed at the top of the market.
10 Changing the image of a brand to attract new market segments.

Listening 1: Introduction to a lecture on branding

🎧 **2.11**

Business view

You are going to listen to a lecture with Dr Sally Hibbert, Associate Professor of Marketing at Nottingham University Business School.

1 Listen to the first part of the lecture. Which slide is correct, A or B?

> 1 brand definitions
>
> 2 brand features
>
> 3 differentiating brands
>
> 4 strategic decisions
>
> 5 benefits of branding

Slide A

> 1 brand definitions
>
> 2 brand features
>
> 3 differentiating brands
>
> 4 strategic marketplaces
>
> 5 disadvantages of branding

Slide B

2 Choose one commonly used product that you have bought, for example a pair of shoes or a music system. Make some brief notes on the following:

- What different brands are on the market for this product, and how can you differentiate between them?
- Why did you choose that particular brand?

Then compare with a partner.

Listening 2: Defining branding

🎧 **2.12**

1 Listen to the second part of the lecture and complete the notes below with the words Dr Sally Hibbert uses. Then compare your notes with a partner.

> **Product**
>
> **1** Anything that _____
>
> **2** Has a _____ value
>
> **Brand**
>
> **3** Goes much _____
>
> **4** A brand is represented by: _____ , _____ , _____ , _____ (or any combination of these)
>
> **5** Identifies _____
>
> **6** Allows manufacturers to have some way _____

2 What are the main differences between a product and a brand?

Listening 3: To brand or not to brand?

 2.13

1 What are some of the advantages of brands for customers and for companies?

2 Listen and take notes on the next (long) part of the lecture using the headings below.

> **Advantages for customers**
>
> 1 _____
>
> 2 _____
>
> 3 _____
>
> 4 _____
>
> **Advantages for companies**
>
> 1 _____
>
> 2 _____
>
> 3 _____
>
> 4 _____
>
> 5 _____
>
> 6 _____

3 Dr Sally Hibbert mentions the 'emotional benefits' of brands, and companies talk about the importance of establishing emotional ties with the customers. What do you think this means?

4 What emotional ties do you have to any brand? What adjectives could you use to describe these brands? Are they *exciting*, *reliable*, *comfortable* or *innovative*? What other words could you use to describe brands that you know well?

5 Dr Sally Hibbert outlines many advantages of brands. Look at the list below. Which of the points do you think are the biggest disadvantages of branding? Are they disadvantages for customers, companies or the wider environment? Can you think of any others?

> high possibility of the brand failing
> a high level of investment
> difficult to distinguish from competition
> brands can have too much influence
> high cost of product
> brand extensions can damage reputation

Output: Own brand or manufacturer's brand?

A sports-shoe manufacturer is considering whether to develop a company brand (manufacturer's brand), or to supply their product direct to a retailer/distributor and let them brand the product as their own brand. Work in two groups and follow the instructions below.

Stage 1

Group A: Prepare an argument for developing a manufacturer's brand and against a retailer's own brand.

Group B: Prepare an argument for developing the retailer's own brand and against developing a manufacturer's brand.

Both groups should consider the potential benefits and drawbacks to the company, retailers, and consumers. Think about cost, risk, competition, quality, market share, profit and identity.

Stage 2

Work with members of the other group and discuss the ideas you have prepared. Try to come to a decision.

You may want to make notes in the table below.

Costs
Benefits
Issues

10.2 Practice: The Havaianas brand

Learning outcomes
- Understand brand value and values.
- Use vocabulary to describe brands and products.
- Be able to participate in a meeting discussing brand extension.

Profile: Havaianas

Havaianas is a Brazilian brand with a strong international appeal. Havaianas are rubber sandals, but as a brand, they are not *any* rubber sandals. These sandals are highly regarded by consumers for their unique design and award-winning publicity campaigns. Their sandal collections change frequently and have included special editions such as a Brazilian World Cup range and a promotional 18-carat gold and diamond model. The company sells more than 173 million pairs of sandals in over 80 countries in the world. It is owned by Alpargatas SA of Brazil, which owns a number of well-known company brands.

Reading: A company with desired brands

Read this extract from the Alpargatas Annual Report and answer the questions below.

1 How does the company explain its success?
A It creates new brands.
B It knows its brands.
C It has quality products.

Introduction

1 Read the profile on Havaianas and look at the pictures. What mood, feelings and associations are being created and communicated here? Choose some of the following words that best describe the brand for you personally and discuss with a partner why you chose them. Can you think of any others?

fun friendly Brazilian Hawaiian international fashionable casual summery stylish exciting passionate joyful youthful simple sophisticated artistic creative intelligent energetic fresh tropical optimistic traditional modern

Would the feelings and associations you identified communicate well in your country market? What about for a country with a cold climate?

2 Discuss the following questions about country branding.

1 What image do you have of Brazil as a country? How important is the image of Brazil to the Havaianas brand? How does the company use its country of origin to communicate Havaianas brand values?

2 What about country branding for other countries? What images and associations do you have of Italy, Germany, Japan or another country you know? How do the companies in these countries use the international image of their country to help sell their products?

Alpargatas brands are well known and desired by millions of consumers in Brazil and abroad. They are at the centre of the company's growth strategy and go beyond the purpose for which they were created, that is, to yield comfort, well-being, pleasure, performance, design and style.

The sales of brands add value to footwear, sports goods and textiles and consequently boost consumers' perception of Alpargatas' value, not to mention the company's results. Brands are product extensions. Although products are manufactured, brands are sold and constitute important elements that guide consumer behavior. A company establishes itself in the market through the values and ideas it wants to transmit and through its brands. These brands become an asset, influenced by feelings, perceptions and ideas that are greater than the value attributed to the product and to the use consumers put it to.

This way of understanding the value of its brands enabled Alpargatas to increase its gross revenues from international sales by over 132% over the previous year.

2 Read the text again. Are the following statements about Alpargatas true or false?

1 Their brands change the way consumers view the company.
2 Their products are brand extensions.
3 Their products guide consumer behaviour.
4 Their brands and products have an equal value.

3 Find words and phrases in the text which have similar meanings to these:

1 further than
2 increases quickly
3 continuations / enlargements
4 communicate
5 valuable property
6 ways of understanding
7 associated with / attached to
8 total value of sales (turnover)

Language focus: Describing brands and products

1 Read this FAQ (Frequently Asked Question) from the Havaianas website and choose from the phrases which follow to complete the gaps.

havaianas

Where did the inspiration for creating the first Havaianas model come from?

The Havaianas design ¹_____ the Japanese sandals known as Zori, made of a thin rice straw sole and ²_____ .
To adapt the Japanese model to the Brazilian market, São Paulo Alpargatas used rubber as raw material and the rice grain format for the ³_____ – one of its many
⁴_____ . And that's how the famous Havaianas were born.

1 A were inspired by   B was inspired by   C was inspired from
2 A fabric belts   B fabric braces   C fabric straps
3 A sole feeling   B sole texture   C sole music
4 A mistakable features   B mistake features   C unmistakable features

2 Which word in each group does not usually collocate with the first word?

Example: *product*
We can say relaxed style, relaxed feel and relaxed look but we tend not to say relaxed product.

1 relaxed – style   feel   product   look
2 vibrant – spirit   colours   pleasure   style
3 versatile – combinations   passion   features   footwear
4 inspirational – feel   pleasure   colours   combinations
5 iconic – brand   comfort   footwear   look
6 affordable – style   colours   brand   footwear
7 uncomplicated – style   comfort   look   message

3 In small groups, choose one of the brand extension products here. Write a short description for the website using some of the language presented above. Exchange information with another group when you have finished.

Intercultural analysis

1 Most of the product names of Havaianas' different sandal collections are standardised in English (Surf, Teams, Trend, Wave, Wind, Fit) for international markets as well as the home market in Brazil. Why do you think this is? Do you think it is a good marketing strategy? Why/Why not? How is English used in your country for advertising? Can you think of any examples?

2 Portuguese is used to name a few of the Havaianas collections (Camuflada and Tradicional, meaning, *camouflaged* and *traditional*) for both the international and home markets. Do you think the company should do more of this? Why/Why not?

Transferable skill: Expressing visual ideas

1 The greatest challenge for the architects of the Havaianas store in São Paulo was to create a space that expressed the feelings and associations people have for the brand. Think about the brand and look at the pictures from the store below. How successful have the architects been? Discuss your answers.

oduct display

Customisable zone

In store – 'Street market stall'

2 The store is divided into different zones and can also be visited through a virtual tour on the company's website. Read the mixed-up captions of two of the zones that appear on the website and put them in the right order:

1 The Cube – who want to know / a space that always / to tell. / For those / has a different story / the latest Havaianas news:

2 Cylinder – and fun / accessories to keep handy. / the Havaianas handbags. / Cheerfulness, happiness / are always the best / Check out

3 Write short captions for the Street market stall and the Havaianas customisable zone (shown in the photos) in one or two sentences.

4 Write a short paragraph to explain the success of the Havaianas brand strategy.

Critical analysis

Retail marketing is about communicating what the brand stands for through the design of the store. Discuss how well-known brands do this in stores you have visited. Think about the following:

shop window   product displays   customer service   lighting
store layout   store location   interior design   use of colour

Output: Brand extension meeting

In small groups, work together in product development teams. It is your job in the Marketing department to extend the Havaianas brand.

Stage 1

Decide on a completely new brand extension, for example a mobile phone, bottled water, an airline, a watch or another product. Think in terms of both product design and communication of brand values to the customer. Make notes during your discussion in order to make a short presentation to another team.

Stage 2

Give a brief presentation to another team about your brand extension, and answer any questions they might have.

Learning outcomes

- Learn how to persuade people to change their behaviour.
- Understand issues in customer care and company image.
- Learn language to direct and persuade.

Introduction

1 In small groups, brainstorm all the jobs you can think of in a hotel, e.g. chefs and waiters. What are the responsibilities of each job?

2 Work in pairs and role play the following situation.

Student A: You recently stayed at an expensive hotel and were very disappointed with the service. Phone the hotel to make a complaint.

Student B: You are the manager of an expensive hotel. Try to deal with the customer in an appropriate way.

3 What problems can you have at a hotel? Have you ever experienced any problems? Were any of these problems connected with the staff? What do you think hotel staff are like in your country?

4 What control does the manager have over these problems? How might managers persuade, or directly force the staff to change?

Critical analysis

Mary Jo Hatch and Majken Shultz have written several studies on organisational management. They believe that the success of a company's brand depends on aligning these three elements:

- Vision (top management's goals and hopes for the company)
- Culture (the organisation's behaviour and attitudes)
- Image (the outside world's overall impression of the company)

1 Which of the following relate to each of the above elements?

- what customers think about the company
- how employees feel about the company
- public opinion
- the way the staff behave
- management strategy

2 Which of the three elements do you think is the most important for the staff of a company?

"This really is an innovative approach, but I'm afraid we can't consider it. It's never been done before."

Listening: Address to the staff at a hotel

2.14

You are going to listen to an extract from a meeting in a luxury hotel. Recently, the Rooms Division (responsible for providing services to hotel guests) received a disappointing score on its standards evaluation (standards compliance). This means the staff have not been consistently following the service standards.

1 If you were the Rooms Division manager trying to persuade your staff to change their behaviour, how could you do this? Discuss this in small groups and then listen to the recording.

2 The manager has divided her talk to the staff into four parts. As you listen, number the order of the parts:

- a story
- practising the standards
- the point of the story
- background to the change

3 Listen to the recording again. Are the following statements true or false?

1 The CEO held a meeting with all the hotel staff.
2 The goal of the company is to decide on appropriate standards.
3 Being a telephone operator is a steady job.
4 Staff must choose when to apply the standards.
5 Staff must always use the guest's name.
6 Management do not need to follow the standards.

2.15

1 One powerful way to persuade people is through contrasts. When using contrasts, stress is very important. Listen to these sentences and underline the stressed words.

1 This is what we do. It's not an extra job. It is the job.
2 Yes, we love our employees but standards are our life.

2 Practise saying the sentences. Also practise the pause – silence can be a powerful and persuasive tool.

2.16

3 The manager's talk contains several examples of management jargon and management speak, for example 'standards are our life'. This language makes the manager sound official and can be used to persuade staff. However, many people believe that 'management speak' often does not have much meaning or hides the real meaning. Listen to the following extracts from the meeting, and fill in the missing words.

1 _____ committed _____ .

2 _____ heart _____ .

3 _____ people _____ .

4 If you were a manager, would you speak like this? Would such language persuade you?

Language focus 2: Using *if* to persuade and direct staff

If is used more frequently in business than in everyday English. It is often used in sentences that try to persuade people or to give orders politely. Sentences of this type often look very different from sentences with the conditional use of *if*. Look at these two sentences and answer the questions below.

1 If she had remembered her account number, she would have been able to pay.
2 If I'm opening car doors at the front door I say 'Welcome'.

1 Which of the sentences uses *if* in a conditional sentence? Which sentence is politely giving an order?

2 In pairs, give instructions to each other using *if* in these situations.

You always have to smile at customers, use their names, offer to carry their bags, ask if they want a drink.

Example: *If you see a customer, you always smile at him or her.*

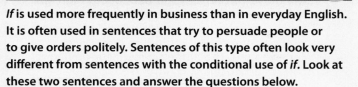

▶ **Watch Sequence 5 on the DVD to find out more about Marketing.**

Output: Persuading staff to change

Your 3-star hotel has been bought by a 5-star hotel chain. It will now try to rebrand itself as a 5-star hotel.

Stage 1
In small groups, brainstorm what changes need to be made. Think about rooms, food in the restaurants, room service, cleaning, uniforms and any other factors that affect the staff.

Stage 2
Now separate into different groups.

Group A: You are the hotel managers. You must communicate these changes to the staff in a way that makes them feel comfortable, while at the same time making them realise these changes are required and not negotiable. Think about how you will do this and what language you will use.

Group B: You are members of staff. You have heard that the hotel is going to upgrade to a 5-star hotel. You want to raise some concerns with the managers about this change. For example, will the salaries be increased? Will training be given? Will contracts be improved? etc. Think about how you can communicate these ideas without putting your jobs at risk.

Stage 3
Have a meeting with the other group and try to reach agreement about all the changes needed. How effectively did the management communicate the changes in your meeting?

Writing 5: Persuasive communication online

Learning outcomes

- Understand key principles behind persuasive communication.
- Use appropriate connectors to change product features into benefits.
- Write persuasive sales copy for online home pages.

Introduction

Business view

> 66 Nobody who bought a drill wanted a drill. They wanted a hole. 99

Perry Marshall, marketing guru

> 66 The people who line up for Starbucks aren't just there for the coffee. 99

Howard Schultz, Starbucks CEO

1 What do these quotes say about what customers really want?

2 How can we use this information to help us communicate with customers to persuade them to buy?

Read this text and answer the questions that follow.

Benefits not features

Most marketing experts agree that when you are writing a product or service description, you need to persuade your customers with benefits and not just describe features. Features are characteristics and specifications of the product. For example, an MP3 player can be said to have '64GB storage'. A benefit, however, will tell customers how this feature translates into solving their problems and meeting their needs. For example, '64GB storage allows you to store 14,000 songs'. It tells customers what the feature can do for them and helps them make sense of the features. Copywriters and branding experts will move further beyond benefits to highlight hidden benefits (in text and visual images) – these are seen as the real underlying reasons why customers buy a product or service. For example, the hidden benefit for having a certain product may be because it is seen as cool or sophisticated.

3 Do you respond more to advertising and web pages which emphasise features, benefits or hidden benefits? Give examples.

4 When do you think it is more appropriate to write the other way round and describe features not benefits?

5 How might the language of 'describing benefits not features' work in a wider context, e.g. internal memos requesting staff cooperation, email responses to requests for product information, giving presentations, negotiations with your boss/teacher/partner, a cover letter for your CV, etc.?

Language focus 1: The language of advertising

1 Read the question below posted on an online forum of small businesses manufacturing and selling T-shirts. How might you answer the question?

May 29, 12:33:07 PM

Reckless Tees

T-Shirt Lover   Location: Phoenix, AZ
T-Shirt Aficionado   Posts: 191
You can call me: Mike   Thanks: 3
Member Since: Feb 2007   Thanked 2 Times in 2 Posts

How to sell 'benefits', not 'features'

I have been doing a lot of reading about marketing/sales and I now understand that you must sell your benefits to the customers, not the features. My question is, how does one convey benefits or sell benefits on a website? I don't want my site to be a sales letter and it most definitely is not structured as so. Any ideas how a website can sell its benefits without sending the 'buy me now' message?

2 Read some of the replies and choose the best answer for each gap from the choices below. The first one has been done for you.

May 29, 12:40:17 PM

People ¹____B____ benefits over features because they want to know: 'What's in it for me?'

As T-shirts are quite simple, they don't have many features, but there are ²_____ benefits.

You need to think about why people would want one of your designs – what's it going to do for them? What human need will it ³_____ ?

'You will make at least three friends with this shirt.' (Although it's funny, this benefit ⁴_____ 'desire for acceptance' _____ .)

If you don't want to go so deep, you can always just have a page listing the physical product benefits, ⁵_____ 'Why buy from us?'

To get a benefit you just put ⁶'_____' after the feature, and explain it.

1 A buy from   B buy into   C buy up   D buy in
2 A plenty of   B considerably   C numberless   D too many
3 A fulfil   B aim   C desire   D request
4 A pulls the … handle   B turns the … switch
     C pushes the … door   D presses the … button
5 A titling   B titles   C title   D titled
6 A gives you   B allows you to   C which means
     D so means that

Language focus 2: Changing features into benefits

As we have seen in the replies, we can use 'which means' to change a feature into a benefit. We can also use the following connecting words:

meaning that	giving you	which gives you allowing you to
which allows you to	and so you will benefit by	
so you will be able to		

Write sentences using these connectors to 'translate' the following features of these products and services into benefits. The first has been done for you.

1 Timberland boots – hard-wearing materials
     Timberland boots are made of hard-wearing materials, so you know they will last a long time.
2 Bose music systems – 0% finance
3 NatWest Private Banking – 24-hour customer service
4 American Express Travel Insurance – 150 years' experience
5 easyJet – no weight limit on hand luggage
6 Cif cleaning product – 'strong yet gentle' cream

Output: Writing persuasive copy for an internet site

Work in pairs. Write and design an attractive web page for 'Phoenix Custom Shirts'. You want to maximise sales by persuading customers to buy the products (up to 200 words).

Start by discussing an outline of the main points, the type of photos, images and colours you want to use, and then make a rough sketch of how the page will look. Finalise the text for the page and then compare with another pair.

INDIRECT COSTS

OVERHEADS

PERSONNEL

CAPITAL

11.1 Theory: Activity-based costing (ABC)

Learning outcomes
- Recognise and actively use vocabulary about cost accounting.
- Learn the language of traditional cost accounting and activity-based accounting.
- Use gerunds more effectively.

Introduction

1 Why might an organisation want to install new software?

2 Imagine that your organisation is considering installing new software. Decide what purpose the software should have. What would the costs be of installing the software? Note down ideas about who you would have to pay and any costs the company itself might have.

Costs
- _____
- _____
- the cost of training staff to use it properly

3 What would be the benefits of installing the software?

Benefits
- _____
- _____
- _____

4 Why do you think that companies do cost-benefit analyses like this before they decide whether to go ahead with a project?

Business view

❝ Cost-benefit analysis seeks to compare the costs and benefits and take decisions on the basis of the findings. The problem is that it is difficult to quantify all benefits and costs, especially the intangibles. ❞

Gopinathan Thachappilly, business writer

5 Look again at the costs and benefits of installing software. Are they all measurable? Is there an advantage to having these things in figures? Which of the benefits and costs are intangible (difficult to measure)?

Language focus 1: Key financial terms

You are going to read a text about activity-based costing activities (ABC). There are different ways of classifying costs: they can be categorised by behaviour (fixed and variable costs) or by type (direct or indirect costs / overheads).

1 Match the terms below to their definitions.

1	Overheads / indirect costs	a	are related to a specific product or department
2	Fixed costs	b	change according to level of activity; usually volume-related
3	Variable costs	c	regular and necessary costs involved in operating a business
4	Direct costs	d	remain the same and are not dependent on level of activity; usually time-related

2 Here are some of the costs incurred when running a building firm. Which of the categories (1–4) above would you put them in? There may be more than one possibility.

rent   raw materials   salaries of staff on a permanent contract
salaries of freelance staff   insurance

Reading: The advantages and disadvantages of activity-based costing

For a company to work profitably, it needs to understand how the costs of providing a product or service occur. Usually, it is clear what the direct costs of a product are but the indirect costs also need to be allocated. Companies which use traditional accounting methods allocate their indirect costs in the same proportion (ratio) as the direct costs. Imagine a company which produces robots and which uses traditional cost-accounting methods. To produce standardised robots, the company needs the same amount of direct labour and material as when it produces customised robots, so the indirect costs of both mass-produced and customised robots will be allocated in the same way even though the customised robot has much higher research and development costs. Many experts feel that this is not an efficient way of calculating costs.

1 Read the text below quickly. What advantages and disadvantages of ABC does it mention? Note them down.

Activity-based costing

Activity-based costing (ABC) is a method of assigning costs to products or services based on the resources that they consume. Its aim, according to *The Economist*, is 'to change the way in which costs are counted'.

5 Introducing activity-based costing is not a simple task. For a start, all business activities must be broken down into their discrete components. As part of its ABC programme, for example, a Swiss–Swedish power company divided its purchasing activity into such areas as negotiating with
10 suppliers, updating the database, issuing purchase orders and handling complaints.

Large firms should pilot a scheme before implementing the system throughout their organisation. The information essential for ABC may not be readily available and may have to be
15 calculated specially for the purpose. This involves making many new measurements. Larger companies often hire consultants who are specialists in the area to help them get a system up and running.

The easy approach is to use ABC software in conjunction with
20 a company's existing accounting system. The traditional system continues to be used as before, with the ABC structure an extra to be called upon when specific cost information is required to help make a particular decision. The development of software programs has made the introduction of activity-based costing
25 easier.

Setting up an activity-based costing system is a prerequisite for improving business processes and for any re-engineering programme.

Robert Kaplan is credited as the founder of ABC. In a book
30 published in 2007, he outlined time-driven activity-based costing (TDABC), which tried to make activity-based costing easier by relating the measurement of cost to time. As Kaplan put it, only two questions need to be answered by TDABC:
- How much does it cost per time unit to supply resources for
35 each business process?

- How much time is required to perform the work needed for a company's products, transactions and customers? ABC has many satisfied customers. The American car manufacturer, Chrysler, claims that it saved hundreds of
40 millions of dollars through a programme that it introduced. ABC showed that the true cost of certain parts that Chrysler made was 30 times bigger than the original estimate, a discovery that persuaded the company to outsource the manufacture of many of those parts.

Source: *Guide to Management Ideas and Gurus* by Tim Hindle

2 Underline the correct phrase in the following statements which reflect what the article claims.

1 One reason why it is (*relatively easy / quite difficult*) to set up ABC is because each activity needs to be analysed into its constituent parts.

2 Bigger companies need to set up a trial (*before / when*) they introduce ABC into all parts of the organisation.

3 One (*simpler / more complex*) way of introducing ABC is to set it up in parallel to the organisation's normal way of costing.

4 It is now possible to implement ABC because companies know (*what each business activity involves / that software for this is available on the market*).

5 Implementing ABC is a condition for the success of strategies (*for the improvement of business processes / for engineering processes*).

Critical analysis

What experience have you had of activity-based accounting as a customer? Many car repair shops provide invoices which are activity-based, i.e. each activity (changing oil, repairing a light, etc.) has a given price as well as the cost of the material (oil, lamp, etc.). As a customer, how do you feel about this? Are there any areas where you think this would not be acceptable, e.g. medical treatment?

Language focus 2: Gerunds

gerund *noun* [C] a word that ends in *-ing* which is made from a verb, and which is used like a noun

1 Underline the phrases which have gerunds in these sentences. The first one has been done for you.

1 I'd be really <u>interested in knowing</u> what those five items are.

2 Jerry is good at seeing how much change the organisation can assimilate.

3 I enjoyed the challenge of managing different groups of staff but what appalled me was my first real experience of seeing the patient areas.

4 He kept on talking so fast.

5 Many consumers who see a promotion online go into a store to buy it as a result of seeing that promotion.

6 Perez will focus on bringing our products into new markets.

7 Our clients have never had a problem in finding us.

2 Gerunds are often used after an adjective and preposition, a verb and preposition or a noun and preposition. Write the phrases you underlined in exercise 1 under the correct heading below. One has been done for you.

Adjective + preposition + gerund
interested in knowing
Verb + preposition + gerund
Noun + preposition + gerund

3 Look at the text on page 101 again and note down other verb and noun phrases which use the gerund form. Add them under the headings above.

4 There are two sentences in the text which use the gerund form as a noun at the start of the sentence:

■ Introducing activity-based costing is not a simple task.
■ Setting up an activity-based costing system is a prerequisite for improving business processes and for any re-engineering programme.

They could have been written in the following way, not using the gerund form:

■ It is not a simple task to introduce activity-based costing.
■ A prerequisite for improving business processes and for any re-engineering programme is to set up an activity-based costing system.

What is the difference in meaning in the styles? How does the emphasis change? Is this the same in your own language?

5 Rewrite these sentences using the gerund form at the start.

1 It is important to allocate costs accurately.
2 It is necessary to break down activities into their individual parts.
3 Chrysler saved hundreds of millions of dollars when it introduced ABC.

6 Write a list of the activities involved in one of the following, using the gerund form at the start.

> Example: *Making a note of useful vocabulary and storing it carefully is essential.*

■ learning a foreign language
■ buying goods and services online
■ selling a product
■ organising an office excursion

Output: Comparing traditional cost accounting and ABC

Stage 1
Work in pairs or small groups. Decide if the following are advantages or disadvantages of ABC.

1 It is more accurate than traditional accounting.
2 You need a lot of resources to do ABC properly.
3 You need to collect a lot of data before ABC can be introduced.
4 ABC looks at the unit cost of a product, not the total cost.
5 You can easily see the true cost of each overhead.
6 It is possible to see how much waste there is.
7 It costs a lot to maintain the system needed to do ABC.
8 It is easier to make comparisons with other companies in the industry.

Stage 2
Work in pairs. You work in a company that is thinking of introducing ABC to replace the traditional accounting methods your company uses at the moment.

Student A should look at page 141 and Student B at page 145. Follow the instructions and have the meeting.

Stage 3
Discuss with another pair whether you decided to implement ABC accounting or not. In your opinion, which has the most advantages – ABC accounting or traditional accounting?

11.2 Practice: Cost and price

Learning outcomes
- Consider the relationship between cost and price.
- Learn and use vocabulary for discussions about costs.
- Learn skills for presenting information visually.

Profile: Ukrainian International Airlines

Ukrainian International Airlines (UIA) was founded soon after independence in 1992 and was one of the first joint ventures in Ukraine which was set up with the help of foreign capital. It was the first airline in the CIS (Commonwealth of Independent States) to use the modern Boeing 737. It offers both passenger and cargo transportation on services from Ukraine and, together with its partners, it flies to more than 3,000 destinations worldwide.

Introduction

1 What factors influence people when they buy an airline ticket? These ideas may help you:

- the location of the airport
- the price of the flight
- the hidden costs (e.g. for luggage, for not booking online, for food and drink)
- the reputation of the airline (e.g. reliability and safety)
- the design of the plane

Have you flown anywhere recently? How did you decide which airline to fly with?

2 How do you feel about very cheap flights? Are you happy or worried? Why?

3 Some people choose to travel by train, for both business and personal purposes, rather than by plane. Why do you think this is? If you had to choose between a one-hour flight or a four-hour train journey, which would you choose?

4 Here are two proverbs about price and value. What do you think of them? What similar sayings do you have in your country?

- What costs nothing is worth nothing. (The Netherlands)
- Take a second look. It costs you nothing. (China)

Listening 1: The business of flying

🔊 2.17

Business view

You are going to listen to Richard Creagh, the Vice-President of UIA, who has been with the company since its early days.

1 In the first extract Richard Creagh talks about the services which UIA offers. Which services do you think an airline might offer? Listen to the first part of the interview. Which of the following does he mention?

1 low-cost flights	2 charter flights	3 freight transport
4 package holidays	5 passenger handling	
6 aircraft maintenance		

2 Listen again and write down the numbers he mentions for the following:

1 the population of Ukraine _____
2 the number of the aeroplane which carries freight _____
3 the number of countries which Swissport operates in _____
4 what percentage of their passenger handling UIA sold to Swissport _____
5 how much the airline industry as a whole lost in the previous year _____

3 Richard Creagh mentions UIA's core business (flying passengers and cargo) but says that they also look for partners for the 'peripheral' businesses which add value to the airline. Which peripheral services does he mention?

Listening 2: Costs and prices

🎧 2.18

1 In the next extract Richard Creagh talks about the factors which influence the price and cost of flights. How would you define 'price' and 'cost'? Listen to Richard Creagh and complete what he says.

'1 _____ is what it costs you to put the 2 _____ in the market, and you have to keep trying to get that 3 _____ down. Price is what the market will 4 _____ you.'

2 Which factor has the most influence on the price of a flight, according to Richard Creagh?

Listening 3: Control over costs

🎧 2.19

1 What costs does an airline have? Listen to Richard Creagh and complete the first column below.

Costs	Controlled by

2 What are the costs controlled by? Listen again and complete the second column.

Business view

66 We may have fantastic ideas in our heads but unless we have a way to show them to others, the value of our ideas will never be known. 99

Dan Roam, expert in visual thinking and business consultant

1 Look at the pictures below. What do they tell you about the visual thinking process? Why do you think that visual thinking is important?

The process of visual thinking

1 Look

2 See

3 Imagine

4 Show

2 In your studies or job, when do you have to be able to visualise ideas? How do you do this? Which of the following have you used?

mind maps   graphs   diagrams   tables   flowcharts   timelines

What are the advantages of using these over using written descriptions? Do you agree with the following statements? Why/Why not?

- Visuals provide a basis for verbal explanations.
- Visuals communicate faster than written text.
- Visuals show the facts and let the listener do some of the thinking.

3 Think again about what factors customers consider when they buy an airline ticket. Which ideas from exercise 1 in the Introduction are represented here visually?

1

2

4 How could you visually represent some of the other ideas mentioned in the Introduction?

5 Look again at the table in Listening 3. How could you represent some of the ideas visually? Prepare a simple visualisation of one of the ideas from the table and discuss it with a partner.

Language focus: Different types of cost

1 Look at these costs which airlines have and match them to the definitions.

1	depreciation	a	guarantee of compensation
2	maintenance	b	decline in value of an asset
3	interest	c	plotting a course
4	insurance	d	provision of food and drink
5	navigation	e	keeping something in good condition
6	catering	f	payment on a loan

A company has direct, indirect and central costs.

- Direct costs are ones that can be identified with a particular project or activity.   Example: *aircraft*
- Indirect costs are not directly accountable to a particular project or activity.   Example: *depreciation*
- Central costs are costs for corporate and regional functions. Example: *head office costs*

2 Which category do these costs belong to? Are they direct costs, indirect costs or central costs?

depreciation   aircraft   airport charges   head office costs
staff   press office costs   insurance   navigation charges
maintenance   fuel charges   interest charges
passenger handling charges   catering charges

3 Think about a business activity which you are familiar with. With a partner, map out some of the different costs and their categories.

Output: Cutting costs

You work for an airline which has a reputation for safety and reliability.

Recently you have been making a loss. Market research shows that passengers are choosing budget airlines rather than your type of medium-price air services. Clearly, the company has to do something to halt this trend. Here are some ideas to help you, but you may like to add some of your own.

- At the moment, you offer a mix of self-service check-in at airports as well as staff support to help passengers with the machines. You could make savings by cutting the number of staff here.
- Passengers can book flights via the Internet as well as through travel agencies. The latter cost the airline more because it has to pay commission to the agencies. If you cut this, you could save money.
- On your short-haul flights passengers receive a drink and a snack as part of their ticket package. If you stopped doing this, you could afford to cut the ticket price on these flights.
- At the moment you offer ticket-holders a luggage limit of 20 kg. You could generate more revenue if you cut this to 15 kg and then charged for luggage over this limit.

Stage 1

Work in three groups. Group A are from the Finance department (page 141), Group B are from Human Resources (page 145) and Group C are from Marketing (page 146). Read your information and discuss together in your group what strategy the company should follow.

Stage 2

How could you visualise the ideas for your strategy? Look at the suggestions in the Transferable skills section and together create a visual of your strategy. (You will each need to have your own copy of this visual.)

Stage 3

Work together with people who were in the other groups. Using your visuals, present your strategies to each other. Then discuss the ideas and come to an agreement. Can you create a visual to show this?

11.3 Skills: Developing internal relationships

Learning outcomes
- Develop a good relationship with colleagues.
- Use polite language and strategies.
- Understand power and communication at work.

Introduction

1 These are four common communication 'channels' within an organisation:

manager to manager   staff to manager

manager to staff   staff to staff

Which of the following actions would probably happen in each of the four categories?

1. pay a compliment about somebody's work
2. gossip about a colleague
3. delegate a task
4. fire somebody
5. promote somebody
6. motivate somebody
7. make strategic decisions
8. make a request
9. complain about a customer
10. criticise somebody in front of their colleagues
11. pay a compliment about somebody's appearance
12. make an official complaint about somebody

2 Which of the actions do you think are the three most difficult to perform? Why?

3 If you had to do the actions above, in which of them would you try to be polite? How?

4 Research shows that in business, managers and staff try hard to be polite to each other when performing many of these actions. Why is it important to be polite?

Critical analysis

One action above involved 'complimenting somebody on their appearance'. In pairs, discuss the following questions.

- When do you think it is appropriate to compliment somebody on their appearance in the workplace? When is it appropriate between male and female staff? What about between a manager and a staff member?
- How about in an international workplace? What problems could there be? Have you ever experienced this or a similar situation?

Listening: Commenting on a meeting

🔊 2.20

Listen to the end of a meeting between Marco, the marketing manager of a luxury hotel chain, and two of his staff, Jenny and Veronique. Jenny is the first person you will hear speak in the meeting.

1. What did Jenny think was going to happen at the meeting? Was she pleasantly or unpleasantly surprised at the end of the meeting?
2. What approach was used in the past, and how successful was it?
3. What will happen in the monthly meetings?
4. Do you think relations in this department are good or bad?

Intercultural analysis

In the meeting, Jenny compliments Marco, her manager, a lot. If you were Jenny, would you say things like this to your manager? If you were the manager, how would you react to these comments by one of your staff? In general, why is the way the manager reacts to such comments important for staff–management relations?

Language focus: Polite language

There are two types of polite language that show we care about people's feelings or 'face needs' (see Unit 6).

Type A: make the listener feel good about him/herself or group (*showing solidarity*)

Type B: show we do not want to impose too much on the listener or his/her group (*showing respect*)

1 Type A politeness involves the speaker boosting the self-image of the listener, whereas type B involves the speaker lowering his/her self-importance. Can you think of one example of each? In the following illustrations, 1 is a normal situation. Which is type A and which is type B?

Speaker	Listener	Speaker	Listener	Speaker	Listener
1 normal		**2** _____		**3** _____	

2 Look at this list of different 'polite' actions. Are they type A or B?

1 complimenting **4** apologising
2 offering praise **5** requesting indirectly
3 joking **6** thanking

3 Listen to the following examples of polite language and match them with the actions in exercise 2.

 2.21

a (*manager to staff*) Can I save this in my folder? Would you mind? Or is this valuable information?

b (*staff to 60-year-old manager*) And I really thought you were in your early fifties!

c (*manager to staff*) Magic! Looking good!

d (*manager to manager*) Thanks for coming in, John.

e (*manager to manager*) Oh, you didn't have to slam it!

f (*staff to boss*) I'm sorry I haven't done a copy of this one.

4 Read through the audio script which follows. Underline examples of polite language.

Audio script
 2.20

Jenny: I was dreading this meeting because I was thinking, 'Oh, we're just going to be hearing all the bad things we didn't do right, blah, blah, blah.' And now we get to the end and I feel great.

Veronique: Well, I can say bad things about you if you want!

Jenny: No, no, I thought it was a good way of leading the meeting.

Marco: Thank you.

Jenny: Because you know. It has to be addressed to us anyway.

Marco: Yes.

Jenny: And, every time we have a meeting with you, I

---

don't know for everybody else, but for me it's very motivating. I really feel like going back to work and doing well.

Marco: That's good to hear. That's what I want.

Jenny: Yeah.

Marco: Really, that's the effect a meeting should have.

Veronique: Yes, that should be how we feel afterwards.

Marco: You know, it's no good sitting here telling everyone off. That's what they did in the past and it didn't work.

Veronique: Yeah.

Marco: And I knew it wouldn't work. We want to come up with solutions but also take responsibility and stick to the solutions that we decide now.

Veronique: Yeah.

Marco: And for me it's like, 'You had your chance to speak your mind. If you didn't say what you think, then you missed the opportunity.'

Jenny: Yeah, then it's your problem.

Marco: Like some of you saying, 'You know, we don't have the right equipment.' You know, the issue should have been raised at an earlier meeting.

Jenny: That's true.

Marco: Speak up – in our monthly meetings we need to speak about our problems and see if we can make improvements. Some things might not happen. Other things might happen, you know, who would have thought that we could have wireless handsets?

Jenny: Yeah.

Marco: We should get wireless keyboards and get proper equipment. Hannah isn't shy about spending money if it's for the guests. If we address it the right way, it will happen.

Jenny: Great.

Marco: OK, thank you both.

Jenny: Cool.

Marco: Thanks for coming.

Jenny: Thank you.

---

5 Research shows that cultures tend to prefer one type of politeness over another (type A is more common in the US, type B is more common in Japan). Which type of politeness is more common in your culture? What other factors are relevant in using type A or type B politeness?

Output: Applying politeness strategies

Stage 1

Work in pairs. Discuss the scenarios below and write a short dialogue for each of them, making sure you use polite language.

- You are a manager and have to gently criticise your employee about his/her recent performance, while trying to motivate him/her.
- You have to tell your boss you want to make a request to transfer to another department, but not because of him/her.
- You want to show your boss your excellent attitude towards your job, because you think it will help get you promoted.

Stage 2

Perform your dialogue for another pair.

12 Microfinance

Beggar (USA)

Millionaire (Hong Kong)

Artisan (Cameroon)

Farmer (Japan)

Farmer (Mexico)

Street vendor (Pakistan)

12.1 Theory: The concepts of microfinance

Learning outcomes

- Understand the scope and characteristics of microfinance.
- Use grammatical structures with *used to, be used to* and *get used to*.
- Evaluate and conduct research into microfinance.

Introduction

1 Which of the following financial services do you have or have you used?

current bank account	savings bank account
long-term bank loan	mortgage
pension plan	short-term bank loan
money transfer	credit card
debit/cash card	emergency loan
PayPal	life/car/house/travel/health insurance

Why are these services useful to you? How would your life be different without them? How easy or difficult was it for you personally to get access to these services?

2 Look at the photos and discuss these questions:

- What financial services might these people most benefit from?
- Why do you think some people are excluded from access to these services?
- Is there a good reason for their exclusion or are banks too conservative?
- Who should pay the highest/lowest level of interest on bank loans? Why?

Business view

UNCTAD (United Nations Conference on Trade and Development) promotes the integration of developing countries into the world economy. It is an institution which aims to help shape current policy debates and thinking on development.

Reading: Microfinance FAQs

1 Read the following FAQs (Frequently Asked Questions) from the microfinance pages of the UNCTAD website and match them to the section (A–G) on page 109 that answers the questions. Question 4 has been done for you.

1 How does microfinance help the poor?
2 Who are microfinance clients?
3 What kinds of institutions deliver microfinance?
4 What is microfinance?   A
5 When is microfinance NOT an appropriate tool?
6 What is microcredit?
7 Why do MFIs (microfinance institutions) charge high interest rates to poor people?

A

Microfinance is often defined as financial services for poor and low-income clients. In practice, the term is often used more narrowly to refer to loans and other services from providers that identify themselves as microfinance institutions (MFIs). These institutions deliver very small loans to <u>unsalaried</u> borrowers, taking little or no collateral. More broadly, microfinance refers to a movement that envisions a world in which low-income households have permanent access to a range of high-quality financial services to finance their income-producing activities, build assets, stabilise consumption, and protect against risks. These services are not limited to credit, but include savings, insurance, and money transfers.

B

Microcredit refers to very small loans for <u>unsalaried</u> borrowers with little or no collateral, provided by legally registered institutions. Microfinance typically refers to microcredit, savings, insurance, money transfers, and other financial products targeted at poor and low-income people.

C

Typical microfinance clients are poor and low-income people that do not have access to other formal financial institutions. Microfinance clients are usually self-employed, household-based entrepreneurs. Their diverse <u>micro-enterprises</u> include small retail shops, street vending, artisanal manufacture, and service provision. In rural areas, micro-entrepreneurs often have small income-generating activities such as food-processing and trade; some, but far from all, are farmers.

D

Most MFIs started as not-for-profit organisations like NGOs (non-governmental organisations), credit unions and other financial cooperatives, and state-owned development and postal savings banks. An increasing number of MFIs are now organised as for-profit entities, often because it is a requirement to obtaining a licence from banking authorities to offer savings services. For-profit MFIs may be organised as commercial banks that specialise in microfinance, or microfinance departments of full-service banks.

E

The impact of microcredit has been studied more than the impact of other forms of microfinance. A harsh aspect of poverty is that income is often <u>irregular</u> and <u>undependable</u>. Access to credit helps the poor to smooth cash flows and avoid periods where access to food, clothing, shelter, or education is lost. Credit can make it easier to manage shocks like sickness of a wage earner, theft, or natural disasters. The poor use credit to build assets such as buying land, which gives them future security. Women participants in microcredit programmes often experience important <u>self-empowerment</u>.

F

Financial services, particularly credit, are not appropriate for all people at all times. For loans that will be used for business purposes, microcredit best serves those who have identified an economic opportunity and can capitalise on it if they have access to a small amount of ready cash. <u>Regardless</u> of how loans are used, MFIs can provide long-term, stable credit access only when clients have both the willingness and ability to meet scheduled loan repayments. Microfinance is particularly <u>inappropriate</u> for the destitute, who may need grants or other public resources to improve their economic situation.

G

Concerns often arise as to why microcredit interest rates are higher than the bank interest rates that wealthier people pay. The issue is cost: the administrative cost of making tiny loans is much higher in percentage terms than the cost of making a large loan. It takes a lot less staff time to make a single loan of $100,000 than 1,000 loans of $100 each. Besides loan size, other factors can make microcredit more expensive to deliver. MFIs may operate in areas that are remote or have a low population density, making lending more expensive. If an MFI wants to operate sustainably, it has to price its loans high enough to cover all its costs.

2 To what extent do you agree or disagree with the following ideas from the text? Give reasons for your answers.

1 'Low-income households [should] have permanent access to a range of high-quality financial services.'
2 'Credit can make it easier to manage shocks like sickness of a wage earner, theft, or natural disasters.'
3 'Financial services, particularly credit, are not appropriate for all people at all times.'
4 'If an MFI wants to operate sustainably, it has to price its loans high enough to cover all its costs.'

Transferable skill: Strategies for understanding unknown words

1 The meaning of a large number of words can be guessed without using a dictionary. Sometimes unknown words can be ignored without reducing your general understanding of the text. Discuss the following questions.

1 What do you do when you come across an unknown word in your own language?
2 Did you match the FAQs to the sections in the text above without knowing all of the words?

2 If you need to or want to understand the meanings of some words, you can do this by studying the word in context (looking at the words before and after the unknown word and guessing the meaning) or you can analyse the structure of the word for any clues such as prefixes or suffixes.

Match the definitions on page 110 to words and phrases in the text above and discuss how you arrived at your answers.

1 sees (A)   2 security guarantee (such as a house) you provide to a bank to get a loan (B)
3 business people who work at home (C)   4 organisations (D)
5 necessity (D)   6 build on or take advantage of (F)
7 extremely poor people (F)   8 number of people per km² (G)
9 do business over the long term without support (G)

3 Match the following meanings to the underlined prefixes and suffixes of the words below, taken from the reading text.

1 not   2 very small   3 without   4 own person

a <u>un</u>salaried (A and B)   b <u>micro</u>-enterprise (C)
c <u>ir</u>regular (E)   d <u>un</u>dependable (E)   e <u>self</u>-empowerment (E)
f regard<u>less</u> (F)   g <u>in</u>appropriate (F)

4 Find the above words, which are underlined in the text, read the word in context and note down the definition of the word.

5 Can you think of any more words with these suffixes and prefixes?

Critical analysis

1 Some commercial banks would like to enter the field of microfinance intending to make profits and not just cover costs. What do you think about this? Could it be a profitable business? What are the arguments for and against commercial banks entering the field of microfinance? Is it right that they should be allowed to profit from poor people?

2 There is an increasing amount of interest in microfinance for poor people in the rich developed world. Why do you think this is the case? Do you think there is a real need for this? What are the chances of success?

Language focus: *Used to, be used to* and *get used to*

■ When *used to* is used as an active verb, e.g. *We used to buy from Compaq*, it describes habitual actions or states that continued in the past but have now stopped – emphasising that the situation has changed.

■ When it is used as an adjective, e.g. *they're used to it, we're getting used to it*, it means that something is familiar or usual. When it is followed by a verb, the *-ing* form is used, e.g. *I'm used to having access to internet banking*.

1 In the following sentences, is *used to* an active verb or an adjective?

1 There's an astonishing number of businesses out there which used to be our customers.
2 She used to run the social group before she got promoted.
3 We used to pride ourselves on quality.
4 Get used to it – the Internet moves at a much faster pace than we do.
5 He isn't used to using the new computer system yet.

2 Correct the errors in the sentences below.

1 The public is used to park illegally in our company car park.
2 I prefer people who are used to work hard.
3 She used to spent a lot of money on holidays.
4 He was used to get money from his parents.

3 Think about your present job/study environment, and about the differences from when you first started. What things did you use to do that you don't do now? What did you use to find difficult, but you have since become used to? What things have you not got used to yet? Is there anything you hope you will never get used to?

Output: Researching microfinance

For microfinance to be successful, high-quality information is needed to improve decision-making. In small groups, first discuss the failure of previous research and then move on to prepare and conduct your own research.

Stage 1
In small groups, read the comments from researchers who used to be employed to carry out research with borrowers. Why do you think previous research failed to provide accurate, reliable and relevant information? What recommendations would you make for conducting future research?

'The clients were very poor people. They seemed to be afraid of us.'
'We weren't given enough computers or training to do the job.'
'The MFI representatives in the field were very knowledgeable, but they were too busy to help us with our research.'
'None of the borrowers said a word during interviews – I used to invent most of their answers!'
'I'm not used to sitting all day long in the heat asking people questions.'

Make notes during your discussion and then present your recommendations to another group.

Example: Some researchers were not used to the difficult and uncomfortable conditions in the countryside and poor areas of the cities. We recommend that we start to employ researchers from a wide variety of backgrounds.

Stage 2
Prepare a new trial study to focus on getting high-quality information. In groups, think of what information a micro-finance bank might want and then prepare a list of questions to ask clients and potential clients.

Example: Who did you use to borrow money from before taking this microfinance loan?

Stage 3
Work with somebody from another group and take it in turns to play the roles of the interviewer and the client of the bank.

Case study

Learning outcomes
- Contrast microfinance with conventional banking.
- Learn word formations about banking.
- Discuss bank lending criteria.

Profile: Grameen Bank

Grameen Bank was founded in 1983 in Bangladesh by Muhammad Yunus, who was awarded the Nobel Peace Prize in 2006. It is sometimes referred to as 'the rural bank', 'the bank for the poor' or 'the microcredit bank' as its operations are focused on making small loans to people on very low incomes living in the 80,000 villages across the country. It has over 7,500,000 borrowers, 97% of whom are women. Unusually for a bank, its client base also includes 100,000 beggars. They have been given small loans to become door-to-door salespeople. Client repayment of loans has been excellent and 10,000 of the beggars have now stopped begging completely. The bank is owned by the borrowers, and the profit that the bank makes goes back to the borrowers as shareholders.

Introduction

> ❝ Banks lend you an umbrella on a sunny day and take it away again the second it starts to rain. ❞
>
> Robert Frost, American poet

> ❝ The less you have, the more attractive you are. ❞
>
> Muhammad Yunus, founder of Grameen Bank

1 What do these quotes tell you about the differences between Grameen Bank and conventional banks?

2 Read the profile of Grameen Bank. What are the differences between Grameen Bank and standard commercial banks?

3 Would a bank offering microfinance to the poor be successful in your country? Why/Why not?

> ❝ A bank is a place that will lend you money if you can prove you don't need it. ❞
>
> Bob Hope, American comedian

> ❝ If you owe the bank $100, that's your problem. If you owe the bank $100 million, that's the bank's problem. ❞
>
> John Paul Getty, founder of the Getty Oil Company

Language focus: Word formations

1 Complete the table below to create different word formations commonly associated with banking.

Verb	Noun	Person
to penalise	1 _____	–
2 _____	guarantee	3 _____
to pay to repay / to pay back	4 _____ 5 _____	6 _____
incentivise	7 _____	–

2 Complete these sentences with the correct form of the words on page 111.

1 Other possibilities to buy a home include asking a parent or a relative to act as a _____ for a loan.

2 Early _____ of the loan is possible and will ensure you avoid penalties.

3 Before you consider moving your mortgage to another bank, check that your current lender won't _____ you with exit charges.

4 If the recession gets very bad, there isn't a lot you can do to force people to _____ the loans.

5 People have little _____ to save when a booming stock market makes them feel wealthier.

Listening 1: How and why Grameen Bank was founded

Business view

Professor Muhammad Yunus is the founding director of Grameen Bank and Nobel Peace Prize winner for his efforts to create social and economic development from the bottom up.

🔘 **2.22**

Listen to the first part of Muhammad Yunus's presentation of Grameen Bank at a book fair in the USA and answer the following questions.

1 What was the situation like in Bangladesh when Muhammad Yunus was teaching economics?

2 Who was causing problems for the villagers?

3 How many people did he help?

4 What did Muhammad Yunus have to do to persuade the bank to finally offer the loans?

5 How much of the money did the people repay on their loans?

6 What was the prediction of the bank about providing loans to poor people?

Critical analysis

Muhammad Yunus mentions loan sharks exploiting people in a ruthless way. What examples of this do you think he could refer to?

Listening 2: Reversing the basic principles of banking

🔘 **2.23**

1 Listen to the next part of Muhammad Yunus's talk and identify the correct definition (A or B below) of the banking term 'collateral'.

> **ⓐ collateral** *noun* SPECIALISED valuable property owned by someone who wants to borrow money which they agree will become the property of the company or person who lends the money if the debt is not paid back
>
> **ⓑ collateral** *noun* SPECIALISED valuable property owned by someone who wants to borrow money which they agree to give the company or person in exchange for a loan

2 What are the reasons why it is such a 'scary thought' for banks to provide loans without asking for collateral from borrowers?

Listening 3: Differences between Grameen Bank and conventional banks

🔘 **2.24**

1 In the table below conventional banks are compared with Grameen Bank. Try to predict the answers before listening.

Conventional bank	Grameen Bank
Require collateral and 1 _guarantee_ for loans	No collateral or 1 _guarantee_ required
2 _____ check contracts	No 2 _____ check contracts
Customer visits 3 _____	3 _____ visits customer
Bank will 4 _____ customers for non-repayment of loans	Bank does not 4 _____ customers
Lower client 5 _____ rates	Nearly 99% 5 _____ rates
6 _____ interest rates if you don't pay back loan in time	No 6 _____ interest rates

2 Listen and check your answers.

Work in groups and have separate meetings to discuss different bank lending criteria. Group A represents commercial bankers who are considering adopting practices from micro-finance banks. Group B represents consultants to a micro-finance bank that is considering adopting some commercial bank lending criteria. Read the information for your group.

Stage 1
Group A

You are a group of executives from a conventional bank. You have just returned from a fact-finding trip to Bangladesh where you have seen how Grameen Bank operates. Your Managing Director has asked you to report back on what you have learnt and how the bank can usefully incorporate some of the philosophy of Grameen Bank, whilst at the same time making a profit. Look at the information below.

Group A

Look at the list of 'freedoms' at Grameen Bank and decide to adopt at least **two** of them for your bank. Choose factors which you believe will increase profits for your bank (increasing business, reducing costs, reducing bureaucracy, creating new opportunities).

- Customers don't have to come in to the bank to see a manager.
- Customers don't need collateral to get a loan.
- Customers don't need a job to get a loan.
- Third-party guarantees are not necessary to get a loan.
- You don't need formal legal contracts for loan acceptance.
- There are no penalties if customers default on their repayments.

After you have finished your discussion, make your choices.

Group B

You are a group of international management consultants. You are preparing a report to review the basic principles of a micro-finance bank you have recently visited in India. They have asked for your help to make it more like a conventional bank, whilst at the same time keeping it a 'bank for the poor'. Look at the information below.

Group B

Look at the list of 'rules' that most conventional banks have and decide to adopt at least **two** of them for the micro-finance bank. Choose factors which you believe will increase profitability for the bank but have the minimal social cost for existing and future clients.

- Customers have to come in to the bank to see a manager.
- Customers need collateral to get a loan.
- Customers need a job to get a loan.
- Third-party guarantees are necessary to get a loan.
- You need formal legal contracts for loan acceptance.
- There are penalties if customers default on their repayments.

After you have finished your discussion, make your choices.

Stage 2
When you have made your decision in your groups, find a partner from the other group and explain your decisions to him/her.

Grameen Bank employees issuing loans to clients

Learning outcomes

- Use techniques to improve your delivery.
- Give a clear and engaging presentation.
- Learn how metaphors can help to improve a presentation.

Introduction

1 'Glossophobia' is the fear of public speaking. Seventy-five percent of people are reported to suffer from the phobia – this is more than the number of people who say they are frightened of death. What about you? Do you enjoy giving presentations and speaking in public?

2 Different cultures can expect different things from a presentation. Which of these are considered important in your culture, and which might be problematic? Which of the points below do you think are most important for a successful business presentation?

- appearing very confident
- making your audience laugh
- maintaining eye contact with the audience
- using good intonation and stressing key words
- being modest
- using linking language, such as 'firstly', 'on the other hand'
- appearing enthusiastic
- anything else?

3 Think of a very impressive speaker you have heard, either in person or through the media. It could be a politician, a lecturer, a business person, or somebody else. Tell a partner what the person talked about, and why they were impressive.

Listening 1: Good and bad delivery

🔘 2.25

1 When presenting, the way you say something is very important. Listen and compare these two ways of saying the same sentence.

- I'm sure you'll agree (that) our product is the best on the market.

2 Which of the presenters do you think is better? How would you describe the delivery of each of the presenters?

3 The second speaker uses effective intonation, speaks slowly and clearly, and breaks her sentence into clear 'chunks' (understandable groups of words separated by short silences). Speaking in chunks is arguably the most important presentation skill, because it makes your speech clear and interesting. Good presenters chunk. In pairs, practise saying the sentence above with clear chunking.

Listening 2: The President

🔘 2.26   🔘 2.27

Barack Obama, President of the United States of America

1 Listen to the whole of President Barack Obama's speech about his visionary plans for the US following his election victory in November 2008, and consider these questions.

1 Why is he easy to understand?

2 How does he sound confident?

3 How does he seem in control of his talk?

2 Listen again to the first part of Barack Obama's speech.

🔘 2.26

1 Does he separate his language into understandable groups of words (chunks)?

2 How does he use pauses?

3 Listen again to the second part of Barack Obama's speech.

🔘 2.27

1 How does he use intonation?

2 Does he stress certain words to show what's important? Which words?

Listening 3: The support manager

🔘 2.28

Listen to a support manager in a telecommunications company talking about how the various departments have been reorganised. Compare and contrast this presentation with Barack Obama's. What are the main differences?

Language focus: Use techniques to improve your delivery (stress, chunking and pace)

1 What conclusions can you draw about these factors when presenting?

- stressing key words
- chunking language
- speed of speech

2 Look at this sentence from Barack Obama's speech. It has been chunked strangely, with the wrong words stressed. The underlined words show the stress and the lines between words show the pauses.

<u>There</u> are many who / won't agree <u>with</u> every decision or policy <u>I</u> / make <u>as</u> / president and <u>we</u> / know <u>the</u> government can't / solve every <u>problem</u>.

🔘 2.29

3 Listen to the original, and correct the mistakes with stress and chunking in the sentence above.

4 Read through the beginning of a talk below. Underline the key words and put pause lines between possible chunks.

Thank you very much for coming here today. We're very glad to have this opportunity to tell you about our products and we hope that by the end of today we'll be ready to move our relationship on to the next stage. So firstly we'd like to talk about the history of our company. Then we'll move on to the suitability of our products for your market.

5 What types of words are usually key words? Why is this? Where do key words usually come in the chunk?

6 What is the maximum number of words in one chunk?

7 Where do the pauses come? Where shouldn't they come?

8 Practise reading the beginning of the talk above to a partner.

Critical analysis: Metaphors

1 A common type of business metaphor is forward movement as progress, e.g. *We're getting there.* Does Barack Obama use this type of metaphor in his speech?

2 Read through the audio script of his speech on page 162 and underline the metaphors.

3 While metaphors can be a good communication strategy when speakers share a culture, in international business they might be unsuccessful. Why?

Output: Short presentation

Stage 1

Prepare a short presentation (one or two minutes) about a project you have been working on recently at work or as part of your studies. Alternatively, you might think about a future work or study project you would like to do. Think about the following questions:

- What is the project?
- Why am I doing it?
- What makes it interesting, difficult, etc.?

Stage 2

Practise delivering it on your own, using the techniques from this lesson: chunking the language, stressing key words in each chunk, using good intonation. You may want to include a metaphor.

Stage 3

Give the presentation to a partner, and offer feedback to each other on your spoken delivery.

▶◀ **Watch Sequence 6 on the DVD to find out more about Accounting and finance.**

Learning outcomes

- Consider relationships and appropriate styles when writing emails.
- Understand and use a variety of functions in emails.
- Write emails to superiors and clients.

Introduction

1

⊖ ⊜ ⊝

Hi Tony,
Really sorry to mess you around, but there's a budgeting issue with the non-HK stuff. Can you put in an invoice for only ¥35,000 this time, and then we'll talk again next financial year. I hope you haven't made the trip to the bank already.
All the best, and apologies again.
John

2

⊖ ⊜ ⊝

No worries – wasn't expecting a reply anyway!

3

⊖ ⊜ ⊝

Dear all,

Please find the revised agenda for our meeting on Thursday and Friday.
You should all have your hotel details, but give us a ring if there are any problems. I'm afraid I can't make it for dinner on the Thursday evening this time. However, we have booked you a nice restaurant on us (Loch Fyne, as you all know it and seemed to like it last time) at 7.30, so it will be a good chance to get to know each other a bit more. Looking forward to a very productive meeting.

Best wishes,

Alex

4

⊖ ⊜ ⊝

Dear Claire,
I have been asked by Sara Quaile to let you know my dates for the meeting in St Petersburg in September. I will be staying two nights: Monday 1st and Tuesday 2nd September.
Best wishes,
Gila

5

⊖ ⊜ ⊝

Dear Mrs Bennett,

15th November is fine with me. Could you come to 12th floor of the Isuzu Building around 9.30? I will collect the material to explain our business and send it to you, probably by tomorrow. Then we should discuss it by phone.

Regards,

Kenji Sato

1 Quickly read the emails. What do you think is the relationship between the sender and receiver of each email?

2 Do you agree or disagree with these tips for writing emails to clients?

1 Be concise at all times.
2 Don't use abbreviations (such as *etc.*).
3 Don't use emoticons (such as :o)).
4 Always check your email for mistakes before sending it.
5 Always start the email 'Dear + title (Ms/Dr) + family name'.
6 Use friendly language.

3 How about for internal emails to colleagues? What differences do you think there are in terms of style, content, directness, openness, negativity, etc.?

Language focus: Formality and functions

1 The following abbreviations may be used in emails. Do you know them or can you guess the meaning?

| cc | e.g. | i.e. | etc. | re | asap | BTW | LOL | FYI | PLS | THX |

2 Some of the abbreviations above should not be used in formal emails. What might happen if you use them with the wrong person?

3 Which of the abbreviations could be used for these functions?

| thanking | requesting | developing a relationship | informing |

4 Match the functions from exercise 3 with the sentences below. Which would be suitable with clients and potential clients?

1 Could you please send us a written version of the agreement?
2 We are very sorry but, unfortunately, we do not think we can send a representative at this time.
3 Please, let us express our gratitude for the offer.
4 Just to let you know, I will be available from 9.30 till 3.00 on Thursday.
5 We are very keen to develop a long-term and mutually beneficial relationship with your company.

5 Make a note of any language from the above sentences that you could use in an email to a client.

Intercultural analysis: Starting and finishing the email

Deciding on the appropriate opening and term of address in emails can be very difficult, especially with people from different cultures.

1 Put the following terms of address in order from the least formal to most formal.

> 1 Dear Director   2 Hi Mary   3 Dear Mary
> 4 Dear Ms Lee   5 Hello Mary   6 Dear Professor Lee

2 Put the following closings in order, with the least formal first.

> 1 Best wishes   2 Cheers   3 Yours sincerely
> 4 Kind regards   5 Regards   6 Best   7 All the best
> 8 Yours faithfully

3 In which situations would you use the different openings and closings in your culture? In what ways may this be different in other cultures? If you don't know the other person well, do you think it is better to be too formal or too informal?

Writing skill: Functions of emails

1 Find examples of the following functions in the emails in the Introduction. Each email may include more than one function.

- informing
- inviting
- requesting
- thanking
- confirming
- apologising
- developing a relationship

2 Underline the language in each email that addresses these functions.

3 Plot each email on this diagram.

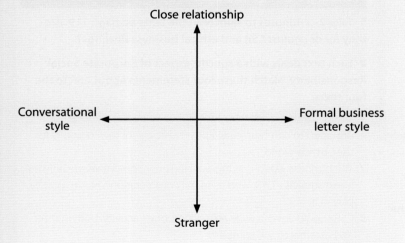

Output: Deciding on the formality of an email

Stage 1

Look at the following email from your manager. Is it written in a formal or informal style?

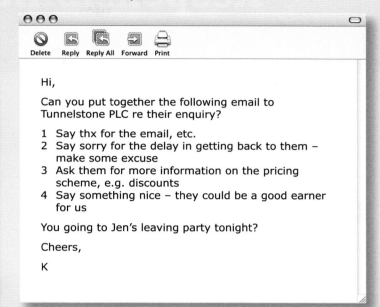

Hi,

Can you put together the following email to Tunnelstone PLC re their enquiry?

1 Say thx for the email, etc.
2 Say sorry for the delay in getting back to them – make some excuse
3 Ask them for more information on the pricing scheme, e.g. discounts
4 Say something nice – they could be a good earner for us

You going to Jen's leaving party tonight?

Cheers,

K

Stage 2

Write a brief response to your manager. Think about how your relationship with your boss will affect the formality of the email.

Stage 3

Write the email as instructed. Consider the different functions you will use in the email, and the appropriate level of formality for this type of email.

Stage 4

Work in pairs. Look at each other's emails, and write a new version combining the best parts of each email. Then read it out to the rest of the class.

13 Corporate Social Responsibility

13.1 Theory: Business ethics and Corporate Social Responsibility

Learning outcomes

- Make connections between ethics and CSR.
- Identify authors' opinions in reading texts and edit writing styles.
- Learn topic vocabulary and debate two sides of an argument.

Introduction

1 What is your personal opinion of the statements below?

1 = strongly agree   2 = agree   3 = unsure   4 = disagree
5 = strongly disagree

Accepting gifts and generous hospitality from clients is acceptable.	1	2	3	4	5
Filling job vacancies internally amongst staff, their friends and family is fine.	1	2	3	4	5
Being open, honest and truthful is always the best course of action in business.	1	2	3	4	5
Companies should decide what is right and wrong in business, not the government.	1	2	3	4	5
A supplier's ethical standards must be checked before doing business with them.	1	2	3	4	5
Maximising profits is more important than acting ethically.	1	2	3	4	5

Discuss your answers in pairs.

2 Many organisations have a Corporate Social Responsibility (CSR) policy which deals with ethical issues such as those outlined above. What decisions regarding CSR do you think the following companies have to make?

- a footwear company
- a supermarket
- a broadcaster
- a government ministry

Reading: Cases for and against CSR

1 Take 2–3 minutes to skim read the texts on page 119. Are they *for* or *against* CSR and ethical business dealings?

2 Each text deals with a specific aspect of Corporate Social Responsibility. Match these four statements about CSR to the four texts.

1 CSR is nothing more than a PR (Public Relations) exercise, designed to communicate a positive image of the company to the outside world.

2 The business world is a dog-eat-dog environment where only the fittest survive – CSR, with its moral considerations, has no part to play in it.

3 CSR should cover a wide area of corporate activity, both internal and external to the company.

4 CSR doesn't turn companies into non-profit-making organisations. The opposite is true – doing the right thing makes money.

A

A businessman from time to time is almost compelled, in the interests of his company or himself, to practice some form of deception when negotiating with customers, dealers, labor unions, government officials, or even other departments in their own companies. By knowingly giving misinformation and hiding important facts – in short, by bluffing – he tries to persuade others to agree with him. I think it is fair to say that if the individual executive refuses to bluff from time to time – if he feels obliged to tell the truth, the whole truth and nothing but the truth – he is ignoring opportunities permitted under the rules and is at a heavy disadvantage in his business dealings.

Source: *Is Business Bluffing Ethical?* by Albert Z. Carr

Glossary
to be compelled: to be forced (to do something)
deception: not telling the whole truth
bluffing: misleading somebody; for example, you pretend to have knowledge that you do not have

B

General Managers need to predict and monitor the effects of corporate policy on environments inside and outside the corporation. One way of understanding the corporation is to divide its transactions into two types. First the corporation acts as a moral agent when its policies and actions affect outside stakeholders such as suppliers, competitors, the local community and the wider environment. Second, when policies affect inside stakeholders (employees and shareholders), the corporation can be viewed as a moral environment and should therefore be managed with a view to the freedom and wellbeing of its members.

Source: *Note on the Corporation as a Moral Environment* by Kenneth E. Goodpaster

Glossary
monitor: to observe and record
stakeholder: person or group with an interest in an organisation
wellbeing: health and happiness

C

Why should these giant corporations, or any company, for that matter – whose primary purpose for existence is to maximise profits for their shareholders, be concerned with becoming good global citizens? Simply, in addition to being the right thing to do, it is good business. A study published by the Institute of Business Ethics of the FTSE 250 companies, provides evidence that those companies with an ethical code in place for over five years generated greater economic value and market value than their peers.

Source: *Corporate Social Responsibility: Are you giving back or just giving away?* by Jim Gus Gustafson

Glossary
primary purpose: main reason
FTSE 250: index of top 250 companies listed in UK stock exchange (Financial Times Stock Exchange)

D

CSR can seem to have taken ownership of a vast number of issues, from work–life balance to procurement policies for suppliers and contractors to customer service. Many companies find themselves trying to cover all the bases and the result can be little more than a giant box-ticking exercise, with very little business value. The reality of CSR for most organisations is that it is only skin-deep and consequently almost meaningless. Its primary function seems to be to maintain outward appearances.

Source: *CSR: More than PR, Pursuing Competitive Advantage in the Long Run* by John Surdyk

Glossary
vast: very large
work–life balance: refers to the relationship between work and personal life. A good work–life balance is when work and personal life are in harmony
procurement policy: policy regarding buying from suppliers
box-ticking exercise: following procedures without really believing in them. It's as if you are just ticking boxes on a form – *done this, done that*, etc.

3 Read the texts again. Which texts do you agree and disagree with the most? Why?

Check that you understand the meaning of the words below taken from the texts. Then use these words to complete a summary of the arguments *for* and *against* CSR.

> work–life balance   wellbeing   bluffing   box-ticking exercise   compelled   vast   primary purpose   deception   generated   procurement policies   stakeholders

Not everyone agrees that companies should be
1 _____ to behave as moral agents concerned with
the 2 _____ of their staff or of society as a whole.
Some writers argue that for the 3 _____ majority of
companies, CSR is simply about image and PR. In other words, CSR
policy is not much more than a 4 _____ . In reality,
business is very much like a game where 5 _____
and 6 _____ are a recognised part of business life.
On the other hand, studies of FTSE 250 companies in the UK have
proved that CSR has 7 _____ high profits for ethical
companies. Having formal 8 _____ for suppliers
to ensure they do not employ child labour, for example, means
companies not only do the right thing but also protect their brand
from negative publicity. Similarly, having guidelines to ensure a
good 9 _____ for staff means that employees
suffer less stress at home and are therefore more productive in the
workplace. In short, your opinion of CSR depends on how you see
the 10 _____ of business – is it simply to satisfy
shareholders and maximise profits or is it about meeting the more
complex needs of a much wider range of 11 _____
inside and outside the company?

Critical analysis

1 Text A was written a number of years ago – why would many people now consider the writing style (not the content) old-fashioned and unacceptable?

2 Underline all the examples of the use of the male gender in Text A when the writer means both men and women.

3 Many people think it is better to use the plural to refer to people in general. For example, we can rewrite the first few words of Text A as follows:

Businesspeople from time to time are almost compelled ...

Change the other examples in the same way.

4 Is this similar in your language? What language structures (if any) can you use to avoid using the male gender when referring to men and women?

> ❝ Ethics has no place in business – CSR in reality is nothing more than words. ❞

Stage 1
Work in two groups to prepare for the debate. Group A are *for* the motion and Group B are *against* the motion. In your groups, first prepare a list of points that support your position. Then consider what the opposition will say and discuss how you can counter their arguments. Make notes about the main points for your discussion.

Stage 2
Group A should start the debate. Take it in turns to speak. Everybody in the group should speak and spend two minutes explaining their points. Group B should then speak, taking it in turns, with each person speaking for about two minutes.

Stage 3
At the end of the debate, have a Q&A session where each group asks the other group questions.

Stage 4
What is your personal opinion on CSR? Has your opinion been changed at all by the debate?

13.2 Practice: The business case for Corporate Social Responsibility

Learning outcomes

- Understand and discuss how CSR works in practice.
- Improve listening skills by using paraphrase.
- Use phrases accurately with the correct dependent preposition.

Profile: The BBC

The BBC is one of the most well-known broadcasting corporations in the world, broadcasting programmes on radio, television and online and employing over 23,000 people across the world. Its aim is to 'inform, educate and entertain'. It is an independent organisation financed mostly by television viewers in the UK who pay a licence fee to watch the BBC's TV channels. The licence fee is set annually in consultation with the UK government. The BBC also generates some of its income from commercial activities – selling programme content to other networks, sales of DVDs, etc. However, the BBC has no shareholders and states in its annual report that it 'does not seek to make a profit from its public service activities'.

Introduction

1 Match the four images to the words below. Then discuss in what ways companies can act with a sense of social responsibility (or not) regarding the people and places represented here.

community   physical environment   marketplace   workplace

2 Read the profile of the BBC and note who the different stakeholders are in the corporation. What do you think the interests are of each of these stakeholders?

Example: Employees have an interest in the long-term success of the BBC to guarantee job security.

Do you think it is possible for an organisation to meet the needs of all its stakeholders or will the interests of these groups always be in conflict?

Listing 1: Defining CSR

 2.30

Business view

Yogesh Chauhan is the BBC Corporate Social Responsibility Director.

1 You will hear an interview with Yogesh Chauhan in which he talks about CSR in general and CSR at the BBC. In the first part he gives a definition of CSR. Read the text below and try to predict what he says.

Corporate responsibility 1 _____ corporate philanthropy. Instead it is a holistic approach that companies and organisations take to manage their business in a 2 _____ manner. The four key components to the BBC's CSR policy focus on the 3 _____ the organisation has on the community, the physical environment, the marketplace, and the workplace. CSR, however, goes beyond just addressing these issues – it's about how these factors are incorporated within the 4 _____ of an organisation, how they are integrated into the company and how 5 _____ it is in disclosing information.

2 Now listen to the interview and complete the summary using the words you hear. Were any of your predictions correct?

Listening 2: The different sides of CSR

 2.31

1 Listen to the next part of the interview and make notes about the four areas of CSR Yogesh Chauhan mentions: *community, physical environment, marketplace* and *workplace*. You might find it helpful to write notes using a mind map or a four-column table.

2 Do you think these four areas of CSR are of equal importance?

Transferable skill: Awareness of paraphrase in listening

To paraphrase means saying one or more words in a different way while also keeping the original meaning. For example, *firm/organisation/business* are all different ways of saying *company*. Being able to identify and understand paraphrase helps you improve your listening skills by helping you locate and identify the answers to questions. It is also an important skill in making your viewpoint clear in spoken and written language.

Look at the underlined phrases in Listening 3 exercise 1 and write down different ways of saying these words.

Listening 3: The business case for CSR

2.32

1 Before listening to the next part of the interview with Yogesh Chauhan, try to predict if the following statements are true or false.

1 It's essential that there are good commercial reasons for CSR.
2 The CSR business case is focused on reducing expenditure.
3 Some CSR initiatives produce real advantages for the company immediately.
4 The owners of the company are the most important stakeholders.
5 Short-term profit is not the only way you can calculate how well a company performs.

Now listen to the interview and check your answers.

2 Listen again and write down the actual words Yogesh Chauhan used that paraphrase the underlined words in the questions.

Listening 4: Is CSR just corporate gloss?

2.33

1 Listen to the final part of the interview with Yogesh Chauhan and choose the best option to paraphrase what you hear.

1 It is _____ for companies to use their CSR activities to promote themselves.
   A acceptable **B** unacceptable **C** vital **D** dangerous
2 The business practices of the Co-operative Bank _____ its marketing.
   A damage **B** match **C** decide **D** contradict
3 A lot of the misleading advertising is _____ by the Advertising Standards Authority.
   A ignored **B** produced **C** edited **D** identified

2 What does the term *greenwashing* mean? Can you give any examples of this kind of misleading advertising?

3 Do you think Yogesh Chauhan gives a good defence of CSR against the attack that: 'CSR is little more than corporate gloss'? Why/Why not?

Language focus: Phrases with prepositions

Dependent prepositions are prepositions that are used with certain words to create particular meanings. They tend to follow nouns, verbs or adjectives, and should be memorised as single items.

1 The following phrases are taken from Listening 1 and 2. Decide which category below they fit in and write them in the table.

the **impact** the organisation has **on** the community

we need to **look at** how these factors are incorporated

are **mindful of** other issues too

Noun + preposition	Verb + preposition	Adjective + preposition

2 Find these phrases underlined in the audio scripts on pages 162–3. Notice what comes after the preposition and write down the whole pattern in the table below. (Note other patterns are also possible.)

(be) incorporated within   amount of   focus on
(be) integrated into   conscious of   aware of

Put the phrases in the correct pattern in this table.

Noun + preposition + noun	Verb + preposition + noun	Adjective + preposition + noun

3 Put phrases from exercises 1 and 2 into these sentences.

1 They should be _____ the broader public interest.

2 It will reduce the _____ repetitive work.

3 NYTimes.com has now _____ these articles _____ its search tools.

4 The company said it would now _____ all its efforts _____ two products.

Output: CSR presentation

Work in small groups. You are going to give presentations on how a supermarket and a government department can improve their CSR. There are two role plays. Look at the following information for your group.

Group A

Role play 1

Look at the information on page 142. You are CSR consultants. You are going to give a short presentation to the management of a large supermarket (Group B) on how they can improve their environmental CSR policies. Prepare your presentation using the topics on page 142 and any others you think are suitable.

Role play 2

You are the managers of a government department and Group B are CSR management consultants. Group B are going to present their ideas about how you can improve your CSR in the workplace. First, predict what you think they will say. After the presentation, report back to them, paraphrasing what they said for confirmation.

Group B

Role play 1

You are the managers of a supermarket and Group A are CSR management consultants. Group A are going to present their ideas about how you can improve your environmental CSR policies. First, predict what you think they will say. After the presentation, report back to them, paraphrasing what they said for confirmation.

Role play 2

Look at the information on page 146. You are going to give a short presentation to the managers of a government department (Group A) on how they can improve their CSR in the workplace. Prepare your presentation using the topics on page 146 and any others you think are suitable.

13.3 Skills: Supporting the speaker

Learning outcomes

- Learn how to be an active listener.
- Improve conversations and be aware of levels of formality.
- Learn how to open conversations and support the speaker on the telephone.

Introduction

Supporting the speaker means being an active listener. This does not mean just concentrating on and being interested in what the speaker is saying, but also *showing* that interest through words and actions. For instance, nodding, asking questions and interpreting what the speaker means are all ways of supporting the speaker.

1 Look at the following list. Which are effective ways for listeners to *support the speaker* in face-to-face conversations? Can you think of any other examples?

1 facial gestures
2 body language
3 intonation
4 summarising what the speaker says
5 letting the speaker know when you don't understand
6 staying silent
7 using response words like 'uh-huh'
8 closing your eyes
9 asking questions

2 Which of the above list are suitable for telephone conversations, and which are not? Why/Why not?

3 In pairs, sit back to back and have a telephone conversation. One person calls the other to book a holiday. Try to support each other through active listening.

4 Some sales trainers recommend that staff should smile on the phone. Do you think you can 'hear' a smile?

Listening 1: Opening telephone conversations

1 Read the dialogue below between the general manager and the owner of a travel company.

Ken: Hi, Sarah. Ken here.
Sarah: Hi, Ken. Good to hear from you. Is everything OK?
Ken: Yes, very good. Just calling about …

 2.34

2 Now listen to the start of a conversation between a sales representative (John) from the same company and a customer.

3 Answer the following questions about both the dialogue and the conversation you listened to.

1 How does the speaker introduce himself? What phrases are used to do this?
2 How does the speaker introduce the topic? What language is used to do this?
3 How much small talk is there? Why do you think this is?

4 Put the following openings to conversations in order from most formal to least formal.

1 Good morning. I'm calling on behalf of Aster Electronics. My name is Jin Peeranut.
2 Hi, Jeanne here.
3 Good morning. This is Ricky from Rococo Constructions.
4 Hi, it's Monica here from Peru Internationals.

5 Who do you think the speakers above are talking to? What type of relationship do you think they have with the person they are calling?

Listening 2: Showing interest on the telephone

2.35

Listen to the phone conversation between the general manager (Ken) of a travel company and the owner of the company (Sarah). Ken is discussing the promotional materials they have been designing together.

1 How enthusiastic does Sarah seem about making changes?

2 How does Sarah show her feelings?

Listening 3: Helping the speaker expand a topic

🔊 2.36

1 What do you think is the difference between *sponsorship* and *support*? Which is more specific?

2 Ken clarifies the company's level of involvement (as sponsorship or support). Listen to the recording and answer these questions.

1 How does Sarah's level of support here differ compared to the first part of the conversation? Why do you think this is?

2 How does Sarah finish the conversation? Does this stage of the conversation sound positive?

Language focus: Supporting the speaker through listener responses

1 Listeners in business often say *yes, hmm* and *sure*. Why do you think listeners use these words?

2 The response that is used depends on the status and the relationship of the speakers. Do you think *sure* is used more by managers to clients, or to subordinates? How about *hmm*?

3 Listener responses can be positive (encouraging and supportive), e.g. *sure*, or neutral, e.g. *hmm*. The listener can show in conversation that they disagree or think there is some problem. Do you think that the following responses are positive, neutral or negative?

absolutely	maybe	uh-huh	sure	oh	(silence)	hmm	yes
really	great						

4 Work in pairs. Ask your partner a question (for example, *What did you do last weekend?*) and then DON'T use any encouraging words or offer any support while listening. The listener must stay silent.

5 Change roles, and once again the listener should not respond. Then discuss how it felt and the effect it had on the conversation.

6 When we listen in a second language we sometimes forget to show we are listening because we are concentrating so hard on understanding the message. How will this make the speaker feel?

7 Repeat the conversations with your partner. This time try to be as supportive as possible by asking further questions and showing that you are listening. What differences were there this time compared to the conversation where there was no support?

Critical analysis

Why are listener responses especially important on the telephone? In what ways can we encourage the speaker to continue in face-to-face communication?

Intercultural analysis

In your first language, what sounds and words do people use to show they are listening? Are they the same as in English in terms of sound and level of support, or do some of the words and sounds convey a different meaning?

Output: Helping speakers get their ideas across

Stage 1
Work individually and take two minutes to think about and prepare a short talk on a newspaper or magazine article you have recently read. Make sure you answer these questions in your talk:

- Where did you see the article?
- What was it about?
- What was your opinion of the article?

Stage 2
Work in small groups. In turns, give the talk to members of your group. This time the listeners should just listen to the speaker and not make any comments.

Stage 3
Give the talk again. This time the listeners should help to support the speaker by showing interest, asking for clarification and asking any follow-up questions to get the speaker to expand on the subject.

Stage 4
Work on your original talk after getting feedback from your group and then deliver the talk to somebody from another group over the phone. Once again, the listener should be very supportive.

14 Strategic planning

14.1 Theory: Corporate strategic planning

Learning outcomes

- Understand the process of strategic planning.
- Learn words and phrases connected with strategic planning.
- Create your own strategic plan.

g. This afternoon

Introduction

1 The strategic planning process starts with five simple questions about the company and the business environment it operates in.

1 Where are we now?
2 Where do we want to go?   **Company**
3 How do we get there?

4 What dangers do we face?
5 What new possibilities are there?   **Environment**

Match the following formal business terms to the five questions.

a Strategy
b Goals and objectives
c Analysis of the company's own internal strengths and weaknesses and its present competitive position
d Analysis of external opportunities
e Analysis of external threats

Note that analysis of strengths, weaknesses, opportunities and threats is known as a SWOT analysis.

2 Answer the questions in exercise 1 about a company or organisation you know well.

1 Match the images (a–h) on page 126 to these guidelines for corporate strategic planning.

1 make forecasts
2 search for information
3 communicate goals and objectives
4 combine detailed analysis with long-range focus
5 set out objectives to aim for
6 measure progress constantly
7 remember action, not just words
8 don't ignore changes in your environment

2 Visualisation techniques such as these are widely used in business to help communicate concepts that can sometimes appear complex and difficult. It works for many people but not everyone. What about you? How useful do you find it?

1 Match the following verbs taken from the text below to their meaning.

1	implement	a	decide if something is good or not
2	monitor	b	go to someone for information
3	evaluate	c	clearly identify someone or something
4	conduct	d	check, observe and record
5	deviate	e	carry out
6	develop	f	make sure
7	specify	g	change direction (from an agreed one)
8	ensure	h	build
9	consult	i	put into action

2 Skim the text below on strategic planning in 2 minutes and then match the headings (1–5) with the paragraphs (A–E).

1 Advantages of strategic planning
2 What is strategic planning?
3 When should strategic planning be done?
4 Monitoring, evaluating and deviating from the plan
5 How do we ensure implementation of our new plan?

A

Simply put, strategic planning determines where an organisation is going over the next year or more, how it's going to get there and how it will know if it got there or not. The focus of a strategic plan is usually on the entire organisation, while the focus of a business plan is usually on a particular product, service or programme. The corporate strategic plan is best seen as an umbrella plan that incorporates departmental plans: marketing plan, financial plan and operational plan. There are a variety of strategic planning models but the most common is goals-based planning.

Strategic planning should be conducted by a planning team. The chief executive and board chair must be included in the planning group, and should drive development and implementation of the plan.

B

Strategic planning serves a variety of purposes in organisations, including the following. 1 Define the purpose of the organisation and establish realistic goals and objectives in a specified time frame. 2 Communicate those goals and objectives to the organisation's main stakeholders. 3 Ensure the most effective use is made of the organisation's resources by focusing the resources on the key priorities. 4 Provide a base from which progress can be measured.

Always keep in mind that the real benefit of the strategic planning process is the process itself, not the beautiful report that is submitted to the boss.

C

The scheduling for the strategic planning process depends on the nature and needs of the organisation and its immediate external environment. For example, planning should be carried out frequently in an organisation whose products and services are in an industry that is changing rapidly. In this situation, planning might be carried out once or even twice a year.

Strategic planning should be done when an organisation is just getting started. It should also be done in preparation for a new major venture, for example, developing a new department, division, major new product or line of products.

D

A frequent complaint about the strategic planning process is that it produces a document that ends up collecting dust on a shelf – the organisation ignores the information set out in the document. The following guidelines will help ensure that the plan is implemented. 1 When conducting the planning process, involve the people who will be responsible for implementing the plan and consult them regularly. Use a cross-functional team (representatives from each of the major departments or work groups involved). 2 Ensure the plan is realistic. Continue asking planning participants: 'Is this realistic? Can you really do this?' 3 Organise the overall strategic plan into smaller action plans. 4 In the overall planning document, specify who is doing what and by when.

E

Monitoring and evaluating the planning activities and status of implementation of the plan is, for many organisations, as important as identifying strategic issues and goals. One advantage of monitoring and evaluation is to ensure that the organisation is following the direction established during strategic planning. Note that plans are guidelines. They aren't rules. It isn't a problem to deviate from a plan. But planners should understand the reason for the deviations and update the plan to reflect the new direction.

Source: managementhelp.org

3 Are the following statements true or false according to the text?

1 The strategic plan covers one part of an organisation's activities. (A)

2 It is essential that top management lead the planning process. (A)

3 The results of good planning mean investment is concentrated on priorities. (B)

4 The final planning document is the most important part of the process. (B)

5 There are no specific times when a company should start the planning process. (C)

6 In fast-changing environments you shouldn't revise/update plans regularly. (C)

7 The problem with the planning process is that plans are not implemented. (D)

8 Don't be concerned with setting highly ambitious goals and targets. (D)

9 Setting objectives is more important than checking and measuring progress. (E)

10 It is OK to change plans (after they are written) and follow a new direction. (E)

4 The statements above express the writer's opinion. To what extent do you agree with the points raised?

Language focus: Verbs for strategic planning

1 Choose the best word to complete this advice about good strategic planning.

1 Keep reminding yourself that [1](*implementing / conducting*) the plan is the most difficult part of the process.

2 Remember that [2](*monitoring / ensuring*) the planning process is more important than [3](*consulting / evaluating*) it.

3 In order to [4](*ensure / consult*) the job is done, you need to [5](*specify / consult*) someone to do it.

4 It's probably not a good idea to [6](*deviate / conduct*) too much away from the agreed plan.

5 To successfully [7](*develop / deviate*) a plan, it is best to [8](*consult / evaluate*) widely within the department.

2 Which is the most important piece of advice in your opinion?

Intercultural analysis

The planning process is not uniform across the world and across all types of businesses and corporate cultures. In certain cultures, decision-making is fast but the implementation stage can take a long time. This is often because not enough time is spent on the consultation stage and developing ideas at the beginning. In other cultures, the opposite is true, as a lot of importance is given to building consensus and getting everyone's agreement and cooperation before implementing the plan.

1 Which of these two timeline diagrams of the planning process suits your personal way of working? Why?

Model A

| Ideas | Consultation | Implementation |

Model B

| Ideas | Consultation | Implementation |

2 Which type of planning process (A or B) best represents what happens in your country or organisation?

Output: Creating a strategic plan

Create your own personal strategic plan. You might find it helpful to draw or visualise images to help you do this task.

- What are your career goals in five years' time?
- What steps do you need to take to get there?
- What are your present strengths and weaknesses?
- What might be the possible outside threats stopping you from reaching your objectives?
- How might you overcome them?
- What opportunities can you take to help you reach these goals?

Make notes in the table below.

Goals	
Steps	
Strengths	
Weaknesses	
Threats	
Opportunities	

When you have completed your plan, discuss it with a partner.

Learning outcomes

- Discuss the key attributes for a successful strategist.
- Understand and apply SWOT information to develop a corporate strategic plan.
- Learn multi-word verbs and expressions.

Profile: Abercrombie & Kent

Abercrombie & Kent is an international travel company, with over 60 offices worldwide and head offices in the UK and US. It specialises in luxury travel to exotic locations, and the client's itinerary is carefully planned to suit his/her personal needs. The company was set up in 1962.

Introduction

1 What plans do you have for the future?

2 What strategy do you have to achieve these plans?

3 Which of the following characteristics do you think a strategist in business needs?

- decisiveness
- aggression
- thoughtfulness
- intelligence
- patience
- a sense of humour
- experience
- listening ability
- honesty

4 What faults might an unsuccessful strategist have?

5 How do you think the travel industry has changed in your country over the last ten years?

6 How do you think the travel industry will develop in the future?

7 How important is the travel industry for your country?

Listening 1: The characteristics of a strategist

🔊 2.37

Business view

Justin Wateridge is Managing Director of Abercrombie & Kent.

1 Listen to Justin Wateridge talk about what makes a good or bad strategist. Note down his key points.

2 What happens if a strategist often changes his/her mind?

3 Are you suited to being a successful strategist? For example, are you good at analysing lots of information?

Listening 2: Company strategy

🔘 2.38

1 Listen to the next part of the interview. Are the following statements true or false?

1 Abercrombie & Kent started off in Africa.
2 They have ground agents in 45 countries.
3 They also offer cheap package holidays.
4 Abercrombie & Kent's holidays are designed for individuals.
5 Abercrombie & Kent rely on brochures to sell their holidays.
6 Justin Wateridge thinks that travel should be an interesting experience for the clients.

2 Listen again and complete the SWOT analysis (Strengths/Weaknesses/Opportunities/Threats) diagram below for Abercrombie & Kent, using the information that Justin Wateridge gives. One has been done for you.

Strengths	Weaknesses
Staff expertise	
Opportunities	**Threats**

Critical analysis

Add your own ideas to the SWOT analysis for Abercrombie & Kent. Use the following questions to help you.

- What are the current issues for the travel industry?
- What social issues does the travel industry have to take into account?
- What impact will the world economy have on the luxury travel industry?
- What environmental considerations are there?

Language focus: Multi-word verbs and collocations

Justin Wateridge uses several multi-word verbs, e.g. *come up with, set up, go back, put into*. Multi-word verbs are very common in spoken English.

1 *Come, get, put* and *take* form several multi-word verbs. Make multi-word webs using these verbs. Use a dictionary to check the meanings. *Come* has been partly done for you below.

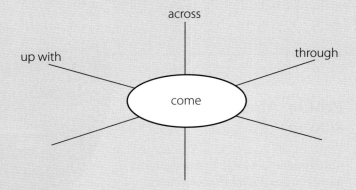

2 Some multi-word verbs occur in fixed phrases. Can you put the fixed phrases that Justin Wateridge used in the correct order?

1 forward in move direction the right
2 ideas practice into put
3 over take a decision time
4 with ideas come up

3 Put the ideas from exercise 2 in a logical order for deciding on and implementing strategy.

4 Here are some other phrases from the interview. Match them to their meaning.

1 the company was set up in 1962	**a** communicate
2 the company got to where it is	**b** establish
3 these qualities have held it in good stead	**c** develop
4 we try to get that across to the customer	**d** support and protect

5 Think of a famous company and its products. If you were responsible for promoting it, what would you try to get across to the customer?

Intercultural analysis

Justin Wateridge says that 'you don't manage by democracy as such'. What do you think he means by this, and do you agree? Are there any situations in business where you should manage by democracy?

Output: Devising a strategy for a travel company

Work in small groups. You are going to devise a business strategy for a tour operator in your country.

Stage 1

1 Discuss the types of tourism that are popular with people of different age groups in your country.

2 Discuss any gaps in the market in your country or the country where you are studying. Are there any unusual forms of tourism you have heard about that might be interesting?

Stage 2

Choose *one* of the following and make a SWOT analysis for it. You may find it helpful to look at the example in Listening 2 and the example of a SWOT analysis of tour operators in India opposite.

- 'fly and flop' holidays where people just want to relax
- active sports holidays
- study holidays where people go to learn a skill (e.g. cooking, a foreign language)
- luxury holidays
- eco-friendly (sustainable) holidays
- holidays for the over-60s

Stage 3

1 Draw up a set of action points (a strategy) that you could give to people who would like to enter the travel industry in your target area.

2 Join another group and explain your proposals to them. Ask for feedback, and then listen to the other group's proposals.

SWOT analysis of tour operators in India

Strengths

- Travel agents are moving from being mere ticket issuers to travel consultants taking complete responsibility for the consumers' needs.
- Travel agencies not only provide the picture of the country to the interested parties but also lure them to visit a country with the attractive packages.

Weaknesses

- Travel agents are most affected by the taxes that are part of the industry.

Opportunities

- As the number of tourists is increasing, there is a need to identify their requirements, and the travel agencies can tap this segment.

Threats

- With the advent of the Internet the role of travel agents is changing and the whole industry faces a threat of extinction unless it changes to meet the needs of tourists.

Source: gourkanjilal.com

Notes

Stage 1
Types of tourism

Gaps in the market

Stage 2
Strengths

Weaknesses

Opportunities

Threats

Stage 3
Action points

Proposals

Feedback

14.3 Skills: Using narratives in interviews

Learning outcomes
- Understand and tell a story or anecdote.
- Describe yourself in a positive light in an interview.
- Use narrative tenses and expressions.

Introduction

1 Spoken narratives (stories) often have the same stages. Put the following stages in order.

> 1 a problem   2 an evaluation   3 a response to the problem
> 4 setting the scene

🔊 2.39

2 Listen to Mike talking about a job interview. What was the problem? What was the result?

3 At work and outside work, people often tell stories. In pairs, make a list of the different situations where people may tell stories. Then compare your list with another pair.

4 In small groups, create a short spoken story using the stages in exercise 1. Your story should be about a funny, pleasant, shocking or embarrassing experience you have had as a customer or shopper or you could make a story based on one of the pictures above.

Listening 1: Conversation with a customer

🔊 2.40

You are going to listen to a conversation between a systems trainer and a manager who both work for a large medical company that provides laser eye surgery. The systems trainer went to one of the company's stores to have laser eye treatment herself and met a customer there. Listen to the first part of the conversation and answer these questions.

1 Why had the customer changed her mind about having the laser treatment?

2 Did the customer know the systems trainer worked for the company? Why might this be important?

Listening 2: Eye test

🔊 2.41

1 Listen to the next part of the conversation.

1 What problem did the systems trainer have regarding her appointment?
2 How was it resolved?
3 Why isn't the systems trainer going to have the eye treatment?

2 Would you consider laser treatment for bad eyesight? Why/Why not?

3 Read through the audio scripts for Listening 1 and 2 on page 165. Does each part of the conversation resemble the narrative structure outlined in the Introduction?

Critical analysis

1 What makes a story interesting or not?
2 Some of the most interesting stories may not be true. Do you think it is acceptable to exaggerate the truth when telling stories at work or outside work? Why/Why not?
3 What examples can you think of when you or somebody you know has exaggerated a story?
4 Do you think it is acceptable to exaggerate or embellish the truth in a job interview? Why/Why not?

Language focus 1: Narrative tenses

1 Look at these sentences from Listening 1 and 2. Match the underlined verbs with these tenses: past simple, past perfect, past continuous, historic present. (The historic present is used to dramatise events in the past by using the present form.)

1 I <u>went</u> to Bond Street …
2 A lady … <u>was having</u> the same tests and things done …
3 She <u>had thought</u> about having laser surgery done before …
4 And <u>she says</u> because we are doing it …

2 The past perfect tense (e.g. *I looked at the information <u>I'd been given</u>*) is used much more in stories than in everyday conversation. Why is the past perfect tense used in these sentences?

1 You thought I'd already done it.
2 It took ages to get here because a lane had been closed.
3 I think she just wanted to know what had been done about it.

3 Complete the following sentences in your own words using the past perfect tense.

1 When I came back home last night, I realised …
2 We heard on the news that …
3 The boss thought that we …
4 It was a really boring presentation because …

Language focus 2: Answering questions in interviews

In many interviews, interviewees are expected to tell stories about themselves. Research shows that interviewees who fail to do this well may not get the job. Look at the following typical interview questions. Which can be answered with a story?

1 Can you tell me about a difficult experience you had, and how you reacted?
2 How long have you worked in your present job?
3 How would your friends describe you?
4 What do you think is your greatest achievement in your life?

Intercultural analysis

1 Look at these typical 'behavioural' questions. Which are the most difficult for you to answer and why?
  - What makes you angry at work?
  - Tell me about a time you had to make an unpopular decision.
  - Tell me about a goal you set for yourself, and how you achieved it.
  - Give me an example of when you showed initiative and solved a problem.
2 Ask each other one question from the list, and try to give a specific answer using the narrative structure in the Introduction.
3 What types of response do you think companies are looking for to such questions? Give examples. For instance, how might a schoolteacher's answers to such questions be different from those of a stockbroker?

Output: Job interview skills

Stage 1
Work in pairs or small groups. Decide on a job each of you would like to be interviewed for.

Stage 2
Look at the questions in Language focus 2 and Intercultural analysis, and write down two or three more questions that you could ask in an interview.

Stage 3
Take a few minutes to prepare some answers to these questions. Make sure you include a story about yourself.

Stage 4
Take turns interviewing each other, and give some feedback after the interview.

▶◀ **Watch Sequence 7 on the DVD to find out more about Strategies and decision-making.**

Writing 7: First contact emails

Learning outcomes
- Write effective emails to people you don't know.
- Distinguish between and make choices about language tones.
- Make a formal and semi-formal request.

Introduction

1 A 'first contact' email is sent to someone you don't personally know yet, and have not contacted before. In the following list, which ones might be 'first contact' emails?

- job application
- complaint email
- request email
- promotion
- reply to an invitation
- invitation

2 The tone of an email concerns how respectful, formal, convergent and direct the language is. Are the speakers trying to appear close, or are they emphasising their differences? Where do you think job applications, complaints and requests would appear on the scales below?

1 respectful ⟷ friendly
2 formal ⟷ informal
3 convergent ⟷ divergent
4 direct ⟷ indirect

3 Which of the points below do you think you should follow when writing a request email to somebody you don't know?

1 Explain who you are very early in the email.
2 Subject headings should be imaginative and playful.
3 Use humour in the email to develop the relationship.
4 Always say thank you at the end.
5 Say why you are writing at the end.
6 State the request in the most direct and friendly way possible.

Writing skill: Analysing emails

1 Which of the emails below is a request for permission and which is a request for information?

2 Write a title for the subject line in each email.

3 What is the tone of these emails and how formal are they?

Email 1

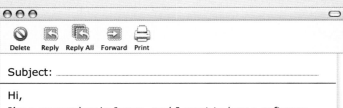

Delete Reply Reply All Forward Print

Subject: ....

Hi,

I'm a researcher in Japan, and I want to buy a software package for recording meetings. I need the software in English, and I was wondering whether you ship internationally. If so, how long would it take to get the package (or possibly two of them) to Japan? And how much would that cost?

Also, I wanted to know if the Olympus AS 2400 recorder would be sufficient for my needs: the files are of communication on a building site between engineers. I have some of the files already.

Many thanks,
Mike Handford

Email 2

Delete Reply Reply All Forward Print

Subject: ....

Dear Sarah,

I am hoping you can help me. I work for Cambridge University Press in the permissions department and we are in the very early stages of planning for a book titled *Business Advantage*. We would like to use information from the Havaianas website. I have attached a very early draft for this book, along with the permissions we would need. Would this be a possibility? We would also like to use images from your site, most notably the two I have put in red. I can give you more details of the print run of the book, etc. but I thought I would use this initial enquiry to see how protective Havaianas are about their brand.

I look forward to hearing from you.

Best wishes,

Chris Doggett

Language focus: Tone through word choice

English has many synonyms which differ in terms of formality. The more formal words often originate from French and Latin, e.g. 'gratitude', whereas the more informal words are originally from Old English, e.g. 'thanks'.

1 Sort the following words into pairs with similar meanings. Which ones come from Old English? How can you tell?

> say appear really get do actually express look good bad perform obtain impressive discuss terrible thanks gratitude talk about

2 Rewrite the following sentence in a more informal and friendly style.

- Obviously, your insights, experiences, and any advice would be extremely beneficial for the trainees.

3 Rewrite the sentence below in a more respectful and formal way.

- Thank you and check out my site (even if you do not buy anything).

4 Phrasal verbs, like 'check out', are usually informal. Match the following phrasal verbs with their more formal (Latin) synonyms.

Phrasal verb	**Formal verb**
1 put forward	a decrease
2 figure out	b understand
3 go down	c analyse
4 look into	d communicate
5 break up	e separate
6 get back	f request
7 pass on	g propose
8 ask for	h return

5 The following stages can be used in request emails. Put them in a logical order.

1 paragraph: explain who you are, and what the email is about
2 paragraph: explain and make the request
3 paragraph: say thank you
4 closing
5 greeting
6 subject line

6 Match the phrases below with each stage from exercise 5.

1 Thanks so much …
2 Please allow me to introduce myself …
3 I want to ask if you can …
4 I would like to express my gratitude …

Critical analysis

Research suggests that communication in many workplaces has become less formal over the past 30 years. Some people argue that this is not because workplaces have become fairer or more democratic, but merely because informal, friendly communication by bosses is the best way to motivate staff, and therefore maintain or increase profits.

1 Do you agree? Why/Why not?
2 Would you feel more motivated in a formal or informal workplace?
3 If you were the boss of an organisation how formal/friendly would you be?

Output: Job application

Stage 1
Look at this list of jobs you could apply for.

- CEO of a financial services company
- Graduate trainee in a small design firm
- Project manager for an oil company
- Office assistant in a legal firm
- Marketing executive in a computer company
- Research assistant in a university
- Human Resources officer in a large multinational company
- Sales person for advertising in the media

Stage 2
Write an email applying for the job you have chosen. Think about the order of the paragraphs and the tone. Decide whether it would be more appropriate to write in a formal or semi-formal style.

Stage 3
Look at the emails on page 142 and compare the styles. Reread your email and make any changes which you think would improve it. Show your email to a partner who applied for a different job. Give your partner feedback on his/her email.

Additional materials

Contents

2.1 Theory: STEEP analysis

Reading: STEEP analysis

Student A: Technological factors

Technological advances have greatly changed the manner in which businesses operate. Technology has created a society which expects instant results. This technological revolution has increased the rate at which information is exchanged between stakeholders (customers, suppliers, employees, government, etc.). A faster exchange of information can benefit businesses as they are able to react quickly to changes within their operating environment. However, an ability to react quickly also creates extra pressure as businesses are expected to deliver on their promises within ever-decreasing timescales. Consumers can now shop online 24 hours a day from their homes, work, or on the move from their phones. Technology will continue to evolve and impact on consumer habits and expectations. Organisations that ignore this fact face extinction.

2.2 Practice: Global consumer goods industry

Output: Launching a new consumer product

Group A

First read the information on page 23. You are going to make a sales pitch for your brand of curry powder. You want to promote its taste and health properties, and there is evidence that curry can help prevent the brain ageing. Think about how you are going to market your product, where you are going to sell it, where you will get the spices, the packaging and any environmental concerns there might be. You should also try to think of a brand name and slogan and an idea for an advertisement (you can decide whether it will be on TV, the Internet or in magazines).

Group B

First read the information on page 23. You are going to make a sales pitch for a new brand of mobile phones. Your target group is the over-50s. You need to think about what the main needs are of this target group and what product features they might value. Think about how you are going to market your product, where you are going to sell it, where you will get the materials, the packaging and any environmental concerns there might be. You should also try to think of a brand name and slogan and an idea for an advertisement (you can decide whether it will be on TV, the Internet or in magazines).

Group C

First read the information on page 23. You are going to make a sales pitch for your brand of skin-care products for the over-50s. You want to use natural products and should decide on three different products in your range. Think about how you are going to market your products, where you are going to sell them, where you will get the ingredients, the packaging and any environmental concerns there might be. You should also try to think of a brand name and slogan and an idea for an advertisement (you can decide whether it will be on TV, the Internet or in magazines).

Group D

First read the information on page 23. You are going to introduce a new fashion line for the over-50s. You want to promote the quality and stylishness of the product. You need to decide if you will concentrate on the male or female market or both, and the type of clothes you want to sell. Think about how you are going to market your product, where you are going to sell it, where you will get the materials, the packaging and any environmental concerns there might be. You should also try to think of a brand name and slogan and an idea for an advertisement (you can decide whether it will be on TV, the Internet or in magazines).

Writing 1: Preparing presentation slides

Critical analysis: Dos and don'ts of presentation slides

Student A

Read the information in the following four slides. Then close your book and tell your partner what you have learnt. After exchanging information, compare slides.

Slide structure – bad

- This page contains too many words for a presentation slide. It is not written in point form, making it difficult both for your audience to read and for you to present each point. It looks very complicated. In short, your audience will spend too much time trying to read this paragraph instead of listening to you.

Colour – bad

- Using a font colour that does not contrast with the background colour is hard to read
- **Using colour for decoration is** distracting **and annoying**
- Using a different colour for each point is unnecessary
  - Using a different colour for secondary points is also unnecessary
- Trying to be creative can also be bad

Fonts – bad

- If you use a small font, your audience won't be able to read what you have written

- CAPITALISE ONLY WHEN NECESSARY. IT IS DIFFICULT TO READ

- **Don't use a complicated font**

3.3 Skills: Negotiating a pay rise

Output: Negotiating a pay rise

Student A

You are the manager of a mobile phone company where PRP is used. You are going to do the yearly appraisal of one of your employees but you want to give him/her the minimum salary increase. This is because:

- your company is not predicted to do as well as expected this year
- the employee is quite competent, but has yet to work on a big project.

First discuss the year's work with the employee. Then try to communicate the news about the pay increase in as motivating and as friendly a way as possible. If absolutely necessary, you can offer a slight increase. Take two minutes to prepare what you want to say.

Negotiate the pay rise with Student B.

4.2 Practice: Innovation in practice

Output: Making a product into a commercial success

Group A
Stage 1

Study the product below from Phonefingers.com.

Writing 2: Describing a process

Output: Writing a short description of a business process

Group A

Write a short description (150 words) of the business process diagram below for an online store. Make sure you include a brief introduction and use both passive and active tenses.

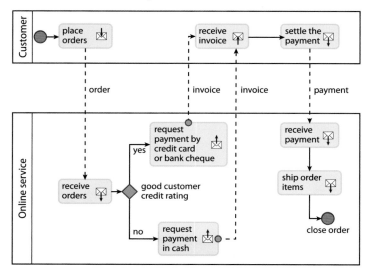

5.1 Theory: Understanding organisations

Introduction

See how many a, b, c and d answers you have and then read the description of the organisational culture that is best suited to you.

Mostly 'a' answers = Role culture
You value stability and long-term job security. You like to know in advance what your job is about and what your objectives are – this is best recorded in a formal job description and an annual job plan. You would probably feel at home in the public sector or a large organisation in a stable business environment, such as life insurance and high street banking.

Mostly 'b' answers = Task culture
You enjoy working creatively in teams on projects where people can exchange views openly and honestly and informally. A high salary is not that important. You like to feel passionate about your job. Your ideal working environment could be in the product development section of a marketing department, a management consultancy firm or the creative side of an advertising agency.

Mostly 'c' answers = Person culture
You are an individual above all else. Your worst nightmare would be to work in an organisation where you had to sing the company song every morning! Organisations are not your friend. They are not your enemy either. Organisations are simply a fact of life and can be useful to you so long as they do not interfere with your work. You would be well suited to working in some academic departments of universities or as a freelance contract worker, such as a software designer or programmer.

Mostly 'd' answers = Power culture

You are a competitive person and like winning. You are happy to take risks and prepared to work very hard to achieve what you want. You like dynamic organisations with strong leaders who are not afraid to take big decisions. You enjoy working environments which have the minimum of rules and regulations and very little bureaucracy. Organisations with this type of culture tend to be small and/or tend to be concentrated in fast-changing business environments such as investment banking, start-up companies and recently restructured companies.

5.2 Practice: Creating a successful culture

Output: Working in a cross-departmental team

Each group should argue the case for the funds to be allocated as follows.

- R&D: You want more money to develop the product – therefore you want 80% of the budget.
- Sales: You want more staff on the ground – therefore you want 40% of the budget.
- Marketing: You need money for promotion – therefore you want 50% of the budget.
- Chair (from Finance): You have to decide where the funds should be allocated.

5.3 Skills: Dealing with problems across departments

Output: Improving communication across departments

In your company, which manufactures electronic books, communication between the R&D (research and development) department and the sales department is very bad. A meeting has been called between the senior staff of the two departments, to see what the problems are and how they can be improved.

Sales managers

You think the R&D department have no understanding of the pressures involved in sales, and do little to support your department. For example, the final price for the product is often much higher than the initial price you were given by the R&D department, meaning that you have to apologise to customers about the price increase. Also, although your department often passes feedback from customers to the R&D department, this feedback is usually ignored. In this meeting, you want these two issues addressed.

6.2 Practice: Multicultural mergers

Output: Managing an alliance

Pair A

You work for a sports shoe company in South America. Try to reach an agreement with pair B, who are from another country, using the points below.

Your position:

1 The other company decided that all meetings should be in English. However, you think that meetings where only locally employed staff are present should be in the local language.
2 The company you are working with has a strong international brand. Your brand is well-known locally, but not globally. You are in favour of joint branding throughout the world.
3 You think that this is a very important stage for the new company and that there should be weekly meetings to discuss new strategy and policies.
4 The new management team is split 60% to 40% in favour of the company you have formed an alliance with. You believe that each company should have an equal amount of managers on the team.

Carry out the negotiation and complete the decision card below.

Language of local meetings – English or local? Decision: _____
Branding – joint branding or use one global brand? Decision: _____
Meetings – how frequent should they be? Decision: _____
New management team – 50/50 split? Decision: _____

7.1 Theory: Dice theory

Output: Planning and evaluating change using DICE theory

Stages 1 and 3

Factor	Details to be discussed	Mark
D	How long will the change project last? Realistically, how frequently can we review progress?	
I	From what departments will we find the right people for this project team? How can we be sure they will have the right skills? How will we choose the team leader?	
C1	How committed are we as senior managers to this change project? How do we plan to communicate the need for change? What benefits do we hope to gain as an organisation/company from making these changes?	

C2	How can we ensure that staff will support the changes proposed?	
E	How can we ensure that the change management team has enough time to do the project and at the same time be able to do their day-to-day work?	

Scores between 7 and 14: The project is very likely to succeed. This is the Win Zone.

Scores between 15 and 17: Risks to the project's success are rising, particularly as the score approaches 17. This is the Worry Zone.

Scores over 17: The project is extremely risky. If a project scores over 17 and under 19 points, the risks to success are very high. Beyond 19, the project is unlikely to succeed. This is the Woe Zone (the Sad Zone).

8.2 Practice: Russian oil industry – Sakhalin-1 Project

Group A

Stage 1	Build temporary living accommodation and offices on site for project workers	2 months
Stage 2	Set up multiple communication links (telephone, Internet, satellite)	1 month
Stage 3	Build basic access roads between the different parts of the site (between the future location of the oil terminals, the warehouses, living accommodation, truck depot, etc.)	3 months
Stage 4	Conduct on-site induction for the first group of long-term project workers who arrive on site (familiarisation with the climate, health and safety requirements and local culture)	1 week

Project management team's notes

1 Already have the start date for the first group of workers and their accommodation must be ready for when they arrive in two months' time.

2 Haven't decided on a company to supply the telephone, satellite and Internet links, but have two companies in mind – have worked with them both before and are confident they can deliver on time.

3 Have already planned all the roads and think that three months is very generous. On the last project, which was very similar, it took two months.

4 Think that one week is enough for induction as have a multinational team of engineers who have a lot of experience of working on similar projects.

Role card – Project managers

Read your project schedule and your notes about the suggested times. You don't really want to change this schedule because you have put so much work into preparing it. However, you are going to have a meeting with health, safety and environmental managers and you imagine they will want to slow things down.

Have a meeting in your team and try to think what HSE will object to about your schedule and then try to think of counter-arguments to protect your schedule. Make a list of points.

Realistically, you know you will need to make some concessions, but you want to keep them to the minimum possible.

When you are ready, have a meeting with the HSE managers and try to reach an agreement about the project schedule.

8.3 Skills: Maintaining relationships

Student A

Scenario 1

You have had meetings today with Student B, a potential client from another country. Your boss is keen to further develop the relationship with this company, and wants you to take him/her out for dinner this evening. It is important for your career to develop this relationship. Invite him/her out this evening. You should speak first.

Scenario 2

You are in a meeting with a company that has been selling your products. The meeting is coming to an end, and you are not very happy with the result of the meeting – you feel the other company is not as professional as it used to be. You therefore do not want to arrange another meeting until you have spoken to your boss. Your partner will start the conversation.

9.1 Theory: The 4Cs of marketing and e-marketing

Group A: KidZ Books

You are a purely 'clicks' operation selling children's books via your web store. Discuss in your group how you can improve your company's e-tail operation. Discuss the questions opposite, take notes and then prepare a 5-minute presentation.

Convenience for the customer (Place)	How can you 'locate' your website to make it convenient for your customers to find?
Customer wants and needs (Product)	What wants and needs do children have that you can satisfy online?
Cost to the customer (Price)	How can you counter the customers' perceptions that the cost of books should be lower online?
Communication with the customer (Promotion)	How are you going to have a dialogue with your customers? Think about both parents and children.

When you are ready, give your presentation to the rest of the class.

9.2 Practice: The benefits of selling on- and offline

Output: E-market research

Student A

Ask Student B the questions below.

1 If you could buy a computer from your local supermarket, would you purchase it?
2 Have you ever bought a computer, mobile phone or MP3 player online?
3 If a branded computer costs 10% more in a high street computer retailer than online, would you still buy it?
4 Do you think that the brand of the computer is more important than which shop you buy it from?
5 If internet penetration levels are high in a country, should a computer manufacturer spend the majority of its advertising budget on online adverts?
6 Do you ever click on online adverts?

Now answer Student B's questions.

Discuss your answers and Student B's answers. How might your results impact on the strategy and e-marketing policy of the computer company?

Present your findings with your partner to the class.

9.3 Skills: Organising a presentation

Listening 2: Developing an e-presentation

5

Thank you

- www.zn.be
- info@zn.be
- +32 123 123

6

How can we help you get started?

7

Challenges of European HQs

- Hub of communication
- Competition
- Demanding a) _____
- Complexity
- b) _____
- Internet

8

Challenges of European HQs

9

How can we help you get started?

- Business objectives
- Start small
- c) _____

11.1 Theory: Activity-based costing (ABC)

Output: Comparing traditional cost accounting and ABC

Student A

You believe that ABC accounting is good for your company for the following reasons:

- You currently produce very standard products, but would like to extend your product range.
- You think that you will be able to see waste more easily.
- If managers understand overheads more clearly, they will be able to cut costs.
- You think ABC will help you make comparisons with other companies and industry standards.

When you are ready, start your meeting with Student B and try to come to a decision about using ABC in your workplace. You can use the ideas above or any others you can think of.

You should start the meeting.

11.2 Practice: Cost and price

Output: Cutting costs

Group A: Finance

Your department is concerned about the costs and is interested in cutting loss-making activities. You feel that staff productivity needs to be raised and you would like to see some incentives for this.

13.2 Practice: The business case for Corporate Social Responsibility

Output: CSR presentation

Group A

CSR in the environment (supermarket)
<ul><li>transport of food to the store</li><li>heating and lighting in the store</li><li>location of the store</li><li>projects with the local community and charity work</li><li>type of products sold (organic, Fair Trade, etc.)</li><li></li><li></li><li></li><li></li></ul>

Writing 7: First contact emails

Output: Job application

Email A

Dear Sir or Madam,

My name is .... , and I am a university student in Madrid. I am studying for a Bachelor's in business administration, and am now in my final year. I am very interested in embarking on a challenging career in international business.

I am in the process of job-hunting, and recently saw your company advertisement in The Guardian newspaper. Having looked at your website, I was deeply impressed by your company philosophy, and the exciting work you are involved in. I would therefore very much appreciate the chance to find out more about your company, with the possibility of having an interview. I think I have a lot of potential, I am ambitious, bright and determined, and I am also good at working in a team. I attach my CV for your reference.

I hope you will consider my request favourably.

Thank you in advance.

Yours faithfully,

Email B

Hi,

I'm .... , and I'm a final-year student at Madrid University. I'm studying business administration, and I'm now looking for an interesting and challenging job in international business.

I recently saw your job advertisement in the newspaper. Your company looks really exciting, and I think that I am the type of person you are looking for. I am a hard worker, and am keen to get a job that allows me to work with other people, but also challenge myself. So I hope you can consider me for an interview.

Thanks very much.

Best wishes,

2.1 Theory: STEEP analysis

Reading: STEEP analysis

Student B: Economic factors

All businesses are affected by national and global economic factors. National and global interest rates and tax policies will be set around economic conditions. The climate of the economy dictates how consumers, suppliers and competitors behave within society. For example, an economy in recession will have high unemployment, low spending power and low confidence. A successful organisation will respond to economic conditions and respond appropriately. In this global business world organisations are affected by economies throughout the world and not just the countries in which they are based or operate from. For example, cheaper labour in developing countries affects the competitiveness of products from developed countries.

Writing 1: Preparing presentation slides

Critical analysis: Dos and don'ts of presentation slides

Student B

Read the information in the following four slides. Then close your book and tell your partner what you have learnt. After exchanging information, compare slides.

Slide structure – good
<ul><li>Use 1–2 slides per minute of your presentation</li><li>Write in point form, not complete sentences</li><li>Include 4–5 points per slide</li><li>Avoid wordiness: use key words and phrases only</li></ul>

Colour – good

- Use a colour of font that contrasts sharply with the background
  – e.g. blue font on white background

- Use colour to reinforce the logic of your structure
  – e.g. light blue title and dark blue text

- Use colour to emphasise a point
  – But only use this occasionally

Fonts – good

- Use at least an 18-point font

- Use different size fonts for main points and secondary points
  – this point is 24-point, the main font point is 28-point, and the title font is 36-point

- Use a standard font like Times New Roman or Arial

Background – good

- Use backgrounds such as this one that are attractive but simple

- Use backgrounds which are light

- Use the same background consistently throughout your presentation

3.3 Skills: Negotiating a pay rise

Output: Negotiating a pay rise

Student B

You have worked in a mobile phone company for two years now. Last year you received the minimum wage increase when you had your appraisal. You felt this was unfair as you had worked hard. You have worked hard this year too, and need to tell your boss this in an appropriate way. You would be disappointed if you did not receive a reasonable pay rise. Think about how you might choose to express this disappointment. Take two minutes to prepare what you want to say.

Negotiate the pay rise with Student A.

4.2 Practice: Innovation in practice

Output: Making a product into a commercial success

Group B
Stage1

Study the product below from Kittywigs.com.

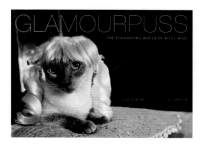

Writing 2: Describing a process

Output: Writing a short description of a business process

Group B

Write a short description (150 words) of the business process diagram below for a software technical support company. Make sure you include a brief introduction and use both passive and active.

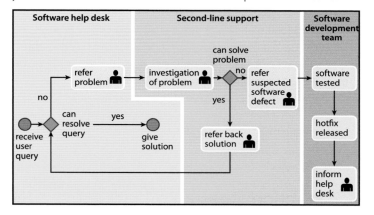

5.3 Skills: Dealing with problems across departments

Output: Improving communication across departments

In your company, which manufactures electronic books, communication between the R&D (research and development) department and the sales department is very bad. A meeting has been called between the senior staff of the two departments, to see what the problems are and how they can be improved.

R&D managers

You think the sales department do not understand your work, and do not try to understand it. All the sales team have insufficient technical knowledge, which means you often have to make adjustments to products after they have been sold, because the sales staff gave the customers the wrong information. Also, the sales staff rarely return your calls or answer your emails. In this meeting, you want these two issues addressed.

6.2 Practice: Multicultural mergers

Output: Managing an alliance

Pair B

You work for a sports shoe company in Asia. Try to reach an agreement with pair A, who are from another country, using the points below. Your position:

1 You are in favour of all meetings being in English. It is the international language and all staff of both companies need to be competent. It is also fair that neither of the languages is favoured.
2 Your company has a strong international brand; the company you are working with has a strong local brand. Therefore you believe that internationally your brand name should be used and the other company should only have its brand name in their country.
3 You think that having too many meetings is a waste of time. You think there should be one big meeting every three months.
4 The new management team is 60% to 40% in your favour. You think that this is generous as your market share was originally 80% to 20% when you and your partners were rivals.

Carry out the negotiation and complete the decision card below.

Language of local meetings – English or local? Decision: _____
Branding – joint branding or use one global brand? Decision: _____
Meetings – how frequent should they be? Decision: _____
New management team – 50/50 split? Decision: _____

8.2 Practice: Russian oil industry – Sakhalin-1 Project

Project management team's schedule

Group B

Stage 1	Build temporary living accommodation and offices on site for project workers	2 months
Stage 2	Set up multiple communication links (telephone, Internet, satellite)	1 month
Stage 3	Build basic access roads between the different parts of the site (between the future location of the oil terminals, the warehouses, living accommodation, truck depot, etc.)	3 months
Stage 4	Conduct on-site induction for the first group of long-term project workers who arrive on site (familiarisation with the climate, health and safety requirements and local culture)	1 week

Health, safety and environmental team's notes

1 The buildings need to be safe from potential fires and suitable for extreme temperatures. It will take two months to build the accommodation and another month to make sure it meets the other safety requirements.

2 The time for setting up the communication links seems fine, if they have already chosen a company.

3 You have had a look at the plans for access roads and think this will take four months. You have also noticed that some of the water crossings could seriously affect the fish in the rivers and streams. This will cause problems with the local population. You are also concerned that some of the roads will not take very heavy equipment.

4 You would like to have three weeks for the induction. The workers need to be briefed on information connected with their work, and also on how to communicate and behave towards the local people. It is important that they are sensitive to the local culture. You also believe that the health and safety information should be provided in English and the workers' first language. This is very important and it will take time to prepare.

Role card – Health, safety and environmental managers

Read the project management team's schedule above and the notes you have made about the suggested times. You think that the project management team are trying to do things too quickly.

Have a meeting in your team and decide how you will get your points across to the project managers.

Realistically, you know you will need to make some concessions, but you want to keep them to the minimum possible.

When you are ready, have a meeting with the project managers and try to reach an agreement about the project schedule.

8.3 Skills: Maintaining relationships

Output: Negotiating sensitive arrangements

Student B

Scenario 1

You have been visiting Student A's company today, with a view to developing an international relationship with them. Tonight, you have to telephone your boss and report back about today's meetings. These telephone meetings are very important, and usually take a long time, so you do not want to go out this evening. You will also meet another potential partner tomorrow. Your partner will start the conversation.

Scenario 2

You are in a meeting with a customer, but you feel the meeting has not gone well. Try to agree on a date for a follow-up meeting with the company, ideally within the next two weeks. This customer is your most important customer. You should speak first.

9.1 Theory: The 4Cs of marketing and e-marketing

Group B: KarlZ Koffee

You are a 'bricks and clicks' operation with a small chain of coffee shops on the high street and a virtual store supporting the high street shops and selling coffee beans direct to the customer. Discuss the questions below, take notes and then prepare a 5-minute presentation.

Convenience for the customer (Place)	How can you better integrate your 'clicks and bricks' operation to make it more convenient for your customers?
Customer wants and needs (Product)	Can you satisfy more customer wants and needs online? How?
Cost to the customer (Price)	Is the customer going to have the same costs buying the coffee beans from you online as in your high street shops?
Communication with the customer (Promotion)	What type of virtual assistant or loyalty scheme would best enable you to deepen your relationship with the customer?

When you are ready, give your presentation to the rest of the class.

9.2 Practice: The benefits of selling on- and offline

Output: E-market research

Student B

Answer Student A's questions.

Ask Student A the questions below.

1 If a computer company set up its own high street shops, would you be more likely to buy their computers?
2 Would you ever buy a computer from an online shop that you didn't know?
3 If you have problems with your computer, would you be happy to contact technical support online or would you prefer to go to a shop?
4 Do you think it is ever possible to provide better customer care online than over the phone or in person?
5 If you were interested in buying a computer and received product information from a computer company by SMS on your mobile phone, would you read it?

Discuss your answers and Student A's answers. How might your results impact on the strategy and e-marketing policy of the computer company?

Present your findings with your partner to the class.

11.1 Theory: Activity-based costing (ABC)

Output: Comparing traditional cost accounting and ABC

Student B

You believe that ABC accounting is bad for your company for the following reasons:

- Your products are very standard, so there is no need to cost each activity.
- Your company produces a lot of waste. If this appears in the accounts you might get a bad reputation.
- You think that the cost of setting up ABC is too high.
- You think that people are too busy and don't have the time to collect the data or maintain the system.

When you are ready, start your meeting with Student A and try to come to a decision about using ABC in your workplace. You can use the ideas above or any others you can think of.

Student A will start the meeting.

11.2 Practice: Cost and price

Output: Cutting costs

Group B: Human Resources

You are aware that recent developments in the airline industry mean staff are very nervous about the security of their jobs and salaries. You think that there is some danger of a strike if staff are asked to do much more than in their current job or if any staff lose their jobs.

2.1 Theory: STEEP analysis

Reading: STEEP analysis

Student C: Environmental factors

Companies and organisations are increasingly aware of the huge impact the natural environment can have on the other STEEP factors and on business in general. Factors include global warming and climate change, increased pollution levels, deforestation, etc. If, for example, there are adverse weather conditions in India, consumers throughout the world will pay more for tea at their local supermarket. Environmental factors are particularly important when it comes to the question of energy and the decreasing availability of natural resources such as oil, fresh water and minerals such as iron and uranium. Rapidly increasing competition for these resources is leading to rising prices and in some cases to wars and large-scale social unrest.

13.2 Practice: The business case for Corporate Social Responsibility

Output: CSR presentation

Group B

CSR in the workplace (government department)
■ child care
■ working hours
■ benefits
■ office environment
■ recycling
■
■

9.1 Theory: The 4Cs of marketing and e-marketing

Output: Improving a company's e-retailing operation

Group C: Carla's Cakes

You are an exclusively virtual store selling cakes to a diverse group of customers ranging from corporate clients' hospitality events to children's birthday parties. Discuss the questions below, make notes and then prepare a 5-minute presentation.

Convenience for the customer (Place)	What extra conveniences can you profitably provide your customers with that a high street store can't provide?
Customer wants and needs (Product)	What additional needs and wants might your customers have, that you could satisfy profitably?
Cost to the customer (Price)	How can you reduce the cost to price-sensitive customers by offering options on delivery charges? (This needs to be done without adding to your costs.)
Communication with the customer (Promotion)	How can you use social media marketing to enable you and your clients to connect?

When you are ready, give your presentation to the rest of the class.

11.2 Practice: Cost and price

Output: Cutting costs

Group C: Marketing

You are concerned about the image of the company. Until now your marketing has been based on an image of safety and reliability and you are worried that if you move towards the low-budget airline image you will become just another cheap airline. At the moment you have some loyal business passengers who regularly use your airline – if you became a low-cost carrier, you could lose these.

2.1 Theory: STEEP analysis

Reading: STEEP analysis

Student D: Political factors

Political factors can create advantages and opportunities for organisations. Conversely, they can place obligations and duties on organisations. Political factors include legislation such as the minimum wage, employment law and environmental legislation. An example of tough environmental laws is California, which became the first state in the USA to regulate emissions of the greenhouse gas carbon dioxide from motor vehicles. Vehicles with high levels of emissions simply cannot be sold any longer in California. Regulations and laws are not just at a national or a local level but are increasingly coming from international bodies such as the EU and the WTO (World Trade Organisation) on issues such as market regulations, trade agreements, import taxes, etc. Failure to conform to these legal obligations can lead to sanctions such as fines, adverse publicity and imprisonment.

9.1 Theory: The 4Cs of marketing and e-marketing

Output: Improving a company's e-retailing operation

Group D: Metropolitan Railways

You are a regional train operator that provides train services mainly to commuters travelling to and from work during the week and leisure passengers at the weekend. You sell tickets at your train stations and on your website. Discuss the questions below, make notes and then prepare a 5-minute presentation.

Convenience for the customer (Place)	How can you improve the website experience so customers want to spend more time on your site?
Customer wants and needs (Product)	What other needs might customers have, apart from buying tickets, which you can satisfy profitably?
Cost to the customer (Price)	How can you improve the online purchase of tickets to make it as user-friendly as possible?
Communication with the customer (Promotion)	How can you make better use of database marketing?

When you are ready, give your presentation to the rest of the class.

Audio scripts

1 Competitive environment

1.1 Theory: Concepts of competitive markets

Language focus 1: Sport as a metaphor and analogy for business

 1.02

Definition 1
Jochen Runde: Well, strictly speaking it's an industry which is dominated by one firm. So a one-firm industry. But the word is used a bit more loosely than that, so you know, it also applies if you have an industry with a really highly concentrated industry of one, two or three firms.

Definition 2
Jochen Runde: Well, this term is used when there's more than one firm in a highly concentrated industry. Strictly speaking, this should be used when there are only two, three or four firms operating in the industry.

Definition 3
Jochen Runde: Well, the railway companies are an example or the network industries would be another example, so is the supply of gas. You know, if you have all the pipes, it wouldn't make sense to have a couple of companies competing in the same field.

Definition 4
Jochen Runde: I'd define it as a market in which there are many firms producing the same product, which means that because there's so many of them in the industry as a whole, none of them has any market power and can't influence the price.

Definition 5
Jochen Runde: Well, I'd understand it as the general context in which a business is operating, like you know, rivals of the firm, the characteristics of the customers of the firm. The regulatory environment, the general economic climate, and so on.

Listening 1: The competitive environment in sport and business

 1.03

Interviewer: What connections are there between the world of competitive sport and competitive business?
Jochen Runde: I think there's certainly lessons to be learnt from professional competitive sports like motor racing and the way it involves people and teamwork. I have a colleague called Mark De Rond who's written a book on the Oxford–Cambridge boat race and preparing for it, and he's drawn all kinds of indications for leadership and managing teams out of that. There are also oligopolies in professional sports. Well, certainly there are some football clubs which have a lot of market power. You know, Real Madrid or Manchester United. It's to do with brand and has to do with lots and lots of support and history and all the rest of it. So, within particular sports,

there certainly are teams that have more market power. It's interesting that the situation is different in American football, where they have rules to make it more competitive, effectively the weaker teams get first choice of the draft every year when they're getting new players in. And that's to make the playing field more level. In football in Europe, the playing field's not very level.

Listening 2: Monopolies, oligopolies and perfect competition

1.04

Interviewer: Let's go back to monopolies and oligopolies – why are they considered uncompetitive and undesirable?
Jochen Runde: Well, the standard argument is that the trouble with monopolies is that because they have market power they will restrict output and raise the price, which obviously is not good news from the consumer's point of view. The reason they do that is they can get higher profits by doing so. However, there are industries in which it makes sense to have a few very large firms and that would be the case in natural monopolies where you can't have a competitive environment simply because there's not enough scope in the market or it's too expensive to set up a number of firms with the upfront investment that's required.
Interviewer: OK, so monopolies and oligopolies are at one end of the spectrum and we've got perfect competition at the other. In your opinion, do you think it's possible to create markets where there is perfect competition?
Jochen Runde: Perfect competition is an ideal and creating perfect competition in the textbook sense with no transaction costs and perfect information and all the rest of it, that's never going to happen. However, I think it is possible to bring markets closer to the perfectly competitive ideal and the way to do that might be to reduce entry barriers, for example, and make it easier for firms to compete. So you get something closer to a competitive environment.

1.3 Skills: Building relationships across companies

Listening 1: Pre-meeting small talk
Listening 2: Judging emotions

1.05

Brian: Tell me, last night …?
Helga: Yeah …
Brian: A good meal out in Aachen …?
Gisella: Yes.
Brian: Was it?
Helga: We went to the same restaurant where we had dinner with Ada and Ton.
Eldric: At the Lycae?

Gisella: Yes.
Helga: Yes.
Brian: Oh, Lycae?
Helga: Yeah.
Brian: Downstairs or upstairs?
Gisella: In the garden.
Brian: Oh, I haven't been there. I must go sometime. Good?
Helga: Very. You should go sometime. It's quite reasonable.
Brian: And great food?
Gisella: Oh, yeah, great.
Helga: Yeah, yeah.
Brian: Little bit jealous, actually. I had a bowl of cereal last night.
Eldric: Oh, I had my mum's wonderful stew last night.
Brian: And only a few more meals to go, Eldric. And then you're all by yourself. Well, I think we should make a start …

Language focus 1: Making your feelings understood

1

4

The audio scripts are in the unit (see page 17).

2 Future uncertainty
2.1 Theory: STEEP analysis

Listening 1: STEEP factors

1 I think people will be more mobile, travelling between countries, and as a result the demand for goods may grow together as tastes across different countries converge, so there may be more global products like Coca-Cola, which is drunk all over the world.

2 We will need to look to Asia if we want to look for future development in an economic field. We have China. We have India. They are extremely large markets and players.

3 Regarding the EU, I believe there is a certain resistance to further increase the size of the EU significantly in the next ten years. It takes time to integrate new countries, to stabilise them. At one point we may even see Russia join the EU but I believe that is something which is some time away.

4 In the field of e-business I believe we are just in the starting phase, or maybe at the end of the starting phase, if you wish. I think in future we will see that marketing and selling online will probably grow much further, particularly in certain fields of business like retail. The only inhibitor may be that we find a certain level where people get fed up with too much technology and want to go back to the previous face-to-face business relationships.

5 I think that the subject of CO_2 emissions will remain very high on the agenda. And it'll probably be the dominating subject over the next few years to come in business boardrooms.

Interviewer: I imagine that future planning must be very important for an industry like the automotive industry where the lead time for product development can be very long.

Dr Hans-Martin Beyer: To develop new models from scratch it takes between two and four years, it may even be a bit more.

Interviewer: The world's going to be a very different place in three or four years' time. So future forecasting and prediction becomes pretty strategic, doesn't it?

Dr Hans-Martin Beyer: That's absolutely right. And that's always the problem with introducing new products in such kinds of industries with complex products. It takes quite some time. It's a much longer lead time than with other highly technological products like mobile phones or things like that. And therefore you always have to look into the future to avoid mistakes and increase the probability of success.

Interviewer: Some companies have been very successful in anticipating future threats and opportunities, and some have not. I wonder if you could give us some examples of when companies have got it right, and when they've got it wrong.

Dr Hans-Martin Beyer: Well, this is a very interesting and difficult question, because if we look at history, there were people who were intuitively dealing with developing certain products. We can now talk about the electronic or micro-electronic industry. Somebody like Bill Gates got it right, with his expectation that every single person wants to have a computer in front of them. And of course there are other important companies in that field such as Apple. They get it right, because they have an understanding of what people basically want, and they have a vision.

And well, there are other companies that have not always made the right decisions. And I have to say that some of the difficulties of some automotive companies are because they have underestimated and misunderstood the potential effects in the field of CO_2 and energy, which have now come higher up the agenda.

Interviewer: They were still producing cars which were producing a lot of CO_2 emissions, which were inefficient.

Dr Hans-Martin Beyer: Exactly, the American automotive industry, for example, has made some misjudgements in that field. There are other automotive companies around the world that may have read the future more correctly, but at the end of the day we need to be clear about one thing, that decisions are made in boardrooms, and it comes down, very often, simply, to the opinions of those who make the decisions. And therefore I believe that the methods which we can apply to forecast the future, or at least get a better understanding of what may happen, and to prepare for that, are one important aspect. But they are not the decision. It comes down finally to the decision-makers in business.

Language focus: Future certainty and uncertainty

The audio scripts are in the unit (see page 20).

2.3 Skills: Presenting a case at a meeting

Listening 1: Upgrading the operating system

 1.12

Alison: OK, we may as well start. So, our Windows operating system. We've been using our present OS in Japan for at least four years and it's time to upgrade. It's more a question of what will happen if we don't upgrade because as many of you know Microsoft has already stopped support for the present OS and we are in the extended support phase.

So, just to give you a bit of background. Mainstream support for the present system expired in the middle of last year. We paid Microsoft fifty thousand dollars for an extended support contract and we still have to pay Microsoft three hundred and fifty dollars an hour if we have any engineering for the present system. And as you can imagine, as time goes by, that figure's going to go up. Obviously, this creates a business risk for us because current software and hardware used by us is no longer supported by our vendors. The vendors are all migrating their products to the new system and they're not supporting the one we presently use any more. The longer we wait, the greater this risk becomes. We've already seen this with certain products on our desktops. And also more recently with our new Dell standard workstation, it doesn't actually give support.

So why do we really want to upgrade besides the impact of not doing it?

Well, we want to reduce the risk of maintaining and the cost of maintaining our outdated desktop environment. There is also the importance of global consistency too. Common desktop build allows the development teams to develop to a common desktop as opposed to what we do now which is we always ask, 'Oh what do they use in that region?' And having to tailor your product or have the support teams tailor their desktop so that your application will work in that place. So what is our basic approach going to be in Japan? On all previous desktop rollouts we've been able to do it in one fell swoop. We've been able to plan for all desktops as a whole, we have bought a big bunch of disks, built the new operating system in advance, and just swapped them all. But we can't do that this time because this time we're being forced to implement the new system on a departmental basis. Some departments simply might say, 'no we cannot afford it,' and some departments might say, 'I wanted one yesterday' and that's exactly what has happened.

But because we're being forced to adopt this approach it really dictates the basic approach that we need to take. So, how do we start? Well, I've already done this. I have solicited the stakeholders, which is you guys and support. Then we need to sit with the department heads and analyse the costs and the risks and decide whether or not to proceed.

And assuming that for a given department we get approval to proceed then we need to get it signed off and proceed as follows – which is to actually begin fixing the applications so that they work.

Listening 2: Q&A session

1.13

Alison: … OK. Any questions?
Nigel: The global implementation of the new OS interests me. Has anyone else done it? So, for example, if our head office in Los Angeles has got some departments on the new OS, are they able to influence the implementation here, or give us some advice?
Alison: So, you mean you want to know about whether other people have experienced any problems that we can learn from, is that right?
Nigel: Yeah, basically.
Alison: I don't think there's a black and white answer to that. It's being funded and deployed globally.
Nigel: OK.

3 Rewarding performance

3.1 Theory: Employee reward strategies

Listening 1: The role and function of pay

1.14

Interviewer: What are the functions and purposes of employee pay from the company's point of view?
Professor Stan Siebert: Well, one could write a book on that. The first function, though, is to attract someone to do the job. There is a demand for labour on the part of the company and the wage is how the company pulls the employees in. And then a second function would be to motivate employees, because we think that employees like money – of course, we all like money – and the more of it we have the harder we work. Of course, the pay scheme has to be structured so that effort is rewarded. So those are the two – to fill the job and to motivate the workers.
Interviewer: What are the different reward systems that companies can use to pay their staff in order to hold and attract workers?
Professor Stan Siebert: Well, we distinguish two basic types of reward systems. One's a reward system based on time, with payment by the hour. The other method is payment according to effort, or on output and performance. We can call this an incentive pay scheme. In this case, people have a basic rate of pay and then the rest of the pay is tied to how much they do. I mean an example that's often in the news is paying chief executives share options which are geared to the share price, which is thought to be in the chief executive's control. And another way would be to pay apple pickers by the apple or coalminers by the kilogram of coal.

Listening 2: Advantages and disadvantages of different reward systems

1.15

Interviewer: What are the advantages and disadvantages of these different reward systems?
Professor Stan Siebert: Well, there are different advantages and disadvantages. There is a cost involved in paying people by time as you have to try to ensure that people work by supervising them. But the advantage of payment by time is that it's simple and also you don't have to think of what to tie the payment to. This brings me to the disadvantage of the payment according to output. You have to find a measure of output that produces the desired results for the company. To take the apple picker, you pay them by the number of apples picked, well then the apple picker might just choose to throw the apples into the back of the truck and bruise them, as he only cares about the number of apples. But that perhaps isn't so bad. The worst case, of course, is when you pay executives according to the share price; they have an incentive to take all sorts of risky accounting decisions to make the share price high.
Interviewer: Yes, as we've seen.

Professor Stan Siebert: So, you can twist incentives to suit your own personal benefit. The advantage of payment by output is that you get more effort. The disadvantage is that you tend to get a sort of 'gaining of the system' if you like, that's inevitable. So I suppose most systems are imperfect and pay systems are too. Many jobs simply don't lend themselves to payment by output and so inevitably payment according to time also needs including. I mean, as a university professor, I am sort of paid by output – the number of articles I write, or the books I write, govern my pay. But I am also paid by the hour. So it's a sort of mix.

🔘 **1.16**

Interviewer: How big a factor is pay in motivating workers?
Professor Stan Siebert: Well, that's one on which I change my mind every day.
Interviewer: Oh, right.
Professor Stan Siebert: There's something called the Theory X view of people and the Theory Y view of people. The Theory X view of people is that they are lazy and good for nothing and they are interested only in pay to make them work. The Theory Y is the opposite, that people are cooperative and kind and they aren't motivated by pay. What they want is a feeling of satisfaction in doing the job well. So, of course, those are the polar extremes …
Interviewer: Yes.
Professor Stan Siebert: Everyone's a mix. So, how big a factor is pay in motivating workers? It's probably surprisingly small. Some people earn enormous sums of money but that simply indicates how good they are. Some of them would probably work for much less.
Interviewer: Yes, but in most offices, factories or shops you will always find some people who feel they are getting paid too little for doing too much. Do you think it's really possible to get reward systems which people feel are fair?
Professor Stan Siebert: Well … Fortunately, the market decides. I don't really worry too much about fairness because if you feel you're being paid too little for doing too much then the answer for you is to quit your job and find a job which suits you better and stop complaining, get moving!
Interviewer: Right.
Professor Stan Siebert: So, in other words the market ensures that we get our reward systems right.
Interviewer: OK. I don't know whether I should ask you this next question … It looks a little bit too personal to me.
Professor Stan Siebert: No, no, no. Go ahead.
Interviewer: Oh, good! The question is: do you feel personally that you are rewarded appropriately for the work you do?!
Professor Stan Siebert: Well, I've been in this job for thirty years. If I'd disliked it …
Interviewer: You would've walked away?
Professor Stan Siebert: That's right. We're always …

3.3 Skills: Negotiating a pay rise

🔘 **1.17**

Leroy: As we get into next year we might have to develop something that's performance-related.
Sophie: Well, I'd really welcome that. I mean, I said that last time and in fact I actually thought that the performance review was linked to salary. I mean, I have no trouble being assessed on my performance at all.
Leroy: OK.
Sophie: Because I know that I'm generating a lot of money.
Leroy: Mmm, mmm.
Sophie: Helping to generate a lot of money for RBC.
Leroy: Yes.
Sophie: So, fine.

🔘 **1.18**

Sophie: The demands of the job mean that I have to take more responsibility than I was probably originally intended to take or to have and I absolutely don't mind that at all. What it does do is sort of eat into the time. You know, like having to be approachable and flexible and having to meet clients earlier in the morning or having to meet them after the working day or having to work through lunch and all that kind of thing. I've found this job to be such a challenge that it's meant that I've had to give up the second job that I was doing that was supplementing my income. And the fact that I came here on the salary that I did, I knew I could manage because I was also doing a second job, if you see what I mean.
Leroy: I wasn't aware of that at the beginning, you know. I didn't know that you had a second job until quite recently.
Sophie: No. Well, it wasn't something that really impacted on this job when I originally came here. I mean, all the way back in February, when we had these sort of early conversations I was only going to be doing three days a week.
Leroy: Right.
Sophie: And another thing, when I went on the course to develop business counselling skills, I think it confirmed that the company sees me as a business advisor. And I was equal to some of the business advisors that were also in the room who were certainly paid probably more than double what I'm being paid. Once I've got through the national standards I would be able to do the job of business advisor. I'd like to get promotion here. But …
Leroy: What are you saying … ?
Sophie: Please don't think I will, because I won't, but I would be able to get a job as a business advisor in other organisations.
Leroy: Within Business Link, for example?
Sophie: Well, starting salaries for business advisors in Business Link are twenty-one thousand a year and I'm paid an awful lot less than that. And I've been in contact with them …
Leroy: OK.
Sophie: I've already talked about it more than I wanted to. It's not a huge issue, but it may become one.
Leroy: Yes, I know.
Sophie: My husband's income is still spent in supporting his ex-wife and putting his daughter through university.

Leroy: Right.

Sophie: Which means that I'm pretty much solely responsible for keeping my kids in designer trainers and allowances and everything else.

Leroy: Yes.

Sophie: I have noticed since I gave up the second job the drop in income.

Leroy: Well, this will get addressed when we said.

Sophie: Yeah, right.

Leroy: It will.

Sophie: So, that's OK. And I wouldn't ever want to be thinking about moving on or doing anything differently without talking about it to you anyway.

Leroy: No.

Sophie: I'm not going anywhere, I'm not interested in another role. I really, really want to develop this one and that's why I'm working as hard as I am.

Leroy: Me too. And I seriously want you to take a long-term view of this because it's not that many years down the line when I want to be thinking of retirement.

Sophie: Yeah.

Leroy: I want to do it in the right way and I want to have a proper exit strategy where other people are in place and that kind of thing.

4 Fostering creativity

4.2 Practice: Innovation in practice

Listening 1: How CETO technology works

 1.19

Interviewer: How does Carnegie's CETO technology work?

Jeff Harding: As you can see from the slide, the waves are moving towards shore and they pass over an array of submerged yellow spheres, quite large spheres that are attached to the top of pumps. As the wave passes over the top of the spheres the water pressure increases because there's a much greater amount of water actually acting on the spheres. It has maybe two or three metres more water acting on it. That activates the pumps, which are shown here in yellow, below the spheres and causes the generation of water pressure by the pumps. The pumps are linked together and they force pressurised water through the blue line that you can see onto the shore. It's pumped on shore through the blue line where it drives the Pelton turbine, an electrical generator generating electricity. The electricity goes into the wires that you see there, the transmission line. And the electricity then goes off to be used. The water, after it has been through the Pelton turbine, has lost its water pressure, so it has no real pressure left in it. The water runs back underground into the ocean, through what is shown in the diagram as a green pipe.

The attraction of CETO technology is that it is under water. But another real advantage is that the electricity-generation part of the process is on shore in a protective environment, so there are no electrical installations or electrical generating equipment actually in the ocean. CETO cleverly combines highly innovative technology under water with proven conventional technology (such as the hydro-electric Pelton wheel turbine) on land. This land-based technology has been used for almost a hundred years meaning that the technical risks, once the water pressure is delivered to shore, are quite low.

Listening 2: How CETO was born, developed and commercialised

 1.20

Interviewer: I understand that Carnegie is now approaching full development of the product with test sites in West Australia. But let me take you back, if I can, to day 1 for a moment. How was the initial idea developed?

Jeff Harding: The initial idea came from a gentleman called Alan Burns. Alan developed the CETO concept. He's been a keen diver for most of his life. He has an enormous understanding, appreciation and respect for the sea as a result of spending so much time in there, and he's also very observant and seems to have a good understanding of the forces that operate in the sea. At a particular time when he was on the bottom of the ocean and he was doing some work, he noticed that fish that were at eye level would suddenly go lower or higher as the pressure of the wave going over the top impacted on them. And I guess that got him thinking about the forces that are applying below the ocean and the fact that we have this extraordinary motion going on in our oceans at all times. So he literally did some sketching of basic design concepts when he got onto his boat, and the rest led onto the development of the project.

Interviewer: OK. What makes the development stage successful?

Jeff Harding: The development stage is all about having the right team and making sure they work together well. Within a team you need an environment that allows for open communication and listening. As the company grows there is a need to introduce new blood, new people with new ideas. So you really need an environment where people feel secure enough to talk about what perhaps might seem crazy. Often crazy ideas can lead onto some amazing breakthroughs.

Interviewer: What about the next stage of the project?

Jeff Harding: Well, commercial stages of course are all important. A new product is absolutely useless if it doesn't have a market. And investors who have put money into developing the technologies are obviously very interested to make sure that the commercial aspects progress so that they can get a return on their investment. Carnegie has established an agreement with a very large French utility company, EDF, to help to distribute the product in the northern hemisphere. The involvement of larger companies is useful as they are often better at commercialising innovations because they have greater skills in distribution, and they also have more finance to allow the product to achieve its full potential.

4.3 Skills: Decision-making

Listening 1: Renewing a contract

1.21

Steve: The gold support contract is kind of a higher-level support contract so if there are any problems our guys'll go in and solve them, and troubleshoot and correct the problem. And that's twenty-four seven isn't it?

Fiona: Yeah. That's a twenty-four hour cover.

Anabel: OK, brilliant.

Fiona: So for example, you may not need to have that high level of cover, in which case we can look at putting a lower level of cover in for you.

Anabel: Yeah. Makes sense.

Fiona: With the gold coverage, if one of those servers goes down at three o'clock on a Sunday morning, one of our engineers gets paged and he goes in and fixes it.

Anabel: Great.

Fiona: So you know, that's the very highest level of service.

Anabel: OK.

Fiona: Which may not be something you need, but you know, these are all just options.

Anabel: Well, the important thing is for us to be able to offer it to customers.

Steve: Yeah.

Anabel: Because customers are increasingly saying 'We want that twenty-four cover.'

Fiona: Absolutely.

Anabel: So?

Fiona: So, I mean that's really us managing your servers as if they were our own.

Steve: Yeah.

Anabel: Great.

Steve: So, I think the main difference really with the gold one and the other contract is the fact that with this gold one, we'll actually go in and find the problem out. With the other one it's pretty much down to you guys to find what the problem is and then get us to correct it.

Anabel: Yeah, no problem.

Steve: That's the main difference really.

Fiona: So it's kind of more like just a pair of the right hands, isn't it really?

Steve: Yeah.

Anabel: OK.

Fiona: It's really down to different levels of engineers that would actually maintain the system. Obviously with the gold one you're getting a senior network engineer.

Anabel: Right.

Fiona: It'd be someone who would understand not only networking issues and internet issues but also the server and your company's issues.

Steve: That's right.

Anabel: OK.

 1.22

Steve: So, with the gold option there's a flat rate of £25,000 per year, plus £50 per incident. So, that will cover all the back-up.

Anabel: But that's quite a serious cost on top.

Steve: This is the biggest cost.

Fiona: Yeah.

Anabel: This is the one that we'd have most issue with.

Steve: OK.

Fiona: Right.

Anabel: Because obviously it's covered by the service we have at the moment.

Fiona: Absolutely.

Anabel: It's something that really sticks in the throat.

Fiona: Well, we've put the standard cost down there. I think that's probably one of the areas that we could negotiate on, if you thought the gold option was the better option.

Anabel: OK.

Fiona: It may well be that, you know, there may be an alternative way of doing it perhaps. You know, we actually have all ours done by automated back-up service I think, and that could be a possibility too.

Anabel: Right.

Steve: But obviously there are costs again, so it's almost getting a balance I think.

Anabel: OK.

Fiona: So it may be that there's just a way around it without having to spend that money.

5 Organisational cultures

5.2 Practice: Creating a successful culture

 1.23

Interviewer: How would you describe Mundipharma, and how has it changed over your time with the company?

Ake Wikström: Oh, we have grown a lot. We have more than trebled in the last eight years. We are today, on a global basis, probably the largest, or second-largest family-owned pharmaceutical company in the world. It still has a turnover of around four billion dollars, so we are not super-small, but we're obviously not a big pharma either. Mundipharma has a culture of sharing, a lot of friendliness, warm welcomes, exceptionally free from politics and backstabbing. Since I joined I have just seen a continuous and actually quite dramatic improvement of the culture and the way we do business. So we have had success, which helps us to be happy. We have, I think, an outstanding leadership team, and the culture is second to none.

 1.24

Interviewer: Do you have separate departments within each of those companies?

Ake Wikström: Yes, we have different associates in different countries, and different departments and functions in our different companies as well. Like in the UK company here we have R&D, we have Production, we have Marketing, Sales, Administration …

 1.25

Interviewer: Are there also perhaps different styles or cultures in different departments?

Ake Wikström: We have some examples of where there is such a buzz, such an involvement from people, that it's almost unreal, for example marketing. People have so much fun, and they love to work together so much that nothing seems to be able to stand in their way in terms of obstacles and challenges. And did I mention a few of the others where we have struggled? It is slightly more difficult in terms of the production units where we have three shifts and they don't travel, compared to the marketing department where they do travel, and they have fun, and they do exciting things all the time, right?

Interviewer: So it's partly related to the nature of the work as well?

Ake Wikström: Partly. I think less so than related to the boss. I think the boss means a lot.

Listening 4: Creating a successful culture

 1.26

Interviewer: How did Mundipharma create such a successful culture?
Ake Wikström: I am a big believer in employee's surveys. I have been working with those surveys for fifteen, sixteen years. Since I came here we run one every year across Europe.
Interviewer: Employee surveys?
Ake Wikström: Basically employee satisfaction surveys, engagement surveys, with a set of questions that are very much linked and correlated with customer satisfaction. And also with the general sort of theory and knowledge about what makes people tick. What makes them engaged and willing to contribute to an organisation. And we have seen an absolutely phenomenal development since I joined the group, in terms of the culture, the spirit. So if you look at ... We started roughly six or seven percent below industry benchmarks, and now we're running seven, eight percent above. So that's the kind of evolution we've had in our company culture and the way we have operated over the last seven or eight years.

Listening 5: Managers and the surveys

 1.27

Interviewer: Why is the process so useful, and what changes have taken place in that period of time?
Ake Wikström: The important thing is that the process forces people to talk to each other. It forces managers to sit down and listen to employees, because they have so much to say and so much to contribute, if you are willing to listen and take the time to do so. I'll tell you, it's remarkable ... I just talked to a guy yesterday who was new on this floor and it is always interesting to speak to new people who have been here for only a couple of months, it's always very interesting to listen to the new eyes. 'What do you see?' 'What surprises you here?' 'What has struck you as odd?' 'What do you particularly like?' And almost without exception, what I get back is that everybody is so friendly, and everybody is so willing to share and help. And it sounds a bit corny, but it is actually true. It is an incredibly positive and welcoming environment.
But it wasn't easy in the beginning, because I had to force people to do this. Because most managers are a bit afraid of this, right, it's a bit scary, it reveals weaknesses.
So initially we heard from the managers, 'Ah, shall we do this? I don't believe in that.' And the year after when I said we were going to do it again they said, 'Well, can we wait for another year? Let's give us an eighteen-month gap so we can really do things.' And I said no.
Interviewer: No?
Ake Wikström: Not up for discussion. It is every year at the same time, get used to it. And if you ask them today I think they would all say that they want to continue the way we're doing it.

5.3 Skills: Dealing with problems across departments

Listening 1: Introducing the problem

 1.28

Laura: Something we need to work forward to is improving the attitude of the technical team. If this is going to happen, to be honest with you, Doz, their attitude's got to be 'customer'. You know, 'Good morning this is your salary talking' is very much going to be the way it'll go forward. Which may be alien to a technical individual because they're very much, 'we know what's best'. You know, arrogance is an unfair word, but they can come across like this as they only focus on the technical and don't help the customer. But the trouble is, if you enter into the world of project management there's a completely different attitude.
Doz: Right.
Laura: All I'm saying is that the attitude has got to slightly change.
Doz: Having discussed it with them, it's mostly about ownership, I think.
Laura: What do you mean?
Doz: You know, the technical people don't feel as if they're really part of this process ...

Listening 2: Specific issues

 1.29

Laura: I think, to be honest with you, Doz, the technical team, if they're going to manage these projects, they've got to be proactive rather than reactive, and I think they've got to be very customer facing and their attitude has got to change, which is what I just said. Is that OK?
Doz: I don't think there's a problem with their attitude because when they do speak to customers, I don't really have an issue with how they speak to them.
Laura: No, I'm not saying that.
Doz: I just kind of feel that they don't ever feel as if it's their problem.
Laura: Yes, that's what I mean. Their attitude is ...
Doz: It's someone else's problem?
Laura: Yes. They've got to now become project orientated.
Doz: But don't forget they're taking calls from customers all the time that they're out there.
Laura: I'm not saying that. I think they're fabulous with customers. What I'm saying is that if the customer doesn't ring them back in ten minutes' time they've got to ring them again.
Doz: Right.

Listening 3: Reaching agreement

 1.30

Laura: I'm just saying that when you do get a change like this it's very important that everybody changes with it.
Doz: OK.
Laura: And that people take problem ownership.
Doz: Yes. I mean that's a big part of this.
Laura: And then you've got a sales-type technical person who will think like a sales person.
Doz: Right.
Laura: And they'll think 'Hang on, the customer's my salary. I'd better think about this.'

Doz: I agree, but I think it's just one of those things here – they'll find lots of excuses not to do it and for some reason there does seem to be a reluctance to speak to customers directly when they're not call controllers.

Laura: It's a mindset change. There's going to have to be a mindset change.

Doz: And, you know, like, you say to Doug, 'Oh, can you phone the customer' and tell him what you've just told me and he'll mail them instead and you kind of think, 'Why don't you just pick up the phone?'

Laura: It's because they don't want to talk to them.

Doz: Well, yes.

Laura: They're two different types of beasts, sales and techies.

6 Working across cultures

6.1 Theory: Culture and individual strategies in business

Listening 1: What is rapport management?

 1.31

Interviewer: So the general question is what is rapport management and in what situations is it important?

Helen Spencer-Oatey: Yes, OK, I see rapport management as managing relations, whether they're smooth or turbulent, whether it's harmonious or problematic. And so rapport is the extent to which you're getting on with the other person and rapport management then is strategies for doing that. Why is it important? Well, it's not just important in intercultural interaction. In any context really you need to be able to get on well with people if you're to work well together.

Listening 2: Face, rights and problems

 1.32

Interviewer: How do you see face and how does it relate to the issue of rapport management?

Helen Spencer-Oatey: How the rapport goes is dependent on a few things, and face is one of them. Because face is an aspect of our identity, the image that we want to convey to others or we want people to perceive us as. And so there are different aspects of our identity and if you think about us all having multiple identities, we want to be competent, we may want to be seen as attractive, it could be a whole range of things slightly different for different people. And so if somebody says something that challenges the quality that we regard ourselves as having or wanting to have and they evaluate us negatively, that is a challenge to our self-image. And of course if it's in front of other people that's even more difficult to take. And then naturally you will tend to have the emotions that go with it, embarrassment and so on, and so that is likely to have some impact on rapport. And the other side of things with rapport is that I think it's not only just face but sometimes, you know, we have expectations as to what is proper behaviour or the things that I have the right to expect, and if I don't get that, it might not be a direct attack on my personal qualities, I don't feel a sense of loss of face, but I may feel irritated or angry because I feel my rights have not been upheld.

Listening 3: Email anecdote

 1.33

Interviewer: Can you give us any examples of where someone has felt a loss of face due to cultural differences?

Helen Spencer-Oatey: Yes, I'll give you one from the eChina programme between British and Chinese universities, so it's an intercultural one as well. What I and most of the other project managers did when we were sending emails, we would copy in or just include in the recipient list all the people to whom that email was relevant and leave out those that we thought it was not relevant for. And we did that for a while and then after about six months or something, one of the Chinese project managers sent me an email and said 'You've been copying everybody into the emails and this in many ways is a good thing to do, but you shouldn't always do this in China. You have copied in the leader and by copying him in you've treated him as if he is the same level as his subordinates.'

Interviewer: That's interesting.

Helen Spencer-Oatey: So he was saying, you know, you shouldn't actually do that because you've caused him to lose face so, he hasn't been given the deference of status he was expecting, so there was both a loss of face but also probably his role rights have been challenged because, in his understanding, he would have the right to expect a different email because of his status.

6.3 Skills: International team-building

Listening 1: The stages of building a team

 1.34

Interviewer: What advice would you give to a new multicultural work team, given the responsibility for developing the guidelines for creating a successful work and social group?

Tim Rabone: The first guidelines you come up with in your kick-off meeting, your first phase of face-to-face meetings, won't be the last guidelines. There's a fairly well-known formula of how teams actually get to a stage where they're working effectively and successfully. And most teams, especially in multicultural teams, go through stages of forming, which generally leads to storming. And storming is when people say, 'Well, I didn't really know that this was going to happen,' or, 'Yes, I agreed with the guidelines at first, but they're not really working for us here now.' So, there's change, or realignment, which has to happen on any guidelines for the team to work effectively. Which leads to norming, when the team makes the realignment official. Which then, finally, hopefully within the first three months, leads to performing. So the quicker you get through storming to norming, the better, which means the first set of guidelines will, if you're going to be successful, have to be looked at again and revised. So expect to get into that kind of realignment work at some point in the team's history. And also, don't make your initial guidelines too strict!

Listening 2: An international team meeting

 1.35

Mark: So I think here I definitely need something to be able to say to my head office we're going to go ahead and do this checking. Peter's my man, is that right?

Ursula: Yeah.

Mark: OK. Because one of the pieces of feedback Peter gave at the last technical meeting was firstly, probably he's not too keen to share this information with us, and I've got to understand why, and he's not here to say 'yes or no' so it's probably a bit unfair to explore that, but I did get the impression that it was like, 'Well, we're not going to be checking this on a monthly basis.' Now for me that immediately scared me. Did we go over the top at Staines by checking it every month? I don't know. You could have probably done it every two months and kept things moving. But you know … You can't just say at the beginning of the year we'll do a quick check and stop there.

7 Change management

7.2 Practice: Implementing change

Listening 1: An overview of the interview

 1.36

A

Charlie Peppiatt: I believe for any senior executive, any manager of an operation or a business unit, this is part of their job, it's not an optional area. So the first thing is, what does it mean? It means it's actually about doing my job every day as an executive within the Laird Group.

B

Charlie Peppiatt: I think this is something that's often over-played, but international differences are something that should be taken into consideration. I think in essence all people respond to an environment where they're treated with respect, they're involved, they're rewarded for good performance, they're given clear direction and strong leadership.

C

Charlie Peppiatt: I believe people generally don't resist change necessarily. What they resist is having change done to them, if you like, change that's forced upon people. But there are various people that are resistant to this, and there is a tough side, my belief here is that one should be hard on the issue and fair on the person.

D

Charlie Peppiatt: I think the critical thing here is that at every stage a lot depends on the commitment of the leadership as to whether a programme will be successful.

Listening 2: Dealing with resistors to change

 1.37

Interviewer: So the need for change is not always welcome or understood. Who and what have been the main resistors to change in your context?

Charlie Peppiatt: I believe people generally don't resist change necessarily. What they resist is having change done to them, if you like, change that's forced upon people. But there are various people that are resistant to this, and there is a tough side, my belief here is that one should be hard on the issue and fair on the person.

Interviewer: Yes.

Charlie Peppiatt: So the first thing is, the most important thing here is the way an organisation communicates, educates and converses with all of the members of staff. Help everybody understand that, if you like, the rules of combat, the requirement of business today, is that we change. But part of this approach is the idea that the people in the organisation need to be part of the change process. In other words, they will be involved in contributing to the change. And when people get some ownership of the change that's taking place, I believe the resistance diminishes.

Interviewer: Right.

Charlie Peppiatt: I think people need to understand the issue that a business needs to change to survive, and if people block that then it does need to be addressed with a firm line. But I believe generally, within the right culture of a company, that there will only be a very small minority who resist.

Listening 3: Successfully implementing change

1.38

Interviewer: How did you successfully implement change and overcome resistance?

Charlie Peppiatt: I think the critical thing here is that at every stage a lot depends on the commitment of the leadership as to whether a programme will be successful. If an organisation doesn't have a genuine belief and commitment from the very top then any form of change programme becomes very difficult.

Also, if I speak about my experience over the three years in Beijing with an organisation of 4,000 people, and some huge improvement activity that's gone on, the first thing that needs to be done is to establish what I call the basic principles, the way of doing business. And if you like, these are codes of conduct so everybody understands how, within the company, we're going to try and behave. And there are five points that I passionately believe in.

The first is to create a blame-free culture, as I said earlier, hard on the issue, fair on the person. The second one is maintaining the self-confidence and respect of others. A better focus on team-working, and here the concept of the internal and external customer becomes critical. Meaning that we all understand the external customer who buys our products or services, but also the idea that each of us are customers to each other within the organisation. A strong focus on action – rewarding and recognising people who get things done, rather than people that talk about getting things done. And then finally, understanding that we try and set the right example. So there is a strong emphasis on all the managers leading by example. But I think this has helped a lot.

And then one other area is to establish some core values within the company. And the critical thing here is that this does not become wallpaper or posters that are put up in conference rooms. So what we did in Beijing was we involved five or six hundred members of staff and employees, down to the operator level, to pool what to them, and all the people in the company, were the core values that they believe they want to find from a company that would mean something to them.

Interviewer: Right.

Charlie Peppiatt: Ultimately, the people in the organisation, the management team and the leaders, down to production supervisors and shift leaders, people that make the improvements and make this happen, need to be encouraged, recognised and rewarded for that. But an organisation must have a genuine belief and commitment from the very top – if it doesn't, any form of change programme can be very difficult.

7.3 Skills: External negotiating

Listening 1: Complaints

 1.39

Ada: … absolutely, we at First Pharma are very happy with that.
Giles: Moving on, the next point is First Pharma complaints. OK, Ada?
Ada: Yeah.
Giles: Right, Karl has told me that we've actually had five complaints here.
Ada: Have we?
Giles: Yes, now that hasn't been picked up in my monthly report so I need to ensure that Karl's feeding in the information. It may be that two or three of them were prior to the beginning of this year but he says there've been five in total. So, for example, there's a compliance complaint. And then the stock out page. Helen, run us through what stock out page means, if you would.
Helen: Basically, it means how many markets have been out of stock for the period.
Giles: Yes.
Helen: How many markets have been out of stock. The total days that they were out of stock. So for the five markets it was forty days in total, so the average is eight days. That's the average.

Listening 2: Discussing the complaints procedure

 1.40

Ada: To be honest, I'm not very happy with the description as 'First Pharma stock out'. That means, from my point of view, that we at First Pharma will be responsible for any stock out. But this will not show if the market information from you at ABC has provided the wrong figures for production.
Helen: Oh. What we used to do at ABC head office was we used to have a number of markets out of stock and then we used to split it down.
Ada: OK.
Giles: I think that's a fair comment from Ada because what we're not saying here is if you know whether or not it's ABC or First Pharma's fault. On a monthly basis, we should be root causing why and understanding is this market driven or is it production driven, you know, something like that. So I think we've got to know the reasons why, and maybe there's got to be a comments column underneath so people don't look at it and get the wrong impression. Because, as you say, your first reaction was 'First Pharma stock outs? What have we at First Pharma done wrong this year?'
Ada: Yeah, but it would be interesting to see what we can do to make it better in the future.

Listening 3: Compliance complaints

 1.41

Ada: Yeah, but it's the same issue with compliance. What does 'First Pharma compliance' mean? It's the same. We have not made any compliance mistakes at First Pharma. There is a reaction from the customer saying they are not happy. I have an example. Today at First Pharma we received material not in a temperature-controlled lorry. I'm sorry, but we are not responsible for that. That is a customer complaint and ABC is responsible for that.
Giles: I'm not sure I …

Ada: Maybe we can make a separate line and write compliance complaint or a complaint by a customer or whatever.
Giles: OK, I think I might have missed something. So we can add an extra line to detail the complaint.
Ada: Yeah, yeah, good.
Giles: When it's our fault there's a complaint, we need to put our hands up and say it was our issue at ABC.
Ada: OK.

8 Project management

8.2 Russian oil industry – Sakhalin–1 Project

Listening 1: Project overview

 2.02

Extract 1
Suleyman Narimanov: To work down where there is building and excavation going on we could only use civilianised military tanks. They are actually like tractors, but are a type of tank – it was quite a funny experience. But for everything else, like going from the office to workshops, we used four-wheel-drive cars – Land Rovers, Land Cruisers, things like that. And of course the Russian Niva – it's unbelievable, and I had never thought that this car could survive in that place, but it did.

Extract 2
Suleyman Narimanov: In the early stage everything connected to the negotiation is relevant, such as negotiation on the price of oil. It's also at this stage when you discuss pre-designs, and when you're actually pre-estimating your costs and budgets and everything. Every single mistake during the early stages will impact hugely on your future project. And also at this time it's very easy to change your mistakes, to repair everything … I mean on paper. It doesn't cost you a lot.

Extract 3
Suleyman Narimanov: A part of the pipeline was built in Malaysia, painted in the Philippines and then reconstructed again at the Hyundai factory in South Korea before being shipped to Sakhalin Island. It was really interesting.

Extract 4
Suleyman Narimanov: In the summer it's about 25 to 30 degrees plus. But in the winter it can be a nightmare, minus 30 with a strong wind, which makes work really hard. The island airport can be closed for up to two weeks because of the snow.
Interviewer: So do you still have to work when it's minus 30 on site?
Suleyman Narimanov: It depends on the type of work.
Interviewer: So what type of work goes on?
Suleyman Narimanov: If it's welding, you can't work. But if it's answering emails in the office you have to work.

Extract 5
Suleyman Narimanov: A big problem we have is the type of materials we need to use in the cold climate. So during operations it can really impact on your facility if you have not ordered the right material in order to work under these conditions. Starting from small bolts right up to massive casts. Everything has to be made for an arctic climate. And of course this makes your project double in costs.

Extract 6
Suleyman Narimanov: Fortunately, during my period there was no major incident because we had a really strong HSE department. For the construction people it was really hard to work in harmony with

HSE people, but fortunately due to their influence on our project there were no major injuries. When they informed us there would be a temperature drop, we closed our facility and brought our people back from site, which helped to prevent a lot of problems.

Extract 7
Interviewer: In the evening, what do you do in a place like Sakhalin?
Suleyman Narimanov: Unfortunately, our site was in the middle of nowhere. There were no leisure facilities. We had only one terrible billiard table. There was nothing there. In our camp we had only one TV with one Russian channel, which was the culture channel of Russia, and about 15 channels in Japanese but we couldn't understand that at all.

 2.03

Interviewer: What problems do you have when you work with multinational teams? Is it just language problems or are there other problems?
Suleyman Narimanov: First of all there is the language problem, but if you avoid this problem by having a bilingual project manager he or she can easily speak with his or her own team. The second issue, funnily, is food. If you've got 15 or 16 nationalities, what food will you give them? The European people would like to have European, etcetera. But when you have a nice set-up, the HR department can assist you and help the project managers.
Interviewer: Can you think of an example where Human Resources really helped a multicultural team work together?
Suleyman Narimanov: Yes, let me give you an example from a BP project I was working on in Azerbaijan. The HR department organised a lot of team parties plus some sort of recreation. But sometimes they organised lunch with different menus. They advised the catering company to bring food for the different nationalities, so you could eat whatever you wanted.
Interviewer: Are there any problems where the senior manager is from a different country to most of the engineers in the project?
Suleyman Narimanov: Well, I don't think so. If the manager is a nice and polite person I don't think there will be a problem.
Interviewer: How can you encourage good teamwork and commitment?
Suleyman Narimanov: By providing good working conditions. Listening to the team, you have brought on board different professionals from many disciplines, you have to listen to them. I'd also say that good team-working culture can come from having a team party at least once a month. Yes, definitely. When you have a team party it makes people socialise and understand each other.

8.3 Skills: Maintaining relationships

 2.04

Charles: … well, I mean we fully support that so it shouldn't be a problem.
Valentina: Right. OK. That might be a cheaper thing for us to do.
Charles: OK.
Valentina: Right.
Liam: So, we need to get those figures to you. We should be able to get those to you this afternoon or tomorrow.
Valentina: Whenever. There's no hurry.
Liam: No?

Valentina: No, just fit them in around what else you do. But it's just useful information for us.
Liam: OK.
Valentina: Yeah.
Charles: No problem.
Valentina: Great.
Liam: So, I guess the best way forward is to just kind of leave you to sort of digest this. And then you know, we'll perhaps wait for you to come back to us about the next stage. I'm sure you're going to have some more questions.
Valentina: Probably.
Liam: You know, really it's just about making this make sense for you and for us.
Valentina: Yes. Thank you.
Liam: And I'm sure with all this stuff there's a way of doing it where it's going to please us all. But I think next time we'll just get together and we'll work everything out then.
Valentina: Great.
Liam: OK?
Valentina: Yeah. That's great. Thanks very much.
Charles: OK. Right.
Liam: And I think we've got a football match the week after next, haven't we?
Charles: Yes, I spoke to Raj.
Valentina: Is that here?
Liam: Yeah.

9 E-marketing

9.2 Practice: The benefits of selling on- and offline

 2.05

Interviewer: What is e-marketing and how is it different to standard marketing?
Alastair Brown: Right, OK, e-marketing's a widely used term used to cover a wide variety of approaches, so there isn't a clear single definition. Essentially though, I would define it as the use of electronic media for marketing purposes. Electronic media usually means the Internet, but it can also tie in to include email, mobile phone marketing, and so on. In one way, it has radically changed marketing because it means you can have a much closer relationship with the customer. In another way though, it's an extension of marketing. You're using the same approaches that you would traditionally use in marketing, but just using them through different channels.

 2.06

Interviewer: Presumably you use online advertising and communication channels in those countries where the Internet is that much more popular?
Alastair Brown: Yes, exactly. A country like South Korea, for example, has huge broadband penetration and, you know, a great usage of IT, versus some of your developing countries where it's not so great. If people are used to receiving communications through their PC you do that through e-marketing because there's a distinct advantage to it potentially. You can move very quickly, you can get a message

out very quickly so you can scale your business very profitably but you can also track the effectiveness of it in a very simple and clear way. But that being said, there is also a place for other traditional marketing even if it's a newspaper ad that drives people to go and buy online, or drives people to pick up the phone and talk to you, or drives people to your shop to go and bang on the door and say 'Hey, I want to buy from you.'

Interviewer: What about sales distribution channels? Dell Computers are famous for being the first PC manufacturer to sell their computers exclusively using an online channel. I mean how does this strategy work?

Alastair Brown: Well, I think to just clarify, Dell has never been exclusively online. What Dell has always been is exclusively direct. And what I mean by direct is it's a PC manufacturer that establishes direct relationships with its customers. So the only place that you could buy a Dell was through Dell. And a large part of that particularly in recent years has been done online, but a lot of the business has also gone on over the telephone. You need to note though that in the last few years Dell have started moving into retail channels as well.

 2.07

Interviewer: OK, so how does it work? I mean how can you buy a PC online?

Alastair Brown: Well, the nice thing about this is that it allows Dell to know exactly what their customers want and then build their customers' needs and wants to order. So you go online and you say, OK, I need a laptop. What do I need that laptop to do? Well, I need it to do X, Y and Z, and then Dell through the website will identify the right type of laptop for you. You might need faster memory because you might do a lot of graphics work or play a lot of games, or you might need a higher grade of memory than that or a bigger screen and so you can actually configure your PC to order and your services to order. It delivers on the classic dream of one-to-one marketing.

Interviewer: OK, you've explained the benefits to the customers but what's the benefit to the company?

Alastair Brown: With this approach, the company does not need to hold stock. In its early days Dell had lost money because they put a lot of stock in place and then realised that they'd invested in some technology that wasn't what the customers wanted. Dell learnt from that and is now very tightly integrated into suppliers, meaning that they don't have to hold stock. So you pick up your phone, you talk to Dell and you say, I'd like this sort of laptop, it's then ordered into the Dell factory who then go off and talk to Intel, AMD or whoever and say, this is, this is the kind of chip that we need, this is the type of screen we need, those guys then send that into Dell, it's assembled, then sent straight out to the customer so they hold no stock.

Interviewer: You mentioned stock – are there any other major advantages for the company selling direct online?

Alastair Brown: Yes. This approach cuts out the middleman so it means that there's no Dell PCs sitting in people's shops. It also means that Dell can use the latest technology for their customers. It also means that Dell can cut costs, which are then reinvested back into the business to make it cheaper for the customers to go and buy a Dell PC.

 2.08

Interviewer: Has this strategy been successful, though? Dell has now changed this strategy and is selling through high street shops. Why are we seeing this change of strategy?

Alastair Brown: Well, the strategy needs to change with the marketplace. So the traditional direct model has been incredibly successful for Dell in its traditional segments. Dell traditionally started off as primarily a business-focused PC manufacturer and service provider. So when they enter into a country, they will go in and they'll go for the biggest companies and then they'll work their way down to the smaller companies. And those sort of businesses are very used to buying things direct and online, because they get the best deal, it's an economic decision, it's not an emotional, psychological decision. Howeve, Dell wanted to continue to grow their market share. By doing that they wanted to get into the consumer space because that's where they were least dominant, and consumers, as we all know, behave very differently from businesses. There is more of a need to touch and feel the product, maybe to have a bit more of an emotional attachment to a product, and also with a lot of people who aren't familiar with PCs and a little bit nervous about buying them, they need the reassurance of being able to look somebody in the eye.

9.3 Skills: Organising a presentation

 2.09

Philip Weiss

Slide 1
Hi, my name is Philip Weiss, and I'm the managing director of ZN.

Slide 2
Over the next five minutes I'll give you a brief introduction of who we are, how we can help HQs meet their challenges and what opportunities the Internet created for them, and how we developed a methodology to think differently and execute online campaigns and, finally, we'll look at how we can help you.

Slide 3
We're an e-marketing agency based in Brussels …

Slide 4
… and we focus specifically on helping international headquarters develop strategies on the Internet. We've been around for ten years, we have a small team of people from all different European countries, and we're really focused on creating and executing e-marketing campaigns for our clients.

 2.10

Philip Weiss

Slide 5
So what are the main challenges facing HQs today?

Slide 6
Well, we've seen a big change in the role a headquarters had over the last ten years. Effectively they've moved from being an administrative

hub to a real nexus of communication activity, and the web has actually played a dramatic role in reshaping the focus and the possibilities of HQ. Now, as everyone knows, there's tremendous competitive and budget pressure on every major international company today, there are also new demands from customers who want to be better informed, who have multiple channels that they want to use to get that information and who really expect a faster response.

There's also a tremendous increase of complexity, and new technology, new players, new customer expectations mean that headquarters have to reinvent their role and have to re-explore opportunities on a constant basis and we look at how we can turn this complexity into an opportunity. Globalisation is also making messages international at the click of a mouse, and mean that your customer can see what's going on not only in the market that they live in but of course across borders, so you need to adapt your messages and your strategy to that. It fundamentally creates a big opportunity because the Internet can really be the instrument that a headquarters can use to meet these challenges.

Slide 7
So how can we help you?

Slide 8
The way we start our work is to focus first on understanding your business objectives and priorities, and really start from your reality. Because we need to understand what IT set-up you have, what resources are in place, what's your current experience and how we can take that and build a campaign that will deliver for your company and for your team in the long run. But we know that we need to start small and build campaigns step by step, but at the same time we like to think big and have a strategic vision of where we're going. So we look at your specific needs in the short term, but fit them in a long-term strategy, and we help you to build that architecture and make your campaigns happen within that framework.

Slide 9
If you're interested in pursuing this conversation, we look forward to hearing from you through email or phone.

10 Branding
10.1 Theory: What is branding?

 2.11

Dr Sally Hibbert: OK, at this point you'll have looked at lots of different brands that you could do for your projects. And the idea is that the symbols that are used to represent brands are so familiar to us and they represent a whole lot of things to us that go beyond just the basic product.

What I want to speak about today regarding branding is to look at definitions of a brand, identify the features of brands and differentiate different types of brands that are there in the marketplace. And then we'll go on to look at the different types of strategic branding decisions that are made and consider some of the advantages of branding and good practice for branding.

Listening 2: Defining branding

 2.12

Dr Sally Hibbert: Now a clear distinction to make is between the basic product and a brand. A product is simply anything that satisfies customer needs. So it's something that has a functional value, a utility that hopes to satisfy our needs as consumers. But a brand goes that much further and it's the name, term, symbol, design or any combination of these which is used to identify good sorts of services and therefore differentiates them from other functional products on the market. OK, so this allows manufacturers, retailers, and so on to have some way of grabbing our attention in these competitive market places.

Listening 3: To brand or not to brand?

 2.13

Dr Sally Hibbert: Now there are a number of branding decisions that need to be made along the way. And we're going to look at each of these. So, first of all you've got the branding decision. Do you brand something at great expense or do you not brand it? And your second decision is about who's going to be identified as the sponsor of the brand. Is it going to be a manufacturer brand, a distributor brand, a private brand or a licensed brand?

Now, there are some distinct advantages to branding not just for the firm but from the customer's point of view as well. From a customer's point of view the fact that things are branded allows us to recognise the brands and the choices that we usually make. If you were to go round a supermarket and everything was unbranded and you had to start weighing up which were preferable products it would be very difficult. From a consumer's point of view it gives us fast recognition but also an assurance of quality and performance. OK, we learn over time that we can trust some brands for certain things. And then there are emotional benefits which add meaning or feeling to the offering. So there are some distinct benefits to consumers, which is why we like brands.

From a firm's point of view obviously the branding process increases profitability quite substantially. It allows them to charge premium prices. Again you only need to look at the supermarkets. You look at the supermarket value range, the distributor's brand as opposed to the manufacturer's brand and there's this big difference in price. Secondly, it tends to give you a higher market share and the ability to build market share. It gives you loyal customers so your income is more stable. The whole idea of brand is that people like what you're offering them, therefore they come back and choose your offering as they regard it as superior and they choose it again and again. And when you talk about brand equity it's about this issue of loyalty. How committed people are to that brand and therefore you know how much it's worth to them. The fourth point is that it gives you avenues for future growth. And this is also linked to the fifth point if it gives you directions for segmenting markets. So if you look at things like confectionery manufacturers, they produce things for children, for women, for men, for different eating occasions. It allows them to pursue alternative segments in markets, to target new groups and to target new occasions. The final point is that there's legal protection for brand names and trade marks. So when you've created some kind of customer alliance because of the brand you are to some degree protected from the erosion of your market. Having said that, competitors come in with similar or superior positioned brands and it can start to erode your market quite dramatically. But it does give you some legal protection.

10.3 Skills: Using persuasive communication in meetings

Listening: Address to the staff at a hotel

2.14

Hotel manager: The standards focus really came into play as a company about a year ago. Our CEO Mr Ford held a meeting in New York with the hotel managers. And they made a commitment that as a company our goal and our aim has to be to improve our compliance with central standards. So we've committed ourselves that this has to happen.

In a lot of our … No, I shouldn't say that. In some of our hotels, especially the long-serving hotels like London, there are employees that have been in their job for a number of years. You know, it's not rare, fifteen, twenty, twenty-five, thirty years in a job, and an example came up of a phone operator who works at one of our California hotels. Because being a phone operator could be a position that a person has for a while. It's a stable job and, you know, here is an example of an employee who the guests love, she's a pleasant enough person. Gets good guest feedback and things, but just refuses to use the guest's name. And you know, as a company, we're a company that manages with our heart first and we're a people company, so we always would say, 'Well, it's Amy, so we'll make an exception. You know she's been here twenty years.'

Well, I'm here to tell you that the company's now saying, 'Yes, we love our employees and we still provide an excellent work environment for our employees. But standards are our life. Standards aren't just if you want to, if it's convenient for you or when you want to do them. This is what we do. It's not an extra job. It is the job.'

And it's all of us. If I walk into reception and answer a telephone, it doesn't say that I don't have to use the guest's name. It says, 'The guest's name will be used, when known, in a natural and discreet manner.' There are no exceptions. It doesn't matter if it's a planning committee member, if it's a reservations agent, if it's Maria, if it's Georgina Powell. They have to do it. If I'm opening car doors at the front door I say, 'Welcome to the Laker Hotel.'These are our standards. Period.

Language focus 1: The language of persuasion

2.15

Exercise 1
The audio script is in the unit (see page 97).

2.16

Exercise 3
The audio script is in the Answer key (see page 184).

11 Accounting
11.2 Practice: Cost and price

Listening 1: The business of flying

2.17

Interviewer: Can you tell me what services UIA offers?
Richard Creagh: Well, we're a low-cost carrier, we're a charter carrier, we're a cargo carrier, so we effectively serve all of those markets. The domestic market's important for us because we have to serve all of Ukraine, and Ukraine is a very big market of forty-six million people. And freight, we make money carrying cargo in the belly-hold of our passenger aircraft. But in addition to that, we want to develop a freighter network. We already have one 737 freighter, and we'll be adding more in the future. Our big question is always: 'How can we turn our skills into a revenue-generating activity?' We set up our own passenger handling because we could do it better. And then we started to serve other customers, for example British Airways, Austrian Airlines, KLM, Air France, so we were effectively then providing passenger handling for all of those companies. Then we had Swissport, the biggest handling company in the world, their head office is in Zurich. They're in about 180 countries. And they came to us and wanted to participate in handling, so we sold 70% of the business and kept 30% and handed over the management of the business to them, and let them grow it with us. So that's been a very successful strategy. Another strategy was we wanted to maintain our own aircraft because we wanted, obviously, to get the cost under control and have the quality under control. And we do all the heavy maintenance on our own aircraft, we're also providing third-party maintenance – that's third-party maintenance for airlines in Russia and the rest of the region, which is very good because it generates a profit stream as well. So, we don't want to divert focus too much from our core business, because obviously you don't have the management resource to be running all these businesses. But what we do is we'll keep bringing in partners, if necessary, for the peripheral businesses that would add value to the airline. But last year, the experts say that the whole airline industry itself lost about, well, they're saying nine to ten billion dollars, and this year's going to be equally tough. So it's a crazy business. An industry in chaos.

Listening 2: Costs and prices

2.18

Interviewer: How would you define price and cost?
Richard Creagh: Cost is what it costs you to put the product in the market, and you have to keep trying to get that unit cost down. Price is what the market will pay you. If the price is too high people can't afford to travel, that's assuming you have a monopoly. If the price is too low we can't make money, so our price is really determined more by competition, you know. And we always have to be competitive on price or we're not in the marketplace.

Listening 3: Control over costs

2.19

Interviewer: And what costs are involved?
Richard Creagh: Well, there are, unfortunately, major costs that are outside our control. Fuel is a wonderful example, fuel is the biggest cost. And the power of suppliers is a huge influence on cost where you have fuel costs where there's more or less a monopoly. And there's aircraft, at the moment we're in a position where the power

is with the airlines in negotiating aircraft leases, or negotiating aircraft purchase. And that's a cyclical thing, sometimes there are troughs, like now, when supply is greater than demand but two years ago, it was almost impossible to find good-quality aircraft, because the demand was greater than the supply. Now, today, if you're negotiating for aircraft you can do very well. So the power of suppliers is a huge issue. What's important is also what is under your control. Under your control is labour costs, labour productivity, aircraft utilisation. So all we've got to keep doing is try to increase the utilisation of the resources under our control, so that we get unit cost down. And then try and create competition where there's more than one supplier – more than one handling company. So we believe competition is very, very important and that's one of the problems for our industry – that there's not enough competition.

11.3 Skills: Developing internal relationships

Listening : Commenting on a meeting

🔊 2.20

Jenny: I was dreading this meeting because I was thinking, 'Oh, we're just going to be hearing all the bad things we didn't do right, blah, blah, blah.' And now we get to the end and I feel great.
Veronique: Well, I can say bad things about you if you want!
Jenny: No, no, I thought it was a good way of leading the meeting.
Marco: Thank you.
Jenny: Because you know. It has to be addressed to us anyway.
Marco: Yes.
Jenny: And, every time we have a meeting with you, I don't know for everybody else, but for me it's very motivating. I really feel like going back to work and doing well.
Marco: That's good to hear. That's what I want.
Jenny: Yeah.
Marco: Really, that's the effect a meeting should have.
Veronique: Yes, that should be how we feel afterwards.
Marco: You know, it's no good sitting here telling everyone off. That's what they did in the past and it didn't work.
Veronique: Yeah.
Marco: And I knew it wouldn't work. We want to come up with solutions but also take responsibility and stick to the solutions that we decide now.
Veronique: Yeah.
Marco: And for me it's like, 'You had your chance to speak your mind. If you didn't say what you think, then you missed the opportunity.'
Jenny: Yeah, then it's your problem.
Marco: Like some of you saying, 'You know, we don't have the right equipment.' You know, the issue should have been raised at an earlier meeting.
Jenny: That's true.
Marco: Speak up – in our monthly meetings we need to speak about our problems and see if we can make improvements. Some things might not happen. Other things might happen, you know, who would have thought that we could have wireless handsets?
Jenny: Yeah.
Marco: We should get wireless keyboards and get proper equipment. Hannah isn't shy about spending money if it's for the guests. If we address it the right way, it will happen.
Jenny: Great.
Marco: OK, thank you both.
Jenny: Cool.

Marco: Thanks for coming.
Jenny: Thank you.

Language focus: Polite language

🔊 2.21

The audio script is in the unit (see page 107).

12 Microfinance
12.2 Practice: Grameen Bank

Listening 1: How and why Grameen Bank was founded

🔊 2.22

Muhammad Yunus: I was teaching economics in the Department of Economics, and we were going through a very rough period in Bangladesh, there was famine. So I was trying to see what little things I could do in the nearby villages. I made a list of people who were borrowing from loan sharks. I had forty-two names on that list, and the total money they borrowed was twenty-seven dollars.

So my first action was to solve this problem by giving loans so that they didn't have to go back to the loan sharks and be exploited by them in a very ruthless way. Once I had done that it created a lot of excitement among the people, and I wanted to continue with this. So I thought one way I could solve this problem would be by linking them with a bank located in my university campus. So when I went to the bank, the bank said they could not lend money to poor people. And it became a big struggle for me to persuade them.

Eventually I offered myself as the guarantor. I said I'll become the guarantor, I'll sign all your papers, and you give the money, I'll take the risk. So that was the first time I got involved with a bank lending money to poor people. I had no idea whether people would pay back the money. I had no experience of that. And when I did that, I was amazed that every single penny came back despite the fact the bank was trying to persuade me that it would never happen. That encouraged me, and I wanted to expand, but the banks didn't want to support me, they said it was a matter of time the whole thing would collapse because it didn't make sense.

Listening 2: Reversing the basic principles of banking

🔊 2.23

Muhammad Yunus: The conventional banks are based on one basic principle: the more you have, the more you can get. So as a result they became an institution which is focused on the bigger and bigger people, so that they can give more money, so that they can grow bigger.

We reversed that principle. Our principle is this – the less you have, the more attractive you are for us. So we have reversed the basic principle of the bank thing itself.

In order to create a completely new bank, we have to get rid of the whole idea of collateral. The whole idea of banking is that you must give something as a guarantee, against which I can give you a loan. So if you don't pay back the loan, you lose that valuable property. But as a result, banks cannot go to the poor people because they cannot give you anything against which you can give the loan. We said I don't need anything, I'll just give you a loan. It's a very scary thought. People get very nervous: how can I give him money if he doesn't give me anything? And that's what we do. We have no collateral. We have no guarantee.

2.24

Muhammad Yunus: And above all, we don't have any lawyers who check our loan contract with the borrowers. Imagine banking without lawyers, it's impossible to imagine, but we don't have lawyers.

In conventional banks you have to go to the bank. We reverse it. We say people should not come to the bank, the bank should go to the people. So we go to the people, all of the time. Every day that's what we do. We have twenty-seven thousand staff in Grameen Bank. They don't sit in the office behind the desk. These twenty-seven thousand staff go to the villages, more than eighty thousand villages in Bangladesh, to meet seven and a half million borrowers at their doorstep every week.

The question everybody asks is 'Why do the people pay back? Are they crazy?' They are not crazy. They are just people like us. They find out it is in their interest to pay back. We organise the system in such a way, it kind of focuses on the interest of paying back, the benefit of paying back. If you pay back one immediate thing, you see the bank is willing to lend you more. Having a credit channel opens doors. You can keep on taking money and move on forward, you pay back one loan, you are ready for another loan, and it goes step by step.

We don't penalise anybody, that's another thing. There is no punishment. We don't sue anybody. That is very strange, we have no lawyers, no collateral and no punishment, but still it works. We have a ninety-eight, ninety-nine percent repayment rate – that's a lot higher than commercial banks! We don't want to scare people. Also we don't have any penalty interest rates. If you don't pay commercial banks within the set period, your interest rate will go up – we don't have that. So then why do they pay back? If they don't pay back, their door gets closed, meaning that they can't take any more loans. But if they do pay back, they don't have to go to the loan sharks. So that's a big incentive for them to keep the door open, and to continue.

12.3 Skills: Delivering a presentation

 2.25

The audio script is in the unit (see page 114).

 2.26

Part 1

Barack Obama: … this is your victory. I know you didn't do this just to win an election and I know you didn't do it for me. You did it because you understand the enormity of the task that lies ahead. For even as we celebrate tonight, we know the challenges that tomorrow will bring are the greatest of our lifetime – two wars, a planet in peril, the worst financial crisis in a century.

....

The road ahead will be long. Our climb will be steep. We may not get there in one year or even in one term, but America, I have never been more hopeful than I am tonight that we will get there. I promise you – we as a people will get there.

 2.27

Part 2

Barack Obama: There will be setbacks and false starts. There are many who won't agree with every decision or policy I make as president and we know the government can't solve every problem. But I will always be honest with you about the challenges we face. I will listen to you, especially when we disagree.

And above all, I will ask you to join in the work of remaking this nation the only way it's been done in America for two hundred and twenty-one years, block by block, brick by brick, calloused hand by calloused hand.

 2.28

Support manager: At the beginning of the year we went through some big changes. I think we're now in a position, I think we're in a position to really make some changes. I think we've got the right number of people, well, not number perhaps, but the right people who are able to really improve what we're trying to do, which is customer satisfaction with support from our operations. There are three of us involved in it, I think there are three.
Participant 1: What about the staffing issue?
Support manager: I'm going to go through it. I'm going to give it to you from the top down and then any questions come at the end. But if you feel strongly about some particular point I've covered, then please shout out. Three guys in this area, myself, Janice Moore and Lisa Ross. Right, so big change. We've got service and restoration in one team. And the advantage is a multi-skilled force. So we've got technicians and we've got installation people working together. The planned project is going to need complex provision.
Participant 2: I have a question. Can you define complex provision?
Support manager: Right. I should have put that at the beginning, shouldn't I? Right, so the field engineers take complex equipment into the …

 2.29

The audio script is in the unit (see page 115).

13 Corporate Social Responsibility

13.2 Practice: The business case for Corporate Social Responsibility

2.30

Interviewer: How would you actually define Corporate Social Responsibility?
Yogesh Chauhan: Well, I guess the starting point is to say what it isn't. Corporate Social Responsibility isn't corporate philanthropy. Instead it's a holistic approach that companies and organisations take to manage their business in a responsible manner. The four key components to the BBC's CSR policy <u>focus on</u> the impact the organisation has on the community, the physical environment, the marketplace, and the

workplace. CSR, however, goes beyond just addressing these issues. We need to look at how these factors <u>are</u> <u>incorporated within</u> the strategy of an organisation, how <u>it's integrated into</u> the company and how transparent it is in disclosing information.

Listening 2: The different sides of CSR

 2.31

Interviewer: Can you give us some examples of how companies might act responsibly in the four areas of community, physical environment, marketplace and workplace?

Yogesh Chauhan: Yes, sure. If we start with the first one, community, most companies tend to address that by doing something in their local community by way of charitable donations. In our case we work and support local communities through employees volunteering, so we share the skills we might have with local communities and local community organisations and allow local communities to come into our business and find out a little bit more about what we are doing.

Interviewer: What about physical environment? Let's talk about that.

Yogesh Chauhan: Yes. Well, that I guess has been the one area that generated the most <u>amount of</u> interest. What companies are doing is looking at their environmental footprint in the round which includes their CO_2 emissions from travel, from the products they might be making, the buildings they might occupy, through to water use, energy use, etc.

Interviewer: Right, what about the marketplace and in the workplace in general?

Yogesh Chauhan: Oh, yes. The marketplace, some companies specifically market their products as ethical products. Other companies are mindful of other issues too, and certainly in our case, how we advertise and promote our products. What impact they might have on younger people or children, for example. The supply chain is also an important part of this, and most consumers are now <u>conscious of</u> and <u>aware of</u> issues like child labour and enforced labour in manufacturing goods.

Interviewer: OK, and the workplace, the final area. I guess as the name suggests it's very much about the employment practices that a company has.

Yogesh Chauhan: I believe it to be correct. One statistic is that nearly 70% of jobs in the UK are not advertised, and they're basically through friends and connections and networks and that is deemed, certainly within Corporate Social Responsibility, as not usually the best practice. Big companies like the BBC and others would have pretty clear guidelines and policies on its recruitment practices, ensuring that jobs are advertised appropriately, that there's a fair selection process and the most talented individuals, and the most suitable individuals are recruited for jobs.

Listening 3: The business case for CSR

 2.32

Interviewer: Let's have a look at the business case. I mean how far is the business case and the need to cut costs the main driving force behind organisations' CSR policies?

Yogesh Chauhan: There has to be a business case for CSR. And it's not necessarily about cutting costs, it's about the long-term survival and health and profitability of the company. I do not think necessarily that companies would enter into a Corporate Social Responsibility activity in order merely to cut costs. Obviously, for initiatives such as, for example, environmental policies, one of the

clear benefits is that if you use less energy, then you cut your costs straight away. But in other examples then there usually is a financial outlay. But in the long term that can repay itself to a company.

Interviewer: So shareholders are only one of many stakeholders?

Yogesh Chauhan: Absolutely, yes. I think that what Corporate Social Responsibility has introduced, is the notion that short-term profit gain isn't the only criteria by which you can measure the success of a company.

Listening 4: Is CSR just corporate gloss?

 2.33

Interviewer: Some people say that CSR is little more than corporate gloss and public relations – what would you say?

Yogesh Chauhan: I can understand that there are arguments for and against a company using its CSR activities as a marketing tool for building reputations. But I think on balance there is a role for companies to do this. And I guess, the Co-operative Bank strike me as one of the foremost examples of where their practices mirror their marketing, and of how you perceive that company. And so I don't think we should necessarily automatically criticise any attempt that a company might make to tell its customers and others about its CSR credibility as mere gloss.

Interviewer: So it's not so much corporate gloss but good public relations to communicate a company's CSR policy?

Yogesh Chauhan: That's right. And I think it's a good thing as long as there is truth in that. So what the company is actually telling its customers and others about is actually a true and accurate reflection of what it's actually doing. And in some cases that might not be the case, and hence the criticism that this is mere gloss.

Interviewer: Right.

Yogesh Chauhan: For example, a car manufacturer suddenly proclaiming that a car that they've manufactured for the last five years is suddenly green, and they've done very little to actually change it but certainly the marketing has got green images and green language associated with the car, but the car itself hasn't substantially changed. Then I think most customers see through it and many of those adverts have been picked up by the Advertising Standards Authority as well for this wrongful advertising or misleading advertising.

Interviewer: The classic case of greenwashing.

Yogesh Chauhan: Precisely.

13.3 Skills: Supporting the speaker

Listening 1: Opening telephone conversations

 2.34

Customer: Hello.
John: Good morning. It's John here, from Latin America Holidays.
Customer: Yes. Hi.
John: I'm calling about your honeymoon trip to Peru and Ecuador. My colleague Eleanor's been communicating with you and I know she's away on holiday this week, lucky girl.
Customer: Oh, very nice too.
John: Congratulations, by the way, on getting married.
Customer: Oh, thank you. I can't believe it's only three weeks away.

Listening 2: Showing interest on the telephone

 2.35

Ken: Hi, Sarah. Ken here.
Sarah: Hi, Ken. Good to hear from you. Everything OK?
Ken: Yes, very good. Just calling about sorting out the brochure.
Sarah: OK.
Ken: It's just that it's not finished at the moment.
Sarah: Oh, OK.
Ken: But, we also need to try and get down on paper what our mission is as clearly as possible. Do you agree?
Sarah: What do you suggest we change? I thought it was ready.
Ken: OK. But there are three headings there. The first one is leadership, then communication and then sustainable tourism, yeah?
Sarah: Yeah.
Ken: OK. So we need to …

Listening 3: Helping the speaker expand a topic

 2.36

Ken: Yeah. I'm not totally happy with the next one which is 'sponsorship with local projects' because that implies to me a greater involvement than we have at the moment.
Sarah: Uh-huh. Sure.
Ken: And I suppose what you're trying to say is that we are just producing guide books, helping raise awareness of areas of national parks. But, you're not actually directly giving money back to the community as such.
Sarah: OK. Good point.
Ken: OK. Well, I'll change that to 'support' if 'sponsorship' is too strong a word. So that's fine.
Sarah: Good. Yes. Absolutely.
Ken: All right. I'll still play around with it and try and send that off to you a bit later.
Sarah: That's wonderful, Ken. Do you think it'll be a success?
Ken: I do. Definitely. Definitely. OK?
Sarah: Thanks, Ken. Great job.
Ken: Cheers, Sarah.

14 Strategic planning

14.2 Practice: Planning within a company

Listening 1: The characteristics of a strategist

 2.37

Interviewer: In your opinion, what makes a good strategist?
Justin Wateridge: Somebody who can listen … you need to listen to the people within a company, but also listen to the signals and understand the signals in that industry as a whole. I think the ability to analyse lots of information and get the answers directly from that information is important. Communication is also important. And I think it's important that you can come up with ideas, and that's a part of strategy, but a good strategist is somebody who can actually communicate all of this and then put it into practice.
Interviewer: Right. So you're saying it's basically listening, analysing and communicating. Are there any qualities that you think a bad strategist would have?
Justin Wateridge: To be uncertain – I think you can take time over a decision but I think once you've decided on a course of action, you

need to take it. You do listen to people but you don't manage by democracy as such, you listen to them and that affects the way you move forward in the right direction. But you can't chop and change all the time, otherwise you lose confidence and confidence is key.

Listening 2: Company strategy

 2.38

Interviewer: How did the company get to where it is now?
Justin Wateridge: Abercrombie & Kent was set up in Africa in 1962 by Jeff Kent and his parents, and it grew because it focused on two things. Firstly, it was innovative, and secondly, it gave great service to its clients. I think they have been two of its core premises and these qualities have held it in good stead over the years.
Interviewer: OK, I see. Can you tell us about the strengths and weaknesses of the company at the moment?
Justin Wateridge: One of the strengths of the company definitely at the moment is its staff. A&K is different from most companies in that it has a network of offices around the world. Many other operators sub-let and sub-contract their services to ground agents, whether they be in Kenya, Peru or China, whereas A&K actually have offices in over 35 countries, and that's a key strength. A high standard of service is maintained throughout the world wherever you go. The weakness is possibly that it's a luxury brand, so A&K are trying to prove that we give value for money.
Interviewer: Right. What are the company's objectives for the next five years?
Justin Wateridge: We're really trying to stress our level of service. So we go back to our clients, our database, the public, and stress that we give the very best service, and it's very personal, in that what we do is all tailor-made, it's all bespoke. And that's going to be one of the key things, delivering service. I think there's a lot of tour operators out there, a lot of companies, but not all of them have the level of service that we can offer and they will not have the expertise that we have or the network that we have.
Interviewer: I see. Is there anything else about opportunities and threats that you can see over the next five years?
Justin Wateridge: I think the Internet's certainly a double-edged sword. On one hand, it gives the user access to a huge amount of travel ideas, travel suggestions, places round the world that just weren't available some ten years ago. That's a threat to us on one side, obviously there's a lot of competition, there are some small niche operators who can set up one-man bands and become very specialist out of their back garden almost and their overheads are perhaps lower than ours, but they don't have the network. On the other hand, the Internet is a cost-effective way of us accessing lots of clients as well. I think in the past, us and other operators have relied heavily on brochures, which are costly in terms of finance to produce, in terms of the opportunity cost, the time that you have to put into them, and also I think costly to the environment in terms of paper, even though we try and do reuse paper that's sourced from sustainable sources.
Interviewer: Do you have anything to say about how A&K can achieve your objectives?
Justin Wateridge: Travel is an amazing industry to work in as travel gives people wonderful experiences that can be wonderfully diverse. And it's trying to get that across, and being more experiential in what we say to people, rather than just having a list of countries or a catalogue of hotels. You sort of say, let's give a bit more to the clients and an idea, a flavour of what they might be able to see and do. I think

it's experience your travel as opposed to just flying and flopping as such.

Interviewer: What's that, flying and flopping?

Justin Wateridge: A fly and flop holiday is where you stay in one place and don't do very much for a week or two.

14.3 Skills: Using narratives in interviews

Introduction

 2.39

Interviewer: Have you ever had an interview for a job that went badly?

Mike: Yes, when I was about 24. I went for an interview as a café manager in London. And so, the morning of the interview I got dressed up in my suit and tie and went along to the interview. And then just before I went in I checked the information I had been given and it said: 'Please dress casually for this interview, don't wear a suit.'

Interviewer: Oh! So did you get that job?

Mike: No, I didn't!

Listening 1: Conversation with a customer

 2.40

Systems trainer: … the only other comment I've got is from when I went to Bond Street.

Manager: Oh, yes?

Systems trainer: For the laser treatment.

Manager: Oh, really?

Systems trainer: There was a lady there that I was talking to, who was having the same tests and things done as me. And it's quite interesting to get comments from somebody who doesn't work for the company.

Manager: Yes.

Systems trainer: To see what other people think about us. She'd come all the way from Eastbourne to Bond Street to have a consultation.

Manager: Right.

Systems trainer: I asked her what she thought about the treatment, and she said she had thought about having laser surgery done before but wasn't sure about how safe it was. She said the thing that made her come was because it was our company.

Manager: Excellent.

Systems trainer: And she says because we're doing it she thought it must be all right. And I thought it was nice to be told that.

Manager: And she didn't know you worked for this company?

Systems trainer: She didn't. Though I did say afterwards.

Manager: Right.

Systems trainer: But she didn't know when she told me.

Listening 2: Eye test

 2.41

Manager: How was it, the whole experience?

Systems trainer: Well, it's supposed to take an hour and a half. When I got there at twenty past one they were already running over an hour behind, which is not very good if you've got a train to catch. Fortunately for me, somebody didn't turn up because I actually wouldn't have stayed for my appointment. I would have had to have come away without the consultation, which I wouldn't have been very happy about. Because there are lots and lots of tests that I had to have done, and at the end of it they put stuff in to make your pupils dilate.

Manager: Right.

Systems trainer: I could only see through a quarter of my eye and I looked 'super scary,' as James put it.

Manager: Oh?

Systems trainer: I couldn't even see my watch to tell the time.

Manager: Oh!

Systems trainer: My sight was so blurry.

Manager: That must have been a weird experience.

Systems trainer: Yeah, it was really weird. I just wanted to close my eyes and go to sleep.

Manager: So you've had all the tests done, but have they said if you can have the treatment?

Systems trainer: They've said yes I can have it done.

Manager: So when do you go and get the treatment?

Systems trainer: Well, I can go when I want, but I can't afford it at the moment.

Manager: Maybe when you get your bonus?

Answer key

1 Competitive environment

1.1 Theory: Concepts of competitive markets

Introduction

2

Suggested answers

Any combination of answers is possible depending on personal attitudes to competition. A highly competitive attitude might produce the answer: 1 C, 2 C, 3 C, 4 D. (Question 4 could be considered problematic: 'at all costs' could technically include acting illegally and unethically.) Alternatively, a 'team player' attitude, emphasising the importance of the team or group, might produce the answer: 1 D, 2 D, 3 D, 4 D.

Language focus 1: Sport as a metaphor and analogy for business

1

1 monopolised **2** acted **3** regulated **4** globalised
5 invested

2

1 largely monopolised **2** acted illegally **3** heavily regulated
4 increasingly globalised **5** invested heavily

3

touch base – baseball; kick off – rugby/football; take it on the chin – boxing; the ball's in their court – tennis; score an own goal – hockey/football

1 the ball's in their court **2** kick off **3** touch base
4 score an own goal **5** take it on the chin

4

touch base = speak (to clarify something); kick off = start; take it on the chin = be strong and accept a difficult situation; the ball's in their court = they have to do something before any progress can be made; score an own goal = make a decision that has the opposite effect from what was hoped for

5

1 monopoly **2** oligopoly **3** natural monopoly
4 perfect competition **5** business environment

Listening 1: The competitive environment in sport and business

1

motor racing, boat race, football, American football

2

1 leadership, managing teams **2** Real Madrid, Manchester United
3 brand, support, lots of history **4** American football
5 The playing field is not very level **6** perfect competition

Listening 2: Monopolies, oligopolies and perfect competition

1

1 restrict output, raise prices
2 not enough scope in the market, expensive set-up costs or upfront investment
3 It's never going to happen.
4 reduce entry barriers and make it easier for films to compete

2

1 b **2** a **3** b **4** c **5** a **6** c

3

1 UK **2** USA **3** EU

Transferable skill: Mind-mapping and note-taking

1

1 comp' sport = competitive sport; int'l strat = international strategy; m. power = market power
2 w/ = with; + = and
3 EU UK USA
4 producing same product = producing the same product; bad for consumer = bad for the consumer; Oxford–Cambridge boat race = the Oxford–Cambridge boat race; make takeover bid for rival = make a takeover bid for a rival
5 lots market power = lots of market power
6 make takeover bid = Companies make a takeover bid; expand abroad = Companies expand abroad

2

 1 one firm industry
 2 dominate the market
 3 gas suppliers
 4 raise prices
 5 perfect competition
 6 Real Madrid or Manchester United
 7 Manchester United or Real Madrid
 8 leadership or managing teams
 9 managing teams or leadership
10 Competition Commission
11 Monopolies and Mergers Commission
12 Federal Trade Commission
13 Register patents
14 Lower prices below costs or Agree common price strategy with rival
15 Agree common price strategy with rival or Lower prices below cost
16 Propose merger with rival

1.2 Practice: A highly competitive company

Introduction

4

All the buildings were constructed using glass from Saint-Gobain.

Reading 1: The history of Saint-Gobain

1665–1789: A workshop goes industrial
1789–1856: From legal monopoly to free competition
1856–1970: Industrial revolutions and modern times
1970–1986: An 'à la française' multinational, then nationalisation
1986 to the present day: Back to the future, or 20+ years evolving non-stop

Reading 2: Sharing information about Saint-Gobain

Student A:
Jean-Baptiste Colbert was the Chief Minister and was responsible for guaranteeing the early success of the company.
Following the French Revolution, the advantages the company had enjoyed were removed, and it had to radically change the way it did business.
Saint-Quirin was Saint-Gobain's main competitor before the two companies merged.

Student B:
The company was nationalised in 1982.
The company was re-privatised in 1986.
By 2006, its sales had increased 350%.

Language focus 1: Adjective and adjective + noun combinations

legal and technical monopoly
sustainable and profitable growth
political and economic agenda
impressive and symbolic order

Language focus 2: Tenses that talk about the past

1
1 past continuous   **2** past simple   **3** present perfect
4 past simple   **5** past perfect
2
1 past simple   **2** present perfect   **3** past perfect
4 past continuous
3
past simple: last week, for one year, recently, already, yesterday, one hundred years ago, in the 1980s
past continuous: when it happened
present perfect: in my life, this is the first time, for one year, recently, already, this century
past perfect: when it happened, already
4
1 was working   **2** joined, had worked (the past simple can be used here as well)   **3** worked, have worked   **4** had done

1.3 Skills: Building relationships across companies

Listening 1: Pre-meeting small talk

1 Last night's meal/food.
2 To develop the relationship.
3 Both – the topic and language are very informal, but the one-sided questions asked by the most senior person make it seem like a meeting.

Language focus 1: Making your feelings understood

1
a 4 **b** 5 **c** 3 **d** 1 **e** 2
3
'Flight' is emphasised as it is the most important information.
4
'Flight' is not stressed much because it is 'given' information, that is the questioner has said it already so there is no need to emphasise it. 'OK' is given some emphasis because this is new information. 'Hotel' and 'terrible' are given more stress because they are new information.

Language focus 2: Sounding friendly in informal situations

1
Words missing: **1** Is it a nice place?   **3** I'm a little bit jealous, actually.
No words missing: **2, 4**
2
1 Just been to the café.   **2** (You) read the report?
3 A glass of water, please?
3
It is difficult to give a general answer to this question, because each relationship is different, but it is worth remembering that too much informality can create a negative impression, as can too much formality.

Listening 2: Judging emotions

1
He sounds friendly and seems to be in a good mood.
2
Brian often uses ellipsis. Examples:
Tell me [about] last night; [Did you have] a good meal out in Aachen?; Oh, [did you go to the] Lycae?; [Did you sit] downstairs or upstairs?; I must go there sometime; [Was it] good?; [I'm a] little bit jealous, actually.
3
Because if intonation is not used effectively questions will not sound like questions.
4
It is effective, but a little one-sided as Brian starts most of the conversations.

2 Future uncertainty

2.1 Theory: STEEP analysis

Introduction

3
No company or individual is able to fully control their own future. However, successful companies and individuals are the ones who are best able to predict the future accurately and take steps to respond in the best way possible – defending themselves from possible threats and positioning themselves to take advantage of opportunities.

Reading: STEEP analysis

1
1 affect / shape   **2** purchase   **3** massive   **4** organic
5 conversely   **6** shortages   **7** reconsidering

2

1 People's attitudes to health and diet are changing.

2 Falling birth rates

3 Calls for greater investment in food production; countries that previously did not want to produce GM food are now having to rethink this policy.

4

1 Political   **2** Socio-cultural / Technological

3 Socio-cultural / Economic   **4** Economic   **5** Economic

6 Political   **7** Technological   **8** Environmental   **9** Political

10 Technological

Listening 1: STEEP factors

1

1 Socio-cultural   **2** Economic   **3** Political   **4** Technological

5 Environmental

2

Suggested answers

Socio-cultural – He believes that more people will be travelling between countries and that this will lead to more global products as tastes converge.

Economic – He believes Asia will become more important especially as India and China continue to develop.

Political – He thinks there will be a resistance to further increasing the size of the EU over the next ten years.

Technological – He thinks that marketing and selling online will continue to grow. However, some people may become fed up with the amount of technology and move back to more face-to-face business.

Environmental – He believes that CO_2 emissions will be the most important issue for business over the next few years.

3

Suggested answers

The global automotive industry will need to consider options such as more standardisation of the product across different country markets, opening up plants in India and/or China to supply new markets (opportunity), watch very carefully for any future environmental legislation that limits CO_2 emissions (threat), continue to invest in greener technologies (opportunity). Finally, they might even consider selling direct to the consumer via their own websites (opportunity).

In the computer industry there will be more demand for mobile devices as more people travel (opportunity). Established companies need to watch carefully for new competitors from China and India making a move onto the international stage (threat). CO_2 issues in the future may mean that computer manufacturers need to focus more on recycling component parts to conform to possible future legislation (threat/opportunity).

4

Suggested answers

Trends that would be relevant for the car industry to monitor include predicting the price of oil and the continued future availability of oil. They need to monitor green legislation in different country markets. For the computer industry, monitoring changes in working and lifestyle patterns will provide key information to companies on future product development.

Listening 2: How industries plan for the future

1 It takes between two and four years.

2 They should always look to the future.

3 He correctly predicted that everybody would want a computer in their home.

4 They have an understanding of what people want and they have a vision.

5 They have underestimated or misunderstood how important CO_2 emissions and energy have become for the business agenda.

6 They are made in the boardrooms.

7 They are important, but the decisions that are made are more important.

Language focus: Future certainty and uncertainty

1

Uncertain ◄─────────────► Certain

3   1 4   2

2

1 B – *may* in B sounds more certain than *guess* in A.

2 B – The intonation in B is more certain than in A. Also the use of a question in A to check that the information is correct makes it sound much less certain.

3 A – The use of *definitely* in A makes this sound very certain and the intonation suggests that it is a fact.

4 A – The intonation and use of *going to* in A sound very certain. In B *suppose* and *might* make this sound less certain.

3

May is stressed, which makes it sound less definite.

4

1 may   **2** will   **3** will definitely, might well   **4** going to, might

5

possible: may, could, guess, might, suppose

probable: looks probable (that), is highly unlikely (that), might well

certain: will, must, will definitely, going to

Remember that the intonation will also affect how certain the person is when they use these words and phrases.

6

Suggested answers

Companies with high debts will definitely benefit with lower interest rates.

Tourism will suffer due to volcanic clouds and higher prices for flights due to higher price of oil.

Publishers of educational textbooks may have opportunities to provide digital editions for textbooks for new online courses.

Pizza home-delivery companies may benefit as more people stay at home with online friends on the computer.

The online advertising industry and e-marketing consultancies would benefit as more people spend time and money online on mobile devices – this will mean that companies will pay more attention to selling online and will require more help from e-marketing consultancies.

Global car manufacturers would reconsider investment in your country if it joined or left a regional trading bloc.

Other possible winners might include importers and retailers supplying ethnic food for new immigrants, organisations running courses for people to follow in their extra free time. Possible losers would include airlines and aeroplane manufacturers as people travel less or switch to high-speed trains.

2.2 Practice: Global consumer goods industry

Introduction

3

Products now have shorter lifespans due to the increasing pace of technological change, ever-increasing consumer demand and greater general levels of consumer affluence. It is also often the case that manufacturers will build obsolescence into their products 'forcing' consumers to upgrade after a relatively short period of time.

Language focus: Consumer goods sectors

1

Procter & Gamble – 3 a
Tesco, etc. – 4 f
Johnson & Johnson – 5 b

Sony, etc. – 2 d
Nestlé, etc. – 1 e
Whirlpool, etc. – 6 c

3

Procter & Gamble (USA)
Tesco (UK)
Walmart (USA)
Carrefour (France)
Metro (Germany)
Johnson & Johnson (USA)
Sony (Japan)
Samsung (Korea)

LG (Korea)
Philips (The Netherlands)
Nestlé (Switzerland)
Kraft (USA)
Whirlpool (USA)
Bosch (Germany)
Electrolux (Sweden)

Transferable skill: Speed-reading

Phase 1

1 The source is 'Global Commerce Initiative'. It is likely that this report will favour the interests of the global consumer goods industry.
2 The text is likely to be about the future trends that will affect the Asian consumer goods market.
3 It is likely to be divided into three or four parts: urbanisation, ageing populations, polarisation of new middle class and the poor. (The last section could consist of two parts: rising incomes, poverty and low incomes.)

Phase 2

2 Four blocks or sections
3 **a** before paragraph 6   **b** before paragraph 2
  c before paragraph 8   **d** before paragraph 3

Phase 3

1 In section on ageing   2 In section on low-income consumers
3 In section on urbanisation   4 In section on rising incomes

Phase 4

1 spicier foods   2 governments and communities
3 500,000,000   4 it has revolutionised consumer aspirations

2.3 Skills: Presenting a case at a meeting

Introduction

4

There tends to be more focus on the individual at a presentation and less time for questions and answers.

	Formal presentation	Q&A session
Turn-taking	Not usually	Yes
Spontaneous speech	No (hopefully!)	Yes
Communication is one-way	Usually	No
Questions and answers	Maybe	Yes
Rhetorical questions (asked for effect, not for an answer)	Yes	Not usually
Active listening (responses, e.g. *yes, uh-huh*)	No	Yes
Immediate responses	Not usually	Yes

5

A presentation requires a lot more preparation and practice, but it is often possible to predict certain questions for a Q&A session.

Listening 1: Upgrading the operating system

1

Suggested answers

The reasons include: having a system that is compatible with the one their clients are using; making sure that they have the right support from their operating system suppliers; protecting the system from attacks and viruses.

2

D E A B C

Intercultural analysis: Presentation styles

Suggested answers

Introducing the main point at the beginning makes the presentation easy to understand, but introducing it later may engage the audience more.

Language focus: Discourse markers

1

1 <u>OK, we may as well start.</u>
2 <u>So, our</u> Windows operating system. <u>We've been</u> using our present OS in Japan for at least four years and <u>it's time</u> to upgrade.
3 <u>It's more a question of what will happen if we don't</u> upgrade … <u>Obviously</u>, this creates a business risk for us <u>because</u> … The longer we wait, the greater this risk becomes.
4 <u>So, how do we start?</u> <u>Well</u>, I've already done this.
5 <u>So, just to give you a bit of background</u>. Mainstream support for the present system expired …

2

1 D   2 E   3 B   4 C   5 A

Listening 2: Q&A session

1

She doesn't give an answer to the question. She rephrases it and then says there isn't a black and white answer.

2

Suggested answer

She might not answer the question because she does not have the information; the change has not yet happened in other departments or countries; she may feel that the information is not relevant for their discussion.

3

She follows the format.

Writing 1: Preparing presentation slides

Writing skill: Creating a strong visual impact

2

Low income – bottom left photo
Urbanisation – top right photo
Ageing population – bottom right photo
New middle class – top left photo

4

It refers to the first bullet point.

5

Possible images

1st bullet: a graph showing increasing price of oil or wheat, etc.
2nd bullet: photo of an overcrowded food market in a developing country
3rd bullet: photo of damage to crops or land caused by the weather
4th bullet: photo of a demonstration in a city with protesters carrying placards about price inflation of basic foodstuffs

Intercultural analysis

Suggested answer

The use of humour will depend on the individual style of the presenter and whether humour is acceptable in the context. You should always ask yourself: 'Who are the audience?' and 'What is the usual way of doing things?' in the particular organisation, industry or country where you are giving the presentation.

Language focus: Summarising information into concise bullet points

1

Suggested answers

Rising costs   Volatile climate
Population spikes   Political instability

2

1 There is / will be a continuing rise in the cost …
2 Population spikes are putting / will put pressure …
3 An increasingly volatile climate is affecting / will affect production …
4 Rising costs are leading / will lead to political …
   … instability on the consumer goods industry?

3

Suggested answers

1 Increasing speed of urbanisation in developing world
2 Large segment of world's population still living on low incomes
3 Ageing populations create challenges and opportunities
4 Big increase in middle-class consumers in Asia

4

Suggested answers

1 What will happen if rapid urbanisation increases even faster?
2 What will be the results of a large segment of the world's population living on very low incomes?

3 What challenges and opportunities does an ageing population bring?
4 How will the increase in middle-class consumers in Asia have an impact on the consumer goods industry?

Critical analysis: Dos and don'ts of presentation slides

2

Slides 3A and 3B

In the first pair of slides, both formats are acceptable, but slide 3B has more impact. Slide 3B should be used if the context is clear and the speaker wants to emphasise the figure of 72%.

Slides 4A and 4B

Slide 4A is better. Slide 4B has too many bullet points and too many colours. Also, at least one of the colours is difficult to read. The image in slide 4A is professional but not very exciting. The images in slide 4B are very basic – they might have come from a standard clip-art software package. It is best to avoid this kind of image.

3 Rewarding performance

3.1 Theory: Employee reward strategies

Introduction

1

Suggested answer

A reward was offered to encourage people to catch Hardin. A higher reward would encourage more people to look for him and it would also give people more incentive to try harder to find him. If a lower reward was offered, the opposite would happen.

3

Suggested answer

Bounty hunters and modern-day executives both get paid by results. The difference is that bounty hunters received nothing if they didn't meet their objectives, while today's executives sometimes receive a large pay packet whether they perform well or badly.

4

1 b   **2** e   **3** c   **4** f   **5** a   **6** d

Listening 1: The role and function of pay

1 To fill the job and to motivate the workers
2 Payment by time (by the hour) and payment by effort, output or performance
3 A chief executive can be paid by share options linked to share price, an apple picker can be paid by the number of apples picked and a coal miner by the kilogram of coal.

Listening 2: Advantages and disadvantages of different reward systems

1

1 supervising people   2 measure of output   3 simple
4 more effort

2

1 They may take risky accounting decisions to make the share price high.
2 He is paid by both output (the number of articles and books he writes) and time (by the hour).

Listening 3: Fair pay and motivation

1 A   **2** B   **3** C   **4** C

1

1 encourages / motivates   **2** make   **3** work   **4** job

2

1 pay   **2** payments   **3** pay   **4** payment

3

1 bright   **2** finance   **3** forecast to   **4** inflation to
5 strong   **6** terms

4

1 financial   **2** bonus   **3** difficult to   **4** investment in
5 performance-related   **6** cut

3.2 Practice: Performance-Related Pay (PRP) in practice

Language focus: Compound nouns

1

1 c   **2** g   **3** k   **4** j   **5** h   **6** f   **7** d   **8** b   **9** e   **10** i   **11** a

2

adjective + noun: operating profit
noun + noun: stretch goals / stretch targets, compensation programme, comparison companies
adjective + adjective or noun + noun: equity-based awards, annual base salary, short-term cash incentives, increased shareholder value, operating cash flow, new product revenue

Does not follow any of the patterns: customer-retention rates (**noun + noun + noun**)

3

Compound nouns tend to be more common in written business English.

Reading 1: Nokia's approach to PRP

1

Companies in general use PRP to try to motivate staff and boost staff performance.

2

Suggested answers
The factors are all important to Nokia, as they see them as a key way of recruiting and retaining executives, while also making sure that executives remain accountable to the shareholders.
Some people may think that balancing rewards between Nokia's and an individual's performance is unfair as outside factors may affect an individual's performance.

3

The executives can directly control factors 2 and 3.

4

Factors 2, 3 and 4 are important for maintaining motivation within the company. Factors 1 and 5 are key to encouraging executives to stay with Nokia.

Reading 2: Understanding PRP in terms of short-term cash incentives

1

1 false   **2** true   **3** false   **4** true   **5** true

Transferable skill: Distinguishing main ideas from supporting information

1

Main idea: Our compensation programme for executive officers includes annual cash compensation and long-term equity-based awards
Supporting information: in the form of a base salary, short-term cash incentives … in the form of stock options and shares
in the form of is used twice to signal the supporting information

2

The main ideas covered in Reading 1 concern how and why Nokia use performance-related pay in their executive compensation programmes. The main ideas in Reading 2 concern the short-term cash component of the executive compensation programme.

3.3 Skills: Negotiating a pay rise

Introduction

1

A manager and the employee are usually involved in pay negotiations. For more senior employees, the board of directors may be involved. Conflicts and problems most often occur when the employee overestimates his/her performance or if the company is unable to offer a pay increase.

2

The factors could include the number of sick days, lateness, general attitude, productivity, relations with colleagues, relations with customers, profits generated.

Listening 1: Performance review

She is in favour of PRP because she thinks she brings a lot of business to the company.

Listening 2: Negotiating for more money

1

In general, win–win strategies are preferred in pay negotiations. Using win–lose strategies can be very high risk.

2

Win–lose strategies: 1, 4, 5, 7
2 This could be a win–win strategy because it shows that you have ambition and commitment to the company. It could be a win–lose strategy if there is little or no chance for advancement within the company.
3 This could be a win–lose situation as it could upset your manager if he/she is unaware that you had a second job. It could also be win–win in that it shows that you are fully committed to the company.
6 This could be a win–win strategy in that it puts pressure on the company to offer you a better deal. It could also be a win–win strategy if the company is very likely to give you a pay rise, as both sides will feel satisfied with the result. It could be a win–lose strategy in that the company may not be able to afford to give you a pay rise or they may feel that you are behaving unreasonably.
8 This could be a win–win strategy in that it shows that you are committed to the company. It could also be a win–lose strategy in that it weakens your bargaining position.

3

She uses strategies: 2, 3, 5, 7, 9, 10

4

In this negotiation the trainee uses more win–win than win–lose strategies.

Language focus: Vague language

2

1 B   **2** A   **3** B   **4** B   **5** A   **6** B

3

1 f   **2** c   **3** a   **4** d   **5** e   **6** b

4

Suggested answers

1 Your sales results could really be improved.

2 I think I've earned a reasonable pay rise.

3 If I don't get a pay rise, I may have to consider my future here.

4 We will probably consider your pay situation quite soon.

6

1 collaborative   **2** competitive   **3** competitive   **4** competitive
5 collaborative   **6** collaborative

4 Fostering creativity

4.1 Theory: Creative thinking and creative management

Language focus: Word formations connected with creativity

1

1 c   **2** a   **3** g   **4** h   **5** d   **6** b   **7** e   **8** f

2

1 imaginative   **2** creative   **3** inventive   **4** interactive   **5** –
6 innovative   **7** convergent   **8** divergent

3

1 imagine   **2** create   **3** invent   **4** interact   **5** implement
6 innovate   **7** converge   **8** diverge

4

Most writers in the creative management field would say that inventors are more creative as they are creating something new. Innovators are also creative but generally work with other people's ideas or inventions. They are generally considered more market orientated in their approach as they are designing products for specific groups of people (target markets).

Reading: Making sense of creativity

3

a entrepreneurs

b affected by peer pressure

c controlled or threatened

d flat (non-hierarchical)

e imaginative thinking that is expansive and divergent

f focus on quality, narrow down choices, make selections

g is driven by (periodic) radical breakthroughs

h is driven by continuous small incremental steps

4

1 Person (false)   **2** Place (true)   **3** Process (false)
4 Product (false)   **5** Person (true)   **6** Process (false)

4.2 Practice: Innovation in practice

Introduction

1

It is located below the water surface so there is less risk of damage.

2

Renewable: solar, wind, wave

Non-renewable: nuclear, gas, coal, oil

Note that nuclear is generally considered non-renewable as it is based on uranium which is a finite mineral. Some people in the nuclear industry, however, state that nuclear fission is inexhaustible and therefore there is no difference between it and other renewable energy sources.

3

Coal, gas and oil have high CO_2 emissions but produce relatively cheap energy.

Solar, wind and wave energy produces high-cost energy and generally needs subsidising by governments, but CO_2 emissions are very low.

Nuclear is politically controversial and there is a lot of opposition to it but it has low CO_2 emissions.

Listening 1: How CETO technology works

2

a increases   **b** on the spheres   **c** high-pressure water
d electrical generator   **e** transmission line   **f** low-pressure water

3

a and c

Listening 2: How CETO was born, developed and commercialised

3

c

1 N   **2** C   **3** C   **4** D   **5** D   **6** C   **7** D   **8** D

Language focus: Past modals

1

1 d   2 e   3 a   4 b   5 e   6 c

2

Suggested answers

b They could have communicated their ideas more clearly. / They should have given the designers more information.

c They should have had more realistic goals. / More clearly defined goals might have led to more success.

d The team should have tried to work together. / Better teamwork could have produced better results.

4

Suggested answer

Detachable dog sack: The sack could have worked as the material looks strong. It could have worked as the dog couldn't run away, but could still breathe. The inventor should have realised that the dog would hurt its head when the driver's door is opened.

4.3 Skills: Decision-making

Introduction

1

b, c, a

2

b, c, a

Listening 1: Renewing a contract

2
1 false   **2** false   **3** true

Listening 2: The costs

1
Anabel is not happy with the extra cost of having to pay £50 for every extra incident as well as the high flat-rate cost.
2
b and c
3
This meeting is concerned with the middle part of the process, discussing options.

Language focus: Evaluative metaphors and idioms

1
1 a   **2** b
2
1 a   **2** c   **3** d   **4** b
3
troubleshoot the problem – find exactly what the problem is
twenty-four seven – 24 hours a day, 7 days a week
high level of cover – excellent level of support
find the problem out – uncover the problem
it's down to you – it's your responsibility
getting a balance – finding a happy solution
there's just a way around it – how a solution can be found
4
Positive:
1 Looking good
5 (That's) a good way forward
7 (These are) solid plans
8 I would really welcome that.
Negative:
2 (the plans were) completely unreal
3 (the rent is) stupid
4 That's absolute madness
6 It eats into the time
5
Because a core responsibility and right of managers is to evaluate. If a subordinate does it, he/she is in danger of upsetting the manager/colleagues. This could lead to big problems in the workplace.

Writing 2: Describing a process

Introduction

1
There is a description of the diagram in exercise 1 of the Writing skill section, which follows the Introduction.
2
The arrows show that one stage follows another. The images help illustrate the meaning. Generally, diagrams and visual information help communicate complexity in a simple, immediate format.
3
1 industrial (and natural?)   **2** business (and technical?)
3 industrial   **4** business (and technical?)
5 technical (and industrial?)   **6** intellectual

Writing skill: Describe a creative problem-solving process

1
1 splitting   **2** stages   **3** main   **4** initial   **5** phase   **6** third
7 followed   **8** Since   **9** overall
2
The colon (:) is used to indicate the start of a list of phases. The semi-colon (;) is used to separate these different phases.
3
The present simple passive is used to describe processes. The passive emphasises the process, not the subject or doer of the action.

Language focus 1: Review of tenses in passive form

1
1 passive   **2** active   **3** mixed: active (*said*), passive (*has been badly planned*)   **4** active   **5** passive
2
1 present simple (passive) x 2
2 present perfect (active)
3 past simple (active), present perfect (passive)
4 present perfect (active)
5 past continuous (passive)
3
1 c   **2** a   **3** b   **4** a   **5** c
4
Suggested answer
Because he/she didn't want to name a particular person at the time he/she was speaking. Maybe the Chief Executive was speaking to a group of people – naming the person(s) who were responsible for the bad planning would be embarrassing or rude.

Language focus 2: Linkers of sequencing, structuring and providing reasons

1
Sequence: initial   third   followed
Structure: main   splitting   overall   phase   stages
Provide reasons: since
2
1 principle   **2** platform   **3** while   **4** firstly   **5** breaking up
6 preceded by
3
1 The emphasis on the initial phase of the project was market-driven, followed rapidly by a technology-based approach. / The emphasis on the initial phase of the project, followed rapidly by a technology-based approach, was market-driven.
2 Firstly, you need to undertake a redefinition of the product to satisfy the needs of the customer better than the competition.
3 I have not used the real data and model, since it is more complex and difficult to follow.

5 Organisational cultures

5.1 Theory: Understanding organisations

Language focus: Vocabulary to talk about organisations

1
1 b   **2** e   **3** f   **4** l   **5** j   **6** d   **7** k   **8** c   **9** g   **10** i
11 h   **12** a

2

Suggested answers

1 reserved, confident   **2** share schemes, sales bonus   **3** uniforms, shirt and tie   **4** subsistence, petty cash   **5** functional, divisional   **6** 'leadership, inspiration and positive change'; 'make the world a better place'   **7** the manager always praises staff for good work; staff give each other cards on their birthdays   **8** formal, aggressive   **9** staff must be at their desk by 9 am, all members must attend departmental meetings   **10** for dealing with complaints, for organising cover for staff who are absent   **11** Human Resources, Marketing   **12** research, marketing

Reading 1: What is organisational culture?

1

1 False – organisations are as different and varied as nations and societies of the world

2 False – organisations are as different and varied … NOT more different

3 False – the opposite is true, i.e. the cultures create the structures and systems

4 True – even *within* organisations, cultures will differ

Reading 2: Types of organisational culture

1

Student A: Task culture

a communication within departments

b communication across/between departments

c communication lines that have more influence

d where the power and influence lies

Student B: Role culture

a departments   **b** interactions   **c** Senior management

3

1 Task   **2** Role   **3** Role   **4** Task

5.2 Practice: Creating a successful culture

Introduction

1

a R&D   **b** Sales   **c** Production   **d** Finance

3

Cultural problems can come from misunderstanding the other group of people. For example, some groups are more direct than others and can be seen as aggressive. Some groups are more relaxed about time-keeping and can be seen as lazy. Some companies have a relaxed dress code and can be seen as unprofessional by clients. Opportunities can arise because of the greater range of perspectives.

4

1 Professional (problem)   **2** National (problem)

3 National (opportunity)   **4** Institutional (opportunity)

Listening 1: Company and culture

1

1 The company has grown a lot in recent years.

2 The culture has got better.

3 No

2

According to Ake Wikström, the company has grown a great deal, it has a vibrant open culture, it is family-owned and it has a turnover of $4 billion.

Listening 2: Company departments

R&D, Production, Marketing, Sales, Administration

Listening 3: Department cultures

1

Marketing: They have fun, They love to work together, Nothing seems to stand in their way

Production: They work three shifts a day and they don't travel

2

The boss is the key factor.

Listening 4: Creating a successful culture

1

They use the surveys to find out what engages staff.

2

1 engaged, organisation   **2** below

Listening 5: Managers and the surveys

1 It makes employees at different levels of the company talk to each other.

2 They were against them at first, but now they think they are a good thing.

Language focus: Asking questions effectively

1

1 This requires a response.   **2** This shows the listener's surprise.

3

More senior people in business have more options than more junior people, so all of these types of question could be used. However, 1, 3 and 6 are more typical of senior people. 6, and to a lesser degree 1, can have a negative effect on relationships.

4

1 a   **2** b   **3** e   **4** d   **5** f   **6** c

Intercultural analysis

1 and 2

Sales: developing/maintaining client relationships, hitting sales targets

The priority usually is to sell as much as possible, as fast as possible. Many salespeople may not have a deep knowledge of the product.

R&D: testing of products, creative thinking

The priority is often to develop products that are efficient and economical. Knowledge of and interest in the sales or marketing aspects are often not the priority.

Marketing: promoting the product, researching the market

The priority is dealing with product promotion, costs and making the product attractive to potential customers/clients. How the product is made, or its contents, may not be the main concern.

5.3 Skills: Dealing with problems across departments

Introduction

2

Suggested answers

a They need to appreciate the importance of customers.

b People should try to solve the problems themselves.

c They need to consider the needs of the customers.

d They should attempt to predict and prevent problems, rather than waiting for them to happen.

e This has a direct relationship to their salary (usually about customers, so similar to **a**).

f They need to change the way they think.

g They need to listen more and see issues from others' viewpoints.

The underlying issue with all these extracts is that the staff need to change their attitude, be more flexible and responsive, and consider the customers' needs more.

Critical analysis

2

Many managers argue that if the different departments in a company are more integrated and understand each other more, efficiency will be improved.

Listening 1: Introducing the problem

1 They are too focused on their technical work.

2 They need to consider the customers more.

3 They don't think they are part of the process (of managing the project).

Listening 2: Specific issues

1 The technical staff don't see the problems as their responsibility.

2 If the customer doesn't call them back they should call them again.

Listening 3: Reaching agreement

1 One who considers sales and the customers.

2 They usually don't call, but send an email. It might be a problem because a phone call is more personal (and they don't want to speak directly to the customer).

Language focus: Strategically summarising a position

1

All the phrases can be used in strategic summaries apart from: What do you mean … ? I don't understand, to be honest …

2

It's mostly about ownership; I think, to be honest with you, Doz; which is what I just said; No, I'm not saying that; I'm not saying that; I'm just saying; I just think.

They enable her to persuade the technical director in a clear but not overly aggressive way.

3

Suggested answers

1 I'm not saying your colleagues are lazy, but what I am saying is they could work longer hours.

2 What I mean is, we don't disagree with your proposal. But my point is that we need some more time to think about it.

3 We're not saying that your staff don't think about sales, but we are saying they could think more.

4 My point is not that your staff don't know about technical issues, but that the company would benefit if they had more understanding.

6 Working across cultures

6.1 Theory: Culture and individual strategies in business

Introduction

1

Quote 1: When you are working in another country you should show respect and interest in the host culture. [opinion]

Quote 2: Cultural barriers can lose you a significant amount of business. [fact] Quote 3: It is important to build relationships with customers. [opinion]

Listening 1: What is rapport management?

1 Rapport management concerns managing the relationships between people.

2 It's important in any situation.

Listening 2: Face, rights and problems

1

A

2

A, C, D

3

Being treated negatively by others and people not meeting our expectations.

4

a personal/social value, sense of worth, credibility, dignity, honour, reputation, competence

b personal/social entitlements, fairness, consideration, social inclusion/exclusion

5

1 sociality rights   **2** face   **3** face   **4** both

Language focus 1: Vocabulary related to culture

1

1 b   **2** g   **3** d   **4** c   **5** e   **6** f   **7** a

2

Suggested answers

trust, synergy, conflict, respect, intercultural awareness

3

Primarily face, but also sociality rights, rapport and dignity

Listening 3: Email anecdote

1 China and Britain

2 He didn't think it was appropriate for him to be sent the same email as his subordinates.

3 Primarily face

Language focus 2: Reporting verbs

1

1 h   **2** f   **3** e   **4** g   **5** d   **6** a   **7** c   **8** b

2

Verb + *to* + infinitive	Verb + obj. + *for* + *-ing*	Verb + *-ing*	Verb + *for* + *-ing*
encourage promise refuse offer agree	thank	deny	apologise

3

1 She agreed to do it.
2 They refused to go to the Liverpool site.
3 He apologised for not realising.
4 She offered to help.
5 They promised to make sure the companies would get a copy of the magazine.
6 She thanked them for cleaning up the website.
7 He denied mentioning a price.
8 She encouraged him to apply for the job.

6.2 Practice: Multicultural mergers

Introduction

2

There are many unsuccessful relationships, such as Volvo/Renault, with Volvo paying Renault £120 million; AT&T and Olivetti also failed. Successful examples include Sony's joint venture with Ericsson and the strategic alliance between KLM and Northwest Airlines. Reasons for failed relationships include communication breakdown, loss of trust and lack of shared opportunities.

Transferable skill: Recognising genres

1

Academic journal articles usually try to inform other researchers and interested people about their findings or persuade them of the validity of these findings. A company report for shareholders should report on certain aspects of the company's performance that are relevant to the shareholders and potential shareholders.

2

Extract 1 is from the Nissan website and Extract 2 is from a journal. The metaphors and positive language of Extract 1 (e.g. *boast a wide variety, All members … build, drive sustainable growth*) contrast with the more academic language (e.g. *provides strong evidence, obstacles can be overcome, employ an intercultural communication framework*) of the journal article. The journal article features many more passive forms, whereas the company website text has more active verbs.

3

The steps include building relationships, sharing experiences, listening to and understanding different viewpoints, recognising, accepting and using cultural differences to create synergy, implementing appropriate structures, and using an intercultural communication framework.

Reading 1: How can cultural differences be reconciled?

1

1 Adopt one partner's culture as dominant.
2 Separate/limit shared activities.
3 Involve all partners at all levels, and work towards better integration.

4

When the different organisations have different values and management styles this can lead to problems. Problems can be avoided if the organisations show respect to each other and work closely together.

Reading 2: The alliance's principles

1

Suggested answers
There is a lot of overlap between trust and fairness.
Trust: 3, 6   Fairness: 1, 2, 4, 5

2

a 1 **b** 4 **c** 3 **d** 5 **e** 2 **f** 6

Language focus: Nouns to make positive and negative judgements

1

Positive: synergy/synergies, opportunity/opportunities, transparency/transparencies, chance(s)
Negative: conflict(s), problem(s)

2

Written: synergy/synergies, opportunity/opportunities, conflict(s), transparency/transparencies
Spoken: chance(s), problem(s)
The written nouns tend to have more syllables and be longer; this is a common feature of written language compared with speech.

3

These are the most common collocations (others are possible too):
create/seek synergy/synergies between/among/with
seize/explore/exploit (an) opportunity/opportunities for/to
give/stand/create/have/get (a) chance/chances to/of
raise/resolve/avoid conflict/conflicts between/of (especially conflict(s) of interests)
solve/cause/have (a) problem/problems with
inhibit/lack/enhance transparency/transparencies in/between

6.3 Skills: International team-building

Listening 1: The stages of building a team

1

Forming: the initial stage where the team gets to know each other and makes some provisional guidelines.
Storming: after forming, the group usually finds that some of the initial guidelines and expectations or behaviour are unsuitable. Conflict is necessary and inevitable at this stage. Following this, the guidelines need to be revised.
Norming: the group begins to work together, having overcome the main issues in the previous stage.
Performing: the group performs effectively and efficiently, and productivity is high.

2

1 To remember that the guidelines you start with may not be the final guidelines
2 (Hopefully) three months

Listening 2: An international team meeting

1 He thinks once a month is best.
2 This is from the storming stage – he is expressing strong concerns about the procedures the team will use and the communication in the team (particularly from Peter).

Language focus: Metaphors of movement

1
'Moving forward' means making good progress; 'going nowhere' means making no progress

2
They are all true. Because metaphors are often indirect and rely on shared understanding, they are a powerful way of developing a good relationship between the speakers (they bring the speakers together). Many metaphors in business show progress, or lack of it, and fulfil the crucial steps of showing and judging how communication is moving towards the goals.

3
1 a desire for progress   2 a lack of progress   3 a lack of progress
4 progress   5 progress   6 a lack of progress

4
go ahead (decide to do it); explore (discuss); go over the top (do something too much); keep things moving (maintain production); stop there (not do any more)

5
Examples include *press ahead … work around* the issue … I think we're there.

Critical analysis

Possible negative aspects might include problems with developing trust, understanding disagreements, and correctly interpreting behaviour.

Writing 3: Argument-led writing

Introduction

3
For: 2, 3, 5   Against: 1, 4

Writing skill: Arguments for and against

Arguments for privatisation	Arguments against privatisation
Easy to raise rates for upkeep	High costs for the poor
Easy to experiment	High profits for a few investors
Governments can use money for other things	Good companies might sell to bad ones
	Concerns over quality of service

Language focus: Reason, result and contrast

1
1 Presents a reason   2 Makes a contrast   3 States a result
4 Makes a contrast

2
Suggested answers
Roads and bridges are public services and so should be free, therefore they should be owned by the state and not private companies.
The more privatisation the better because a free market is necessary for economic growth.

Governments should raise funds by selling services to private companies even though some people believe that the state should control services like roads, education and healthcare.
Governments consider the least well-off, private companies do not since the government has a duty to the whole public while private companies only need to consider their shareholders.
Lower taxes are better than free roads and bridges, so I believe that they should be privatised.

7 Change management

7.1 Theory: DICE theory

Language focus 1: Idiomatic language

1
1 h   2 g   3 e   4 f   5 c   6 a   7 b   8 d
2
1 at the coal face   2 peter out / run into trouble
3 crave the limelight   4 run into trouble

Reading: DICE theory – the hard side of change management

1
4, 6, 7, 8
3
1 False ('Companies make the mistake of worrying mostly about the time it will take to implement change programs.')
2 False ('Executives often make the mistake of assuming that because someone is a good, well-liked manager, he or she will also make a decent team leader.')
3 True
4 False ('Ideally, no one's workload should increase more than 10%. Go beyond that, and the initiative will probably run into trouble.')

Critical analysis

Suggested answers
1 It can be very difficult to measure the different factors in DICE theory. 'Duration' is perhaps the easiest to measure, but integrity, commitment and effort can be very difficult to measure and may vary across time and from individual to individual.
2 Soft factors are perhaps best measured by the results that they achieve over the duration of a project.

Language focus 2: Cohesion and referencing

1
1 c   2 e   3 f   4 b   5 a   6 d
2
1 d   2 c   3 b   4 a   5 e   6 f
3
Suggested answers
1 … it is very important to try to explain clearly why the company is doing it.
2 … there are hard factors which focus on measurable indicators such as time and cost, and soft factors such as motivation and culture that are difficult to measure but are just as important.
3 … sometimes change can be very damaging to a company's day-to-day business.

7.2 Practice: Implementing change

Introduction

3

Punish those workers who make mistakes.

Listening 1: An overview of the interview

1 A **2** C **3** D **4** B

Listening 2: Dealing with resistors to change

1 Companies need to involve employees in the change process, and it needs to be well managed.

2 Only a very small number will be resistant.

Listening 3: Successfully implementing change

1 It's important to see colleagues as customers as well as those people who buy the product, i.e. internal and external customers.

2 By asking 500–600 employees from all levels in the company what type of company they wanted Laird to be.

Transferable skill: Non-verbal communication

Suggested answers

1 There are various forms of NVC, including touching, kissing, shaking hands, bowing, head movements, facial expressions, smiling, hand movements, gestures and the distance between speakers.

2 Different forms of NVC across cultures can have very different meanings. For example, slapping someone on the back is seen as aggressive in some cultures and friendly in others.

3 NVC is different between cultures, and this can often be the cause of failure to communicate effectively, and can lead to misunderstandings.

6 In business it is essential that people show sensitivity towards and understanding of other cultures in order to develop good relationships.

Language focus: Present perfect simple and present perfect continuous

1

The present perfect continuous cannot be used to talk about a single action. The present perfect simple is used to focus on a result.

2

(PPS = present perfect simple; PPC = present perfect continuous)

a both **b** PPC **c** PPS **d** PPC **e** both **f** PPS

3

1 d **2** f **3** e **4** a / e **5** b **6** c

4

been buying cranes – repeated action; have never ever paid – single action

5

Suggested answers

1 We've been coming here for years, and we've never had a problem.

2 We've been shopping there since 2009 and have met the manager once.

3 I've been buying these products since I was a child, and I've only made a single complaint.

6

1 How long have you been working here? ('have you worked' is also possible)

2 How many items have you produced since last week?

3 You've received three complaints since last month.

4 How many sick days have you taken in the past six months?

5 The company's been losing money since last year.

7.3 Skills: External negotiating

Listening 1: Complaints

1 Five

2 The number of markets that have been out of stock for a period of time

Listening 2: Discussing the complaints procedure

1 She disagrees.

2 He agrees that the current way of recording complaints should be changed.

Listening 3: Compliance complaints

1 She disagrees.

2 Perhaps because the present system seems unfair, and by agreeing now it may be easier to get Ada to change her mind about other points (a win–win approach).

Language focus: Organising spoken language – head, body, tail

1

But / the figures are already in a database anyway / aren't they?

So / the document will have a final review before it's sent / you mean?

3

Heads: Right, You know, Well, I see what you mean but, I mean, OK, As far as I'm concerned, But, So, Yeah, I'm sorry to trouble you, Erm, Basically, In my opinion

Tails: Right, OK, Yeah (all with rising intonation), you know what I mean, do you see what I mean, as far as I'm concerned (up-down intonation)

Both: Right, OK

4

True: 1, 2 ,3 , 4   False: 5

5

Ada: … absolutely

Giles: Right, Yes, now,

Helen: Basically

Critical analysis

Suggested answer

Speaking in a written style can come across to the listener as too formal and may cause confusion if you are speaking to non-native speakers.

8 Project management

8.1 Theory: The principles of project management

Introduction

1

deadline – specific timescales; budget – cost constraints; quality objective – particular benefit

3

Suggested answer

If you make the deadline tighter then either quality will suffer or costs will increase. For example, you would need to bring in more staff or outside contractors to finish in time. If the budget was cut, either quality would suffer or the time taken to complete the project would increase. For example, you would need to spend more time finding alternative lower-cost suppliers and contractors.

4

Suggested answer

In all cases, project managers would need to design a fully costed plan, put a team together of people with the right skills, and consult and involve a number of external organisations to realise the project.

Language focus 1: Project stages

1

1 a **2** b **3** e **4** c **5** d **6** g **7** f

2

Suggested answer

It is very expensive to make changes when the project is in operation. It is therefore much better to spend longer on the planning stages, where, by comparison, changes on paper are not problematic.

Transferable skill: Engaging with the text

2

Author agrees: 5, 6, 7, 8, 9, 10
Author disagrees: 1, 2, 3, 4

Reading: The principles of project management

2

Suggested questions and answers

1 When is the best time to screen out unwanted projects? – As soon as possible. (Part 1)
2 Why is it a good idea to use the same generic stages for all types of project? – The process is familiar and easier – there is no need for people to learn a new approach. (Part 3)
3 What kind of benefits can creative solutions produce? – They can result in dramatic cost savings and reduce delivery times by half. (Part 4)
4 What can happen if you ignore stakeholders? – The project can fail. (Part 5)
5 How important is risk management? – It's fundamentally important. (Part 7)
6 What's the reason why many projects are late or not completed? – Too many ideas are added. (Part 8)

Language focus 2: Verb/noun combinations for project planning

1

screen out unwanted projects, gather information, increase confidence, slash delivery times, cut costs, engaging the stakeholders, encourage teamwork

2

1 slash delivery times **2** encourage teamwork
3 engaging the stakeholders **4** cut costs **5** gather information
6 increase confidence

Critical analysis

Suggested answers

1 One of the dangers of spending a lot of time on planning is that too much time can be spent on planning rather than implementing the project. If a lot of time is spent on planning, members of the team may start to feel demotivated and feel that the project is not moving forward. It should also be remembered that you can't plan for every eventuality.
2 Many companies have social events to build teams. Some managers also feel that if you have a clear set of goals at the start of the project and choose the right people, frequent meetings will not be necessary.

8.2 Practice: Russian oil industry – Sakhalin-1 Project

Reading: Sakhalin – the place and the project

3

1 g **2** l **3** f **4** a **5** i **6** b **7** e **8** k **9** h **10** d **11** j
12 c

Listening 1: Project overview

1

1 Moving around the site **2** Initial project planning issues
3 Logistical complexity **4** Working conditions
5 Technical and engineering issues **6** Health and safety issues
7 Living conditions

2

Health, safety and environmental

4

1 false **2** false **3** false **4** false **5** false **6** false **7** true
8 false **9** true **10** false

Listening 2: Focusing on teamwork

3

1 There are language problems and differences in the type of food different nationalities want to eat.
2 The company / HR can organise team parties, different types of recreation and bring in catering for the different nationalities.
3 This is not a problem if the manager is nice and polite.
4 Provide good working conditions, listen to the team and have a team party once a month.

Intercultural analysis

1

Suggested answer

There is sometimes conflict between project managers and health and safety inspectors because they have different goals. Project managers will want to finish a project on time and to budget. Health and safety measures can take time and money which can lead to extra costs and time for the project manager.

2

1 project managers **2** health and safety officers
3 project managers **4** health and safety officers

Language focus: Future perfect and future continuous

1

1 future perfect **2** future continuous **3** future perfect
4 future continuous

2

1 future continuous **2** future perfect

3

Suggested answers

I will have written a report by the end of the day.

This time next week I will be studying English.

I will have paid all my bills by the end of the month.

In a year's time I will be working for another company.

My country will have elected a new government by the end of the year.

I will be working in Paris in a month's time.

This time next year we will be working on a new project.

4

1 will be working **2** will have gone **3** will have found
4 will be seeing **5** will have finished **6** will be feeling

8.3 Skills: Maintaining relationships

Introduction

2

Suggested answers

If possible, I think it might be worth considering changing my salary …

If it's not a bad time, perhaps we might have a talk about my salary?

A friend of mine who has the same post at company X gets a 25% higher salary than me, and was saying the other day they were looking for people …

3

Indirect language in bold:

So **I guess** the best **way forward** is **just** to **kind of leave you** to **sort of digest** this. And then **you know,** we'll **perhaps** wait for you to **come back to us** about the next stage …

The functions include showing respect, avoiding conflict, not being too direct in requests, and showing that you are working together. A direct way to say this would be: 'It is now your responsibility to contact us when you are ready.'

4

Directness in international business can be useful as it makes sure that the message is clear.

Listening: A sales meeting between IT companies

2

1 By this afternoon or tomorrow
2 That there is no hurry
3 Perhaps to emphasise indirectly that the two companies have a good relationship

Critical analysis

2

In the recording, the participants tried to build a relationship by showing that they were flexible ('Whenever. There's no hurry'), being indirect ('So I guess the best way forward …') and showing that they are working together ('… we'll just get together and we'll work everything out then').

3

The speakers are indirect because they are building a business relationship and want to show that they are working together and support each other.

Language focus: Signalling identities through 'we'

1

1 exclusive **2** inclusive

2

1 c **2** b **3** d **4** e **5** a

3

All uses are exclusive until Liam says '… where it's going to please us all'. After that they are all inclusive.

4

Better relationships increase the chances of long-term business success, for example through customer loyalty, more trust, and more support when needed.

Intercultural analysis

The listener may feel that the speaker is saying that the British are polite and is suggesting that people of the listener's nationality are not polite. A better way of saying it would be: 'I think in Britain, as in other countries, it is important to be polite.'

Writing 4: Describing graphs

Introduction

4

1 e **2** d **3** b **4** c **5** a

The highest to the lowest industry sectors for carbon emissions are: power, manufacturing, transport, agriculture, waste disposal.

Writing skill: Describing graphs

1

1 The graph shows us how the level of carbon emissions will change if governments are willing to follow regulations.
2 It tells us that the changes are categorised by industry.
3 The Y axis shows the level of emissions in gigatonnes of CO_2. The X axis shows the timeframe between 2000 and 2050.
4 Emissions steadily increase, peaking around 2030, and then steadily decrease.
5 The highest level of emissions is around 2020 and 2030. The lowest is around 2000 and 2050.
6 *Suggested answers*
Power is consistently the biggest cause of emissions over the period and also shows the biggest amount of changes.
Manufacturing rises from 2000 to 2025 and then decreases steadily.
Transport remains at roughly the same level across the time period, although there is a slight decrease.
Land use remains at the same level until 2025 and then decreases steadily.
Agriculture remains at roughly the same level across the period; however, there is a slight increase from 2030 to 2050.
Waste remains at almost the same level across the whole time period.

2

Suggested answer

Even though emissions rise considerably over the first 25 years, by 2050 they are lower than 2000 levels.

Language focus: Comparisons and contrasts

1

1 The percentage of male and female executives is ~~particularly~~ exactly the same.
2 The company faced a considerably ~~low~~ lower return once it didn't sell enough to break even.

3

1 A is considerably / somewhat / slightly / a great deal bigger than B.
2 A is approximately / virtually / exactly / about the same as B.
3 A is totally / completely / quite / not very different from B.
4 A is approximately / virtually / about as big as B.
5 A is approximately / virtually / about / by far / slightly the biggest.

4

1 By far the ~~The considerably~~ biggest producer of carbon is power.
2 The power industry produces considerably ~~exactly~~ more CO$_2$ than other industries.
3 The building industry is not unique in reducing its carbon emissions over the 50-year period.
4 In 2020, the power industry will have the highest CO$_2$ emissions. Furthermore ~~On the other hand~~, it will have greatly increased compared to 2000.

5

1 In the graph, CO$_2$ emissions in the waste industry rise very slightly ~~and then fall~~ over the 50-year period, whereas they rise and fall considerably ~~steadily~~ in the power industry.
2 Overall, CO$_2$ emissions gradually increase from 2000 to 20~~40~~50 in the agricultural industry.
3 Both the ~~agricultural~~ transport and manufacturing industries' emissions peak at around 2025, and then decline steadily.

9 E-marketing

9.1 Theory: The 4Cs of marketing and e-marketing

Introduction

3

Suggested answer

High street shops may turn into demonstration showrooms where people can try out the products, but the purchase, delivery and initial customer research would be done online.

4

Suggested answers

Advantages: The virtual assistant can give instant responses to customers' questions. All calls can be logged by the company which means that they can use this information to develop the service with regards to what their customers are asking for.

Disadvantages: Some customers will prefer to speak to a real person, so they are more likely to buy their tickets from a telephone service. If customers have an unusual request it is unlikely a virtual assistant will be able to answer it.

Language focus 1: Marketing terms

1

Online store: e-retail shop, e-tailer, dot.com, virtual store
High street store: retail outlet, bricks retailer, physical store
Combined online and high street store: multi-channel retailer, bricks and clicks operation

2

1 product   2 place   3 price   4 promotion
5 target customers   6 marketing mix

3

1 customer's perspective   2 producer's perspective   3 cost to the customer   4 customer wants and needs   5 communication with the customer   6 convenience to the customer

Reading: The 4Cs of e-retail and retail

1

C1 3 6   **C2** 4 8   **C3** 2 7   **C4** 1 5

2

1 Web atmosphere such as music and video clips
2 The perception is that prices should be lower online
3 Multi-channel
4 Good feelings and/or solutions to problems
5 Retailers are closer to the customer and can get more feedback
6 Location for a retailer is where to set up shop to minimise travel times for customers, provide convenient parking, etc.; for the pure e-tailer, the location is virtual but needs to be easy to find using search engines
7 High costs of carriage
8 An e-tailer (they can provide a wider and deeper range)

Language focus 2: E-marketing terms

1

Communication with the customer: 1, 2, 4
Convenience for the customer: 3

2

Suggested answers

Database marketing: analysis of web traffic visiting company site
Customer relationship marketing: sending targeted direct emails, monthly newsletters, special offers, online surveys, virtual assistants. (Note that all the quantitative information flowing from this is analysed using Database marketing.)
Web optimisation: fast download speeds, minimising time that customers have to wait for information, cross-linking website to other parties
Social media marketing: setting up a profile of a product on a social networking site, using mobile phones and sending emails with games and prize competitions

Transferable skill: Developing critical thinking skills

1 Pro 4Cs. There is an implicit criticism of the 4Ps in the first sentence of each of the four sections, where a feeling is created that the 4Ps are something a 'company does to a customer'. There is an implication that this is simplistic and an old-fashioned 'hard sell' approach.
2 Many people would find this assumption invalid. For example, someone might simply see an advert, buy the product and not want any more contact with the company. Direct mail is often described as 'junk mail'.

3 A possible criticism might be: 'The 4Cs is exactly the same as the 4Ps. There is no real difference. A 4P approach is just as customer focused as the 4C. False differences are being created.'

4 You could say that different industries have different dynamics and that in your experience certain industries are customer centred (such as retail) but some are not, such as educational institutions perhaps.

9.2 Practice: The benefits of selling on- and offline

Listening 1: A definition of e-marketing

1 email **2** mobile phone **3** relationship **4** approaches
5 channels

Listening 2: Online communication and sales channels

1
1, 3 and 4
2
1 false **2** false **3** true

Listening 3: The benefits of online selling

1 exactly what their customers want **2** faster memory
3 stock **4** the middleman

Listening 4: Problems with online sales channels

1
1 biggest companies **2** smaller companies **3** direct and online
4 it's cheapest (best deal) – buying is an economic decision
5 Many people need to touch and feel the product – buying is not just an economic decision, it is also psychological and emotional.

Language focus 1: Review standard conditionals

1

Type of conditional	Grammar	Use
Zero	If + present simple in both clauses	To talk about a general truth
First	If + present simple / will + infinitive	To talk about a likely result in the future
Second	If + past simple / would + infinitive	The hypothetical conditional – to talk about a result if the present or future was different
Third	If + past perfect / would + have + past participle	The past conditional – to talk about the hypothetical unreal past

2
1 First **2** Zero **3** Third **4** Second

Language focus 2: Mixed conditionals

1
Suggested answers
2 … it would be difficult selling to first-time customers who didn't have a computer.
3 … they wouldn't be so successful in this market.
4 … they would not be making many sales to business customers.

2
Suggested answers
2 … they would have risked losing customers to their competitors.
3 … Dell wouldn't have changed their e-marketing strategy.
4 … customers wouldn't have to wait long for their computers to be delivered.

9.3 Skills: Organising a presentation

Introduction

2
Content: 1, 3, 5, 8   Style: 2, 4, 6, 7

Listening 1: Beginning an e-presentation

1 Correct order: 3, 2, 1, 4
2 The presentation is aimed at prospective customers, i.e. large companies with HQs in Europe
3 'HQs' refers to Headquarters

Listening 2: Developing an e-presentation

2
Correct order: 8, 7, 6, 9, 5
Missing information on slides: **a** customers **b** Globalisation
c Think big

Critical analysis

1 *Suggested answer*
The e-presentation is excellent on a number of points. Philip Weiss keeps things simple, sounds enthusiastic and presents the information in a logical order. He doesn't speak too quickly and sticks to his time limit. As this is an e-presentation, it is impossible to judge the level of eye contact and the use of body language.

Language focus: Introducing and linking slides

1
1 f **2** d **3** e **4** b **5** h **6** g **7** i **8** c **9** a
2
1 … Managing Director of ZN.
2 … who we are, how we can help HQs meet their challenges and what opportunities the Internet created for them …
3 … Brussels …
4 … helping international headquarters develop strategies on the Internet.
5 … today?
6 … the last ten years.
7 … you?
8 … understanding your business objectives and priorities …
9 … to hearing from you through email or phone.
3
Suggested answers
1 Who are the customers of tomorrow?
2 So what do we expect our sales to be looking like over the next two years?
3 How will our sales break down in our major country markets?
4 Why did we fail to break into the Asian markets last year?

10 Branding

10.1 Theory: What is branding?

Introduction

2

Possible answers

Car: Porsche

Sunglasses: Prada, Ray-Ban

Keyboard and mouse: Apple

Sound system: Bang & Olufsen, Bose

Language focus: Branding expressions

1

brand image, licensed brand, brand awareness, brand equity, brand extension, manufacturer's brand, own brand, brand positioning, brand repositioning, luxury brand

2

1 brand awareness **2** brand image **3** brand equity

4 brand extension **5** manufacturer's brand **6** own brand

7 licensed brand **8** brand positioning **9** luxury brand

10 brand repositioning

Listening 1: Introduction to a lecture on branding

1

Slide A

Listening 2: Defining branding

1

Product

1 satisfies customer needs **2** functional

Brand

3 further **4** name, term, symbol, design **5** good sorts of services

6 of grabbing our attention

2

A product is something that aims to satisfy the needs of consumers. A brand also tries to satisfy consumer needs; however, it also tries to differentiate itself from similar products by its use of symbols and images which try to grab the attention of the consumer.

Listening 3: To brand or not to brand?

2

Advantages for customers

1 can be easily and quickly recognised by consumers

2 gives consumers assurance of quality and performance

3 builds trust

4 emotional benefits

Advantages for companies

1 increases profits substantially because of price premiums

2 gives higher market share and ability to build market share

3 provides loyal customers

4 provides avenues for future growth

5 allows for segmenting markets

6 provides legal protection

10.2 Practice: The Havaianas brand

Reading: A company with desired brands

1

B – Understanding its brands enabled Alpargatas to increase its gross revenues by over 132%

2

1 T **2** F **3** F **4** F

3

1 beyond **2** boost **3** extensions **4** transmit **5** asset

6 perceptions **7** attributed to **8** gross revenues

Critical analysis

2 *Suggested answers*

There is a general perception among many consumers (knowingly or unknowingly) that branded products cost more, are better quality, have a more favourable image, give better customer service and leave the customer with a feel-good sense of well-being in comparison to non-branded products. Many customers are happy to pay more for these extras. Customers are buying feelings and emotions more than a simple functional product when they choose a brand.

Language focus: Describing brands and products

1

1 B **2** C **3** B **4** C

2

1 product **2** pleasure **3** passion **4** pleasure

5 comfort **6** colours **7** comfort

Transferable skill: Expressing visual ideas

2

1 The Cube – For those who want to know the latest Havaianas news: a space that always has a different story to tell.

2 Cylinder – Cheerfulness, happiness and fun are always the best accessories to keep handy. Check out the Havaianas handbags. / Check out the Havaianas handbags. Cheerfulness, happiness and fun are always the best accessories to keep handy.

3

The descriptions on the Havaianas site:

'Street market stall – Similar to those on an ordinary street market, it is a tribute to Havaianas' popular origins.'

'Havaianas customisables – You pick the sole, strap and pin and your Havaianas are ready in minutes.'

10.3 Skills: Using persuasive communication in meetings

Critical analysis

1

Vision: management strategy

Culture: how employees feel about the company, the way staff behave

Image: what customers think about the company, public opinion

Listening: Address to the staff at a hotel

2
1 background to the change   **2** a story   **3** the point of the story
4 practising the standards
3
1 false   **2** false   **3** true   **4** false   **5** true   **6** false

Language focus 1: The language of persuasion

1
Stressed words
1 extra, is   **2** employees, standards, life
3
1 We've committed ourselves that this has to happen.
2 We're a company that manages with our heart first.
3 We're a people company.

Language focus 2: Using *if* to persuade and direct staff

1
Sentence 1 – a conditional sentence; sentence 2 – politely gives an order
2
Suggested answers
If you see a customer, you always smile at him or her.
If you see a customer you recognise, you greet him or her by name.
If you see a customer with luggage, you offer to carry their bags.
If a customer is sitting in reception, you ask them if they want a drink.

Writing 5: Persuasive communication online

Introduction

1
Customers are looking for the benefits of the product, i.e. what the product can do for them and how it can make them feel. They are not necessarily interested in the product itself.
2
We need to focus on the benefits in the product descriptions and not give a long list of 'wonderful' features and facts about the product.
4
Describing features not benefits is appropriate for a technical audience or when the writer or speaker knows that the customer is very familiar with the product technology, characteristics, etc. and knows the benefits of these things.
5
To persuade people to come round to your point of view, it is more effective to look at things as if you are 'in their shoes'.

Language focus 1: The language of advertising

2
1 B   **2** A   **3** A   **4** D   **5** D   **6** C

Language focus 2: Changing features into benefits

Suggested answers
2 Bose music systems come with 0% finance, so you will be able to enjoy great quality music today and spread your payments over 12 months at no extra charge.
3 NatWest Private Banking has 24-hour customer service, which means you can call us any time day or night at a time convenient to you.

4 American Express Travel Insurance has over 150 years' experience, which means you can trust that we will always be there for you.
5 With easyJet there is no weight limit on hand luggage, giving you the freedom to bring back more purchases from your holiday or trip without the worry of checking them in.
6 Cif cleaning products are a strong yet gentle cream, allowing you to clean through dirt but not damage or scratch your kitchen or bathroom surfaces.

11 Accounting

11.1 Theory: Activity-based costing (ABC)

Introduction

1
Suggested answers
To be up to date with technical developments in their field; so that they are working on the same platform as other institutions and clients they work with; to ensure that the software they are using does not become redundant
2
Suggested answers
- the cost of purchasing the software
- the cost of installing the software
- the cost of training staff to use it properly
3
Suggested answers
- being up to date with technical developments
- ensures that the organisation is working on the same platform as their clients
- speeds up processes in the long term
4
Companies do cost-benefit analyses to see if the project is worthwhile. If the benefits are not higher than the costs then the project is probably not worth pursuing.

Language focus 1: Key financial terms

1
1 c   **2** d   **3** b   **4** a
2
Overheads: rent, insurance, salaries of staff on a permanent contract, salaries of freelance staff
Fixed costs: rent, insurance, salaries of staff on a permanent contract
Variable costs: raw materials, salaries of freelance staff
Direct costs: raw materials

Reading: The advantages and disadvantages of activity-based costing

1
Advantages: The development of software has made ABC easier, ABC can improve business processes, it is needed for any re-engineering programme, it can also save the company a lot of money
Disadvantages: ABC is not easy to introduce, the information that is needed might not be readily available
2
1 quite difficult   **2** before   **3** simpler
4 that software for this is available on the market
5 for the improvement of business processes

Language focus 2: Gerunds

1

1 interested in knowing   **2** good at seeing
3 (the) challenge of managing, experience of seeing
4 kept (keep) on talking   **5** (as a) result of seeing
6 focus on bringing   **7** (a) problem in finding

2

Adjective + preposition + gerund: interested in knowing, good at seeing
Verb + preposition + gerund: kept (keep) on talking, focus on bringing
Noun + preposition + gerund: (the) challenge of managing, experience of seeing, (as a) result of seeing, (a) problem in finding

3

Verb + preposition + gerund: pilot a scheme before implementing
Noun + preposition + gerund: (a) method of assigning, a prerequisite for improving

4

There is no difference in the meaning in these different styles, but a little in the emphasis. We put the things which are most important right at the start of the sentence; this puts more emphasis on it.

5

1 Allocating costs accurately is important.
2 Breaking down activities into their individual parts is a necessity / is necessary.
3 Introducing ABC saved Chrysler hundreds of millions of dollars.

6

Suggested answers
Making a note of useful vocabulary and storing it carefully is essential; attending lessons regularly is important; speaking English whenever you have a chance can help you learn; watching films in English is a good way to learn more vocabulary; speaking and writing to friends in English can improve your fluency.

Output: Comparing traditional cost accounting and ABC

Stage 1
Advantages: 1, 4, 5, 6, 8
Disadvantages: 2, 3, 7

11.2 Practice: Cost and price

Listening 1: The business of flying

1
1, 2, 3, 5, 6
2
1 46,000,000   **2** 737   **3** 180   **4** 70%   **5** $9 to $10 billion
3
UIA have a 30% stake in passenger handling with Swissport, and they provide aircraft maintenance for other airlines.

Listening 2: Costs and prices

1
1 Cost   **2** product   **3** unit cost   **4** pay
2
competition

Listening 3: Control over costs

1 and 2

Costs	Controlled by
fuel	suppliers
aircraft	supply and demand
labour costs	airlines
labour productivity	airlines
aircraft utilisation	airlines

Transferable skill: Visualising ideas

1
Visual thinking can be a very useful way of communicating ideas when it's hard to find the correct words. It can also form the basis of describing a process using diagrams and visuals in a way that is more real for the listener than simply using words.

3
1 the hidden costs   **2** the location of the airport

Language focus: Different types of costs

1
1 b   **2** e   **3** f   **4** a   **5** c   **6** d
2
Direct costs: aircraft, staff, airport charges, passenger handling charges, catering charges
Indirect costs: depreciation, insurance, navigation charges, maintenance, fuel charges
Central costs: head office costs, press office costs, interest charges

11.3 Skills: Developing internal relationships

Introduction

1
Any type of communication is possible, but these are the more common patterns:
manager to manager 3, 7
staff to manager 8, 12
manager to staff 1, 4, 5, 6
staff to staff 2, 9, 10, 11

2
Suggested answer
Numbers 4, 10 and 12 all threaten a person's 'face' (see Unit 6) and are probably the most difficult to perform.

4
Suggested answer
Many of these actions involve potential 'face threats', that is they can hurt the other person's feelings and sense of worth. Therefore, people use politeness to lessen the force.

Listening: Commenting on a meeting

1 Jenny thought that she was going to be criticised in the meeting, but was pleasantly surprised as she found it motivating.
2 The old approach was to criticise and threaten the staff, and it was unsuccessful.
3 They will discuss their problems and see how they can make improvements.
4 They appear good at the moment, but were probably not in the past.

Intercultural analysis

Perhaps Jenny wants Marco to have a positive opinion of her, or she thinks he lacks confidence, or she wants to be promoted. Reacting to such comments is a sensitive issue because managers often have to balance having good relations with maintaining the respect of the staff.

Language focus: Polite language

1
2 type B 3 type A
2
1 A 2 A 3 A 4 B 5 B 6 A
3
1 b 2 c 3 e 4 f 5 a 6 d
4

Jenny pays compliments to Marco: 'And now we get to the end and I feel great';' … it was a good way of leading the meeting'; 'every time we have a meeting with you … it's very motivating'
Marco shows solidarity: 'We want to come up with solutions'
Marco ends the meeting on a positive note: 'If we address it the right way, it will happen'
Marco thanks Jenny and Veronique at the end of the meeting: 'OK, thank you both'; 'Thanks for coming'

12 Microfinance

12.1 Theory: The concepts of microfinance

Reading: Microfinance FAQs

1
1 E 2 C 3 D 4 A 5 F 6 B 7 G

Transferable skill: Strategies for understanding unknown words

2
1 envisions 2 collateral 3 household-based entrepreneurs
4 entities 5 requirement 6 capitalise on 7 the destitute
8 population density 9 operate sustainably
3
1 a, c, d, g 2 b 3 f 4 e
4
Suggested answers
a no monthly income b very small business c not regular (for example, not every month) d not dependable or not reliable
e sense of taking control of your life f not being affected by something g not appropriate or not correct for a particular situation
5
Suggested answers
unlikely, microchip, irresistible, unbelievable, self-employed, meaningless, indecisive

Language focus: Used to, be used to and get used to

1
1 active verb 2 active verb 3 active verb
4 adjective 5 adjective
2
1 The public used to park illegally in our company car park. / The public is used to parking illegally in our company car park.
2 I prefer people who are used to working hard.
3 She used to spend a lot of money on holidays.
4 He was used to getting money from his parents. / He used to get …

12.2 Practice: Grameen Bank

Introduction

1
Suggested answer
Conventional banks will only lend you money when you don't need it desperately, i.e. if you have money already. (You are seen as low risk with a good credit rating.) However, if you find yourself in a difficult financial situation and need to borrow money, the banks won't lend to you. (You are considered high risk.) Grameen Bank, on the other hand, takes the opposite approach.
2
Suggested answers
Grameen Bank's clients are 97% women, they lend to beggars, the bank is owned by its borrowers, the profits are returned to borrowers, it focuses on small loans.

Language focus: Word formations

1
1 penalty 2 to guarantee 3 guarantor 4 payment
5 repayment 6 payee 7 incentive
2
1 guarantor 2 repayment 3 penalise 4 repay 5 incentive

Listening 1: How and why Grameen Bank was founded

1 It was a very rough period and there was famine.
2 Loan sharks caused the problems.
3 He helped 42 people.
4 He had to become the guarantor.
5 They paid it all back.
6 They thought that the whole thing would collapse and people wouldn't repay the loans.

Critical analysis

Suggested answer
He could refer to illegal or unregulated lenders who lend money at very high interest rates. They use threats and often physical aggression to force people to repay loans. Families can remain in debt to these people for generations and in extreme cases it can constitute a form of slavery.

Listening 2: Reversing the basic principles of banking

1 A
2 There is no guarantee for the bank if borrowers do not repay their loans.

1 guarantee **2** lawyers **3** bank **4** penalise/sue
5 repayment **6** penalty

12.3 Skills: Delivering a presentation

Listening 1: Good and bad delivery

2

The second presenter is better, as she seems more authoritative and confident.

Listening 2: The President

1

1 Barack Obama speaks clearly and pauses to add emphasis to key points.
2 He sounds confident by sounding believable and not hesitating.
3 He has obviously organised and planned his talk and this makes him sound in control.

2

1 Yes
2 Barack Obama uses pauses between groups of words to add emphasis, create impact and make it easier for listeners to follow his meaning and have confidence in his authority.

3

1 Barack Obama varies the rise and fall of his voice far more than speakers would in a conversation. This reinforces the weight and importance of his message.
2 He stresses the following key words: setbacks, starts, agree, decision, policy, president, problem, honest, face, listen, especially, ask, remaking, nation, America, two hundred, block – block, brick – brick, calloused hand – calloused hand

Listening 3: The support manager

Suggested answer
The manager here sounds nervous and clearly hasn't organised what he is going to say. He has prepared badly and sometimes this shows, as his speech loses coherence and there is hesitation that makes him sound as if he doesn't know what he is talking about. Chunking and pausing are not used effectively.

Language focus: Use techniques to improve your delivery (stress, chunking and pace)

1

They are all very important to consider when giving a presentation.

3

There are many who won't <u>agree</u> / with every <u>decision</u> or <u>policy</u> / I <u>make</u> as <u>president</u> / and we <u>know</u> the <u>government</u> / can't <u>solve</u> every <u>problem</u>.

4

Thank you <u>very</u> much / for <u>coming</u> here <u>today</u>. / We're <u>very</u> glad to have this <u>opportunity</u> / to <u>tell</u> you about our <u>products</u> / and we <u>hope</u> / that by the <u>end</u> of today / we'll be ready to <u>move</u> our <u>relationship</u> / on to the <u>next</u> stage. / <u>So</u> / <u>firstly</u> / we'd like to <u>talk</u> about / the <u>history</u> of our <u>company</u>. / <u>Then</u> / we'll <u>move</u> on to / the <u>suitability</u> of our <u>products</u> / for <u>your</u> market.

5

Nouns and verbs are often the key words as they contain the content. Over 90% of key words come at the end of the chunk.

6

Seven is usually the maximum.

7

The pauses come after chunks, not in the middle of them. They shouldn't come between words that are part of a phrase. Example: NOT Thank you very / much.

Critical analysis: Metaphors

1

Barack Obama uses this type of metaphor in several places.

2

lies ahead; The road ahead will be long; Our climb will be steep; We may not get there;
we will get there; we as a people will get there; There will be setbacks and false starts;
remaking this nation … block by block, brick by brick, calloused hand by calloused hand

3

The problem is that people may not understand the metaphor at all, or they may misunderstand it. For example, *to have a thick skin* in the UK means that you can cope with criticism, but in Japan it means that you are insensitive.

Writing 6: Formal and informal emails at work

Introduction

1

Suggested answers
1 This is probably to a colleague who the writer knows quite well.
2 This could be between friends.
3 This could be from somebody who is working on a project with people from another company.
4 This could be to a secretary who the writer doesn't know well.
5 The writer probably doesn't know the person he is writing to very well.

2

Points 1–4 are probably appropriate in most emails to clients, but 5 and 6 are more difficult to generalise about.

3

Internal emails tend to be more informal and more open and can include more negativity; however, it will also depend on the relative seniority of the reader: if the email is to the company CEO, you may have to use very formal and respectful language.

Language focus: Formality and functions

1

cc – carbon copy (i.e. somebody else is copied in to the email)
e.g. – for example
i.e. – that is
etc. – et cetera
re – regarding
asap – as soon as possible
BTW – by the way
LOL – laugh out loud (funny)

FYI – for your information
PLS – please
THX – thanks

2

Using language that is too informal may damage the relationship. The reader may think the writer is unprofessional.

3

thanking – THX
requesting – asap, PLS
developing a relationship – LOL, PLS, THX
informing – i.e., re, BTW, FYI

4

1 requesting   **2** informing   **3** thanking   **4** informing
5 developing a relationship

All of the sentences could be used with clients and potential clients.

Intercultural analysis: Starting and finishing the email

1

2, 5, 3, 4, 6, 1

2

2, 6, 7, 5, 4/1, 1/4, 3, 8

Writing skill: Functions of emails

1 & 2

Email 1: apologising (Really sorry to mess you around …, and apologies again), requesting (Can you …)
Email 2: confirming (No worries), developing a relationship (wasn't expecting …)
Email 3: informing (Please find …, we have booked …), apologising (I'm afraid …), developing a relationship (Looking forward to …)
Email 4: informing/confirming (my dates …)
Email 5: confirming (15th November is fine with me), inviting (Could you come …), informing (I will collect …), requesting (Then we should …)

3

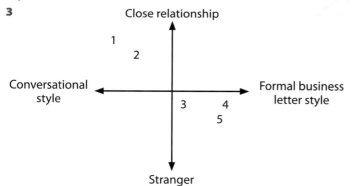

13 Corporate Social Responsibility

13.1 Theory: Business ethics and Corporate Social Responsibility

Introduction

2

Suggested answers

A footwear company has to consider where it sources its materials and the working conditions in its factories.
A supermarket needs to consider monitoring the living conditions of animals in farms which supply its meat and eggs.
A broadcaster needs to consider the effect its programmes have on the audience and for news programmes, whether it is biased or not.
A government ministry needs to think about the reputation of the companies it does business with.

Reading: Cases for and against CSR

1

For: B, C Against: A, D

2

1 D   **2** A   **3** B   **4** C

Language focus: CSR topic vocabulary

1 compelled   **2** wellbeing   **3** vast   **4** box-ticking exercise
5 deception/bluffing   **6** deception/bluffing   **7** generated
8 procurement policies   **9** work–life balance
10 primary purpose   **11** stakeholders

Critical analysis

1

The writer uses the male gender 'he', 'man' and 'his' to refer to both men and women. This is not considered acceptable in many countries today.

2

A businessman, his company or himself, he tries, to agree with him, if he feels obliged, he is ignoring, his business dealings

3

their company or themselves   they seek   agree with them
if individual executives refuse   if they feel obliged
they are ignoring   in their business dealings

13.2 Practice: The business case for Corporate Social Responsibility

Introduction

1

community: bring corporate expertise and know-how to benefit local community (Photo d)
physical environment: commission 'green buildings' powered by renewable energy sources (Photo a)
marketplace: provide honest information about company products and services (Photo c)
workplace: provide good working conditions for staff including good lighting and adequate space (Photo b)

2

The stakeholders are the employees, the licence fee payers in the UK, the UK government and the BBC's commercial clients. Their interests are as follows:

employees: to be valued by the organisation, to be paid appropriately for the job they do, to do interesting and worthwhile work where possible

UK licence fee payers: to watch BBC TV programmes and listen to BBC radio shows that are entertaining and informative and match the viewers'/listeners' interests. In particular, programmes should not just cater for mass markets which can be catered for by commercial broadcasters, but also address the needs of minority groups

UK government: to get value for money from the BBC, to ensure that it meets the needs of the whole UK population, to ensure that it is impartial and objective in news coverage

commercial clients: to be treated fairly, to have equal access to contract work

'Conflict of interest' often happens between different stakeholders. Senior managers will have to try and solve these conflicts in a way that satisfies all stakeholders. At the same time they need to protect the interests of the organisation as a whole.

Listening 1: Defining CSR

2

1 isn't **2** responsible **3** impact **4** strategy **5** transparent

Listening 2: The different sides of CSR

1

community: charitable donations to local communities, employee volunteering, skill-sharing, open doors of business to the local community

physical environment: they need to look at their environmental impact and CO_2 emissions regarding: travel, products they make, emissions from their buildings, how much water and energy they use

marketplace: ethical products, responsible advertising, supply chain issues, e.g. child labour

workplace: responsible recruitment and career development policies

2

Suggested answer

The relative importance of these four factors will depend on factors such as: what industry the company is in, the geographic location of the company, etc. For example, an oil company would probably be far more concerned with environmental CSR issues than a PR company.

Transferable skill: Awareness of paraphrase in listening

1 There (have to be / must be / need to be) good business reasons
2 cutting costs, spending less money, lowering costs
3 clear benefits now, definite results straight away
4 shareholders (UK) / stockholders (US)
5 way of measuring a company's success, means of assessing the worth of a company

Listening 3: The business case for CSR

1

1 true **2** false **3** true **4** false **5** true

2

1 There has to be a business case **2** cutting costs
3 clear benefits **4** shareholders
5 criteria by which you can measure the success of the company

Listening 4: Is CSR just corporate gloss?

1

1 A **2** B **3** D
2

Greenwashing is misleading marketing or promotion that falsely claims that the product, service or company is environmentally friendly. Examples may include beauty products that claim to be 'truly organic' when only a small percentage of the ingredients are actually organic; non-renewable energy companies that promote themselves as 'green' but contribute to global warming and environmental destruction.

Language focus: Phrases with prepositions

1

Noun + preposition	Verb + preposition	Adjective + preposition
impact on	look at	mindful of

2

Noun + preposition + noun	Verb + preposition + noun	Adjective + preposition + noun
amount of interest	focus on the impact (be) incorporated within the strategy (be) integrated into the company	conscious of issues aware of issues

3

1 mindful of **2** amount of **3** integrated/incorporated, into/within
4 focus … on

13.3 Skills: Supporting the speaker

Introduction

1

The answers to this will depend on your cultural background, but in general, all apart from 6 and 8 are effective.

2

3, 4, 5, 7 and 9 are all useful on the telephone.
1, 2, 6 and 8 aren't useful as the other speaker cannot see you.

Listening 1: Opening telephone conversations

3

1 In both conversations the person making the call introduces themselves. In the recorded conversation the caller gives more information, probably because the person they are calling does not know them and is not expecting the call. Phrases used: 'Hi, Sarah. Ken here' and 'Good morning. It's John here from Latin America Holidays.'

2 They both go straight into the topic. However, in the recorded conversation John is more formal and uses fuller sentences as he does not know the person he is calling. Phrases used: 'Just calling about …', 'I'm calling about your honeymoon trip' and 'My colleague Eleanor's been communicating with you.'

3 There isn't any small talk in the first conversation. On the recording there is a lot more small talk, as John doesn't know the client and wants to offer a friendly service.

4

Most formal first: 1, 3, 4, 2

5

1 The speaker is probably calling another company for the first time. The company they are calling could be a client or a potential client.
2 The speaker knows the other person fairly well. It is probably a colleague from the same company.
3 This is quite informal and friendly. The caller is perhaps phoning a client that they have had previous contact with.
4 The speaker is probably calling somebody in another company, as they say which company they are from. However, it is quite informal, so the person they are calling is probably at a junior level or they have met each other before.

Listening 2: Showing interest on the telephone

1 She doesn't sound very enthusiastic.
2 She shows this through pauses and intonation and not asking for more information.

Listening 3: Helping the speaker expand a topic

1

'Support' is a general term that can mean helping at many different levels, whereas 'sponsorship' specifically means ongoing financial help.

2

1 She sounds a lot more enthusiastic by showing she is listening and asking questions.
2 She tells Ken he has done a great job. This is positive.

Language focus: Supporting the speaker through listener responses

2

Sure is used more by managers to clients, whereas managers use *hmm* more when listening to subordinates. This is because *sure* sounds very positive and encouraging, whereas *hmm* is usually more neutral.

3

Positive: absolutely, uh-huh, sure, yes, really, great
Neutral: maybe, uh-huh, hmm
Negative: oh, (silence)
Note that many listener responses with rising intonation are positive, but neutral or negative with flat intonation.

14 Strategic planning

14.1 Theory: Corporate strategic planning

Introduction

1

1 c   2 b   3 a   4 e   5 d

Transferable skill: Using visualisation techniques

1

1 g   2 a   3 f   4 b   5 c   6 h   7 d   8 e

Reading: Strategic planning

1

1 i   2 d   3 a   4 e   5 g   6 h   7 c   8 f   9 b

2

1 B   2 A   3 C   4 E   5 D

3

1 false   2 true   3 true   4 false   5 true   6 false   7 true
8 false   9 false   10 true

Language focus: Verbs for strategic planning

1

1 implementing   2 monitoring   3 evaluating   4 ensure
5 specify   6 deviate   7 develop   8 consult

14.2 Practice: Planning within a company

Listening 1: The characteristics of a strategist

1

Suggested answers
Good strategist: somebody who can listen, who is good at analysis and getting answers from the analysis; he/she should be a good communicator and good at having ideas
Bad strategist: somebody who is uncertain and frequently changes his/her mind

2

They lose confidence.

Listening 2: Company strategy

1

1 true   2 false   3 false   4 true   5 false   6 true

2

Strengths: staff expertise, A&K has offices in over 35 countries
Weaknesses: it is seen as a luxury brand
Opportunities: the Internet provides a cost-effective way of reaching clients
Threats: the Internet has increased competition

Critical analysis

Suggested answer
The travel industry is sometimes accused of not supporting the local social or physical environment of the host countries. For example, waste and pollution can be issues. This in turn can make the place itself less attractive, which may mean fewer visitors want to go there and jobs are lost. Companies that actively support the local environment may increase their opportunities and develop a good reputation. Environmentally, the costs of luxury travel may be high, for example, business/first class plane travel. Given the issue of depleting oil reserves, the cost of flying may rise in the future.

Language focus: Multi-word verbs and collocations

1

Suggested answers
come: come up with, come across, come through, come over, come on, come up against
get: get up, get over, get on, get on with, get away, get away with
put: put on, put up, put up with, put away, put across, put off, put down, put into
take: take off, take on, take away, take out, take in, take over, take up

2

1 move forward in the right direction   2 put ideas into practice
3 take time over a decision   4 come up with ideas

3

4, 3, 2, 1

4

1 b **2** c **3** d **4** a

14.3 Skills: Using narratives in interviews

Introduction

1

4, 1, 3, 2

2

He wore a suit to the interview, but the instructions said that applicants should not wear a suit. He didn't get the job.

Listening 1: Conversation with a customer

1 Because the systems trainer's company does the treatment, and she trusts this company.

2 No, the customer didn't know that the systems trainer worked for the company. It is important because it means the customer has no hidden reason for giving her opinion.

Listening 2: Eye test

1

1 There was a long delay.

2 Somebody cancelled their appointment.

3 She doesn't have enough money at the moment.

3

The first listening sets the scene; however, there isn't a problem or resolution. There is a clear evaluation of the customer's opinion. The second listening has a clear resolution to the problem of the delay, but there is no clear evaluation.

Language focus 1: Narrative tenses

1

1 past simple **2** past continuous **3** past perfect **4** historic simple

2

The past perfect can be described as the 'past of the past'. In each of the sentences it is used to describe something that happened before something else.

3

Suggested answers

1 … I had left my glasses at work.

2 … the stock market had collapsed.

3 … had over-run the budget.

4 … the presenter had designed the slides badly.

Language focus 2: Answering questions in interviews

Questions 1 and 4 could definitely be answered with a story. It would also be possible to answer question 3 with a story. You could not answer question 2 with a story.

Writing 7: First contact emails

Introduction

1

They could all be first contact emails except the reply to an invitation.

2

Suggested answers

Job application: The style of the email will depend on the job you are applying for. It could be friendly and semi-formal or respectful and formal. All job applications should be in the middle on the convergent–divergent and the direct–indirect scales.

Complaint: Complaints tend to be in the middle of the respectful–friendly scale, and formal, divergent and direct.

Request: It depends on what the request is for and who it is made to. The only rule is that requests need to be fairly direct, as the person you are writing to needs to know what the request is for.

3

Points 1, 4 and 6 are good general rules. Points 2 and 3 might be misunderstood by the reader, and 5 should come earlier in the email.

Writing skill: Analysing emails

1

Email 1: a request for information   Email 2: a request for permission

2

Suggested answers

Email 1: Enquiry about recording software   Email 2: Request for permission

3

Suggested answers

Email 1: This is semi-formal and direct (although notice that the writer uses 'Hi' to open the email – a more friendly opening than 'Dear Sir or Madam', which would be too formal for an email like this).

Email 2: This is more formal (notice the opening and closing 'Dear …; Best wishes'). The request is worded quite indirectly: 'I am hoping you can help me … permissions we would need. Would this be a possibility?' Notice how, even in this formal email, the writer uses the addressee's first name. In some cultures this would not be appropriate.

Language focus: Tone through word choice

1

Old English words first:

say – express, look – appear, really – actually, get – obtain, do – perform, good – impressive, bad – terrible, talk about – discuss, thanks – gratitude

The Old English words are all single-syllable words (except *really* and *about*), and tend to be more informal, whereas the French/Latin words are longer and therefore more formal.

2

Suggested answer

If you could give the trainees any advice, or share your experiences and thoughts with them, that would be great.

3

Suggested answer

I am truly grateful for your assistance, and if you had the opportunity to glance briefly at my website, I would appreciate it very much.

It goes without saying that there is no compunction to purchase anything.

4

1 g **2** b **3** a **4** c **5** e **6** h **7** d **8** f

5

6, 5, 1, 2, 3, 4

6

1 3 **2** 1 **3** 2 **4** 3

Acknowledgements

Because of confidentiality issues, some company names have been changed in the Skills lessons.

The authors and publishers acknowledge the following sources of copyright material and are grateful for the permissions granted. While every effort has been made, it has not always been possible to identify the sources of all the material used, or to trace all copyright holders. If any omissions are brought to our notice, we will be happy to include the appropriate acknowledgements on reprinting.

Saint-Gobain for the case study on pp. 13–14. Reproduced with permission of Saint-Gobain; The Consumer Goods Forum and Capgemini for the cartoon on p. 26 © The Consumer Goods Forum and Capgemini; Nokia for the case study on pp. 31–32; Sage Publications for the text on p. 37 'Making sense of creativity' from *Creative Management* by Dr Jane Henry © Sage Publications, 1991. Reproduced with permission; Penguin for the text on pp. 47–48 from *Understanding Organizations* by Charles Handy (Penguin Books 1976, Fourth edition 1993)) Copyright © Charles Handy, 1976, 1981, 1985, 1993, 1999; Renault–Nissan for the case study on p. 57. Reproduced with permission of Renault–Nissan; Sophie Cacciaguidi-Fahy and James Cunningham for the adapted extract 2 on p. 57 and the adapted paragraphs 1 and 2 on p. 58 © Sophie Cacciaguidi-Fahy and James Cunningham; Harvard Business Review for: the texts on p. 65 'The hard side of change management' by Harold L. Sirkin, Perry Keenan and Alan Jackson. Copyright © 2006 by the Harvard Business School Publishing Corporation; extract A on p. 119 'Is Business Bluffing Ethical?' by Albert Z. Carr © 1968 by the Harvard Business School Publishing Corporation; extract B on p. 119 'Note on the Corporation as a Moral Environment' by Kenneth E. Goodpaster © 1989 by the Harvard Business School Publishing Corporation; all rights reserved. Reprinted by permission of Harvard Business Review; A & C Black for: the text on p. 73 'The project workout' by Robert Buttrick from *Business: The Ultimate Resource*, 2006 © A & C Black; extract C on p.119 'Corporate Social Responsibility: Are you giving back or just giving away?' by Jim Gus Gustafson from *Business: The Ultimate Resource*, 2006 © A & C Black; extract D on p. 119 'CSR: More than PR, Pursuing Competitive Advantage in the Long Run' by John Surdyk from *Business: The Ultimate Resource*, 2006 © A & C Black. Reprinted with permission. Charles Dennis, Tino Fenech, Bill Merrilees, 'Sale the 7 Cs: Teaching/training aid for the (e-)retail mix', *International Journal of Retail & Distribution Management*, 33:3 (2005), pp.179–193 for the text on p. 83; Havaianas for the case study and text on p. 93. Reproduced with permission; Profile Books for the adapted extract on p. 101 'Activity-based costing' from *Guide to Management Ideas and Gurus* by Tim Hindle. Economist Books, 3rd Edition, 2008. Reproduced with permission of Profile Books.

The publishers are grateful to the following for permission to reproduce copyright photographs and material:

Key: l = left, c = centre, r = right, t = top, b = bottom
www.123rf.com /© for p. 75(tl); Alamy /©image100 for p. 49(tr), /©Denkou Images for p. 49(cr), /©DCPhoto for p. 49(br), /©JG Photography for p. 49(cl), /©AWPhoto for p. 60(r), /©Adam Jones/ImageState for p. 68(bl), /©Jake Norton for p. 72(tr), /©Alistair Laming for p. 72(br), /©ITAR-TASS Photo Agency for p. 75(tr), /©Caro for p. 80(cr), /©apply pictures for p. 84(t), /©Holger Burmeister for p. 85(t), /©Bubbles Photolibrary for p. 87, /©Oleksiy Maksymenko for p. 90(bc), /©Vladislav Kochelaevskiy for p. 90(br), /©Brt Photo for p. 108(tr), /©Eightfish for p. 108(tl), /©Chuck Place for p. 108(bc), /©Danita Delimont for p. 111(b), /©IS195/Image Source for p. 114(tr), /©67photo for p. 126(e), /©Sergio Pitamitz/Robert Harding Picture Library Ltd for p. 129(t), /©foto-begsteiger/vario images GmbH & Co.KG for p. 132(tr); Dr Hans-Martin Beyer /© for p. 19; Courtesy of BITC /©Alastair Fyfe for p. 121(b); Alastair Brown /© for p. 85(b); Anne Marie Bulow /© for p. 34(l); Carnegie /© for p. 41; Cartoonstock /©Tim Cordell for p. 18, /©John Morris for p. 78, /©Aaron Bacall for p. 96, /©Dan Reynolds for p. 97; Yogesh Chauhan /© for p. 122; Corbis /©Bettmann for p. 28, /©Radius Images for p. 52; Richard Creagh /© for p. 103(b); Getty Images /©Philippe Lopez/

AFP for p. 10, /©Jules Hardouin Mansart/The Bridgeman Art Library for p. 13(tr), /©Alan Levenson/Time Life Pictures for p. 16(l), /©Dick Luria/Taxi for p. 16(r), /©Eightfish/Reportage for p. 21(t), /©Yamini Chao/The Image Bank for p. 21(b), /©PhotoAlto/James Hardy for p. 24, /©Alex Mares-Manton/Asia Images for p. 26(tl), /©PhotoAlto/James Hardy for p. 26(cr), /©Bounce/UpperCut Images for p. 27(t, c), /©Martti Kainulainen/AFP for p. 31, /©Peter Dazeley/Photographer's Choice for p. 33, /©Kimimasa Mayama/Bloomberg for p. 57, /©Gary Vestal/Photographer's Choice for p. 68(tl), /©Digital Vision for p. 70, /©Odile Noel/Redferns for p. 72(l), /©Abrahm Lustgarten/Aurora for p. 75(b), /©Universal Images Group/Eco Images for p. 80(br), /©George Frey/Bloomberg for p. 86, /©Getty Images for Havaianas for p. 93(t), /©Getty Images for Havaianas for p. 94(t), /©Paul Kane for p. 94(b), /©Getty Images for Havaianas for p. 95(tc), /©Randy Brooke for p. 95(br), /©Thomas Barwick/Lifesize for p. 106, /©Pierre-Philippe Marcou/AFP for p. 108(tc), /©Paolo Negri/Digital Vision for p. 108(cr), /©ChinaFotoPress for p. 108(b), /©Mark Wilson for p. 114(b), /©Seth Joel/Photographer's Choice for p. 121(tc), /©Moxie Productions/Blend Images for p. 121(bc), /©Headhunters/Photodisc for p. 126(a), /©Brigitte Sporrer/Cultura for p. 126(d), /©Eric Audras/PhotoAlto Agency RF Collections for p. 126(f), /©Image Source for p. 126(h)/ ©Altrendo Images for p. 132 (l)/©Manfred Rutz/Photonica for p 132 (br); Photograph by Elizabeth Handy /© for p. 47; Jeff Harding /© for p. 40; By permission of www.havaianas.com /© for p. 93(b), /© for p. 95(bl), /© for p. 95(tl); Jane Henry, The Open University /© for p. 37; Dr Sally Hibbert /© for p. 91(t); iStockphoto.com /©AlbanyPictures for p. 15, /©Don Bayley for p. 26(cl), /©Pali Rao for p. 27(b), /©Amanda Rohde for p. 36, /©Darren Wise for p. 45, /©Andresr for p. 46, /©Kristian Sekulic for p. 48, /©Ryan Klos for p. 53, /©Diogo Basílio for p. 56, /©PIKSEL for p. 59, /©Joe Potato Photo for p. 62, /©Dirk Freder for p. 64, /©Nicolas Loran for p. 65, /©Ben Blankenburg for p. 80(tr), /©Dave Hughes for p. 80(cl), /©Nadya Lukic for p. 80(bl), /©photovideostock for p. 81, /©Konstantin Shevtsov for p. 90(tr), /©Christina Solodukhina for p. 90(bl), /©mediaphotos for p. 91(b), /©ranplett for p. 99(b), /©Skip ODonnell for p. 100(t), /©Dmitry Kalinovsky for p. 100(c), /©Nicolas Hansen for p. 102, /©AdamGregor for p. 105, /©Kristian Sekulic for p. 114(tl), /©ohdesign for p. 118, /©gstudio for p. 124, /©Mark Evans for p. 126(b), /©Joe Gough for p. 126(c), /©Peter Booth for p. 134, /©YinYang for p. 135; www.kittywigs.com /© for p. 143(l), /© for p. 143(r); Laird PLC /© for p. 67(t), /© for p. 69; Frank Lane Picture Agency /©Michael Dietrich/Imagebroker for p. 68(tr); Suleyman Narimanov /© for p. 76; Charlie Peppiatt /© for p. 67(b); www.phonefingers.com /© for p. 138; Photolibrary.com /©Jochen Tack/Imagebroker.net for p. 23, /©Jon Feingersh/Blend Images RF for p. 54(t), /©Eric Baccega/Age fotostock for p. 68(br), /©Brand X Pictures for p. 84(b); Tim Rabone /© for p. 60(l); Rex Features /©F1 Online for p. 26(tr), /©Ilyas J Dean for p. 108(bcr), /©ITV for p. 126(g); Jochen Runde /© for p. 11; By kind permission of Saint-Gobain /©Polish Radio Krakow, Poland. Architect Mankowski Wrobel. Photo Moryc for p. 13(l), /©Nanjing Olympic Centre, Nanjing, China. Photo Zou Pei Jun for p. 13(c), /©Glasinform, Vienna, Austria. Architect Gerischer Wolf. Photo Eckelt Glas for p. 13(br); Martin Sanders /© for p. 82; Shutterstock /©Dmitriy Shironosov for p. 34(r), /©Athanasia Nomikou for p. 38, /©Ilin Sergey for p. 89, /©leungchopan for p. 99(t), /©Tomasz Trojanowski for p. 120, /©Dan Breckwoldt for p. 131, /©StockLite for p. 133; Stanley Siebert /© for p. 29; Helen Spencer-Oatey /© for p. 54(b); Still Pictures /©Ron Giling/Lineair for p. 111(t), /©Shahidul Alam for p. 112, /©Ron Giling/Lineair for p. 113, /©Silke Reents/VISUM for p. 121(t); Gopinathan Thachappilly /© for p. 100(b); Ukrainian International Airlines /© for p. 103(t); Justin Wateridge /© for p. 129(b); Philip Weiss /© for p. 88; Ake Wikström /© for p. 50.

Photos sourced by: Suzanne Williams/Pictureresearch.co.uk

Proofreader: Marcus Fletcher

The publisher has used its best endeavours to ensure that the URLs for external websites referred to in this book are correct and active at the time of going to press. However, the publisher has no responsibility for the websites and can make no guarantee that a site will remain live or that the content is or will remain appropriate.